Sara M. Saz
Indiana University

STRATEGIES FOR
LEARNING
SPANISH

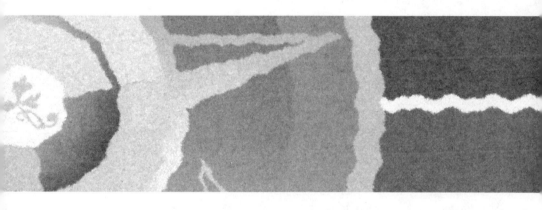

PRENTICE HALL   UPPER SADDLE RIVER, NJ 07458

Library of Congress Cataloging-in-Publication Data

Saz, Sara M. (Sara Madeleine), 1945–
    Strategies for learning Spanish / Sara M. Saz.
      p.   cm.

    ISBN 0–13–107160–2
    1. Spanish language—Textbooks for foreign speakers—English.
    2. Spanish language—Grammar.
  I. Title.
  PC4129.E5S29   1996
  468.2´421—dc20

96-8442
CIP

PARA CARLOS, CARLOS ROBERTO, FERNANDO, PABLO Y ZULEIKA,
COMO SIEMPRE

Editor-in-Chief: *Steve Debow*
Director of Development: *Marian Wassner*
Assistant Editor: *María García*
Editorial Assistant: *Karen George*
Managing Editor: *Deborah Brennan*
Cover and Interior Design: *Ximena de la Piedra*
Manufacturing Buyer: *Tricia Kenny*

©1996 by Prentice Hall, Inc.
A Simon & Schuster Company
Upper Saddle River, New Jersey 07458

Printed in the United States of America
10 9 8 7 6 5 4 3 2 1

ISBN   0-13-107160-2

Prentice Hall International (UK) Limited, *London*
Prentice Hall of Australia Pty. Limited, *Sydney*
Prentice Hall Canada Inc., *Toronto*
Prentice Hall Hispanoamericana, S.A., *México*
Prentice Hall of India Private Limited, *New Delhi*
Prentice Hall of Japan, Inc. *Tokyo*
Simon & Schuster Asia Pte. Ltd, *Singapore*
Editora Prentice Hall do Brasil, Ltda., *Rio de Janeiro*

CONTENTS

PREFACE

CHAPTER 1
Why Should I Learn Spanish?   *1*

CHAPTER 2
Understanding a Different Culture   *17*

CHAPTER 3
Grammar, and Nonsense, and Learning   *38*

CHAPTER 4
Homo Grammaticus   *51*

CHAPTER 5
Learning Vocabulary   *71*

CHAPTER 6
Approaching Reading   *81*

CHAPTER 7
Listening with a Purpose   *102*

CHAPTER 8
Speaking Our Mind   *120*

CHAPTER 9
Writing to Communicate   *140*

CHAPTER 10
Verbs with a Temper   *162*

CHAPTER 11
Could We Talk about the Past?   *177*

CHAPTER 12
Expressing Spatial and Temporal Relations   *196*

CHAPTER 13
Looking to the Future   *214*

ANSWER KEY   228

INDEX   233

PREFACE

When Executive Editor Steve Debow visited Indiana University in the spring of 1993, as a result of our decision to adopt a Prentice Hall textbook, I had not even considered writing a book on *Strategies for Learning Spanish*. However, during that visit, Steve and I sat down to talk in my office about our basic Spanish program and some of the difficulties I have encountered in teaching Spanish to American students since coming to this country in 1988. I remember that, in spite of it being a Friday afternoon and the fact that Steve had other commitments, we talked for hours about language teaching, and possible ways in which students could be helped to learn more efficiently. I was impressed by Steve's interest and enthusiasm. He suggested that I put some of my ideas into writing and this book is a result of that conversation. I am grateful for Steve's support and encouragement, without which the work would not have been written.

This is not a textbook, neither is it a solution for all the problems beginning students of Spanish are likely to find. In recent years there has been an increasing interest in learning strategies and ways in which to help students take charge of their own learning process in order to become more autonomous. There are books on the subject for teachers of languages, and for language students in general. However, to my knowledge there is, no specific work on strategies for learning Spanish. While general advice on language learning may be useful to all students, students of Spanish need content-specific material, and this book tries to fill the gap.

One of the biggest problems we have in the classrooms is that of motivation. Many students are not in Spanish classes because they have a real love for the language, but because they need to fulfill a requisite. Those of us who teach these students also often have to deal with the well-meaning but erroneous advice of advisers, non-Spanish-speaking of course, who funnel students into the language because they tell them that it is easier to learn than French or German. Hence the frustration and even anger when students discover the Spanish verb system. It also means that we frequently have students who have previously tried other languages and failed, so begin Spanish with a low self-esteem.

In this book I first get students to look at their reasons for learning Spanish and to think about their goals. I emphasize the importance of long-term goals and short-term objectives. I then sensitize them to a different culture by getting them to consider their own culture and values, perhaps for the first time. This is followed by chapters on specific aspects of language learning: grammar, vocabulary, reading, writing, and oral expression, in which I show, among other things, that ambiguity and uncertainty, which frequently hinder the learner of a foreign language, are part and parcel of our dealings with our own language, and that we all have the mechanisms to cope with them. These chapters are followed by ones on specific grammar topics such as the expression of the present, the future, the past, etc., but in a way that tries to get the student to reason and understand the concepts, as opposed to merely learning a list of rules and exceptions. In some cases, such as the treatment of prepositions, the topics may not even appear in basic language textbooks, yet are fundamental for the student's understanding of the language.

The book is meant to be used in conjunction with the student's class textbook. Many of the exercises throughout the chapters should be done in pairs or groups because one of our tenets is that peer collaboration can and should be an important factor in helping the student to learn. Other exercises can be done on an individual basis. Answers are provided at the back of the book for those exercises that are not open-ended. This should help students to work on their own. In all cases, it is hoped that the book will help instructors to forge closer links with their students and to bring out into the open some of those factors which impede language learning and which we know are there, such as anxiety, but are not often openly dealt with.

I would like to warmly thank the many people who have seen this book at various stages of its development and offered suggestions for improvement. I would particularly like to thank my friends and colleagues Katy Ratcliff, Stephanie Thomas, and David Wren for their constructive criticism of several chapters. They managed to locate a number of Briticisms, as well as several cases of infelicitous prose. A special thank you goes to Alberto Kelso who read the entire manuscript and made a number of suggestions. Needless to say, the imperfections that remain are my own.

Lastly, I would like to thank the Prentice Hall Foreign Language staff for all their efforts throughout the various stages of this project: Steve Debow, Editor-in-Chief; Debbie Brennan, Managing Editor, Ximena de la Piedra, Designer and, Isabel Picado and the staff at Hispanex. Thanks also to the following reviewers for their invaluable comments and suggestions: Susan Bacon, *University of Cincinnati;* Jorge Cubillos, *University of Delaware;* Scott Despain, *North Carolina State University;* Carol A. Klee, *University of Minnesota;* April Koch, *University of Texas at El Paso;* Barbara Lafford, *Arizona State University;* Roberta Lavine, *University of Maryland at College Park;* Karen L. Smith, *University of Arizona;* Judith Strozer, *University of Washington;* and Janice Wright, *College of Charleston.*

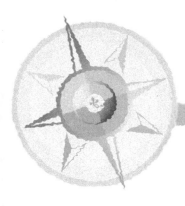

CHAPTER ONE

WHY SHOULD I LEARN SPANISH?

Tiempo no aprovechado, viento que ha pasado.
Time that is not well spent, is like a wind that has blown through.

> Spanish proverb

➤ BEFORE WE BEGIN

In this chapter we will talk about some of the reasons that make learning Spanish worthwhile. We will discuss the areas in the world where Spanish is spoken and the importance of Spanish in the United States. We will mention some of the careers in which knowing Spanish is a definite advantage. You will also try to define your own motives for learning Spanish and decide whether these need to be modified. You will start to establish long-term goals and short-term objectives in your language learning process and think about how to start getting organized. Finally, in the *Nuts and bolts* section you will learn a few useful phrases to use in class from the first day, and start thinking about some of the differences and similarities between Spanish and English.

By the end of this chapter you should have a clearer idea about the following:

- Where Spanish is spoken and who speaks it
- Why Spanish is useful for you in the United States
- What your own motives are for learning the language
- How you can start organizing your work
- Some practical tips about starting to learn Spanish

¡Suerte!   (Good luck!)

If you agree with the Spanish proverb that time is precious and needs to be well spent, then you want to be sure you are not wasting your time studying a language that will be of no use to you. You may already have had some experience with Spanish or you might be learning it for the first time. Whatever your situation, there are a number of things about the Spanish language and the people who speak it that you already know, perhaps more than you realize. As a start, do the following activity.

 Å Activity 1 ···

Quickly look down the following list of statements and mark them true or false. If you don't know the answer, it doesn't matter; go on to the next one. When you have finished, check your answers with at least four more people before commenting on them with your teacher.

1. Spanish is spoken in parts of mainland Africa.
2. People in Brazil speak Spanish.
3. Portuguese is a variety of Spanish.
4. Spanish is spoken on certain islands off the coast of Africa.
5. It is spoken on some islands in the Mediterranean Sea.
6. There are more than 300 million speakers of Spanish.
7. There are more Spanish speakers in the United States than in Venezuela.
8. There are more Spanish speakers in Argentina than in Spain.
9. Mexican Spanish is totally different from the Spanish spoken in Spain.
10. Spanish is the official language in twenty countries.
11. The Spanish spoken by Hispanics in the U.S. would not be understood by a visitor from Chile.
12. Lima is the capital of Uruguay.
13. Barcelona is the capital of Spain.
14. Mexico City has more inhabitants than all of Peru.
15. Spanish is only spoken in countries with tropical climates.
16. Paraguay doesn't have a coastline.
17. Bogotá is the capital of Ecuador.
18. Los Angeles was founded by Spaniards in the eighteenth century.
19. Lisbon is the capital of a Spanish-speaking country.
20. Almost a third of the population of Argentina lives in Buenos Aires.

When you have checked your answers, look at the maps of the Spanish-speaking world on page 4 and make sure you can locate the places mentioned. Discuss your answers with your instructor. Knowing where Spanish is spoken will help you better appreciate the fact that you are learning a language that is spoken over an extremely wide geographical area. When you study aspects of some of these countries in class you will already know where they are located and the places will sound familiar to you. Make a list of the Spanish-speaking countries and write their capital city by the side. These are a lot of names to learn, so you need to decide what is the best way to help you learn them.

One way to learn them is to group them in threes or fours and invent a new word with the first couple of letters of each. To remember, for instance, that the islands of Cuba, the Dominican Republic, and Puerto Rico are located in that order you could write down CUDOMPUR. Or to remember that Colombia is north of Ecuador which, in turn, is north of Peru, you could write CEP. You may find it easier to associate names with an English word that looks or sounds similar and put it into a sentence which may make nonsense to everyone except you. For example, to remember the capital of Peru (Lima), you can think of lima beans; for the capital of Ecuador (Quito), you can say to yourself, "I won't *quit*," or that of Spain (Madrid), "We're all *mad* about Spanish." Some Spanish cities can be translated into English and it may help to put the translation into a phrase. La Paz means *peace* so you could say, "Bolivia is a *peaceful* place." It doesn't matter which system you use as long as what you produce is meaningful to *you*.

For some people, just visualizing a map can be very helpful. When they try to recall it, they can actually see in their mind the position of countries or cities, but you may not be a particularly visual person. Try concentrating on the map of South America for a couple of minutes, then close your eyes and see whether you can visualize it. It may help to notice certain patterns such as Chile, Argentina, and Uruguay forming the base of a triangle with Bolivia at the point (diagram A), or the Tropic of Capricorn passing through Paraguay. Alternatively, you could trace or imagine a large letter S, starting with Venezuela, going through Colombia, Ecuador, then Peru, Bolivia, and Paraguay, followed by Uruguay, Argentina, and ending up in Chile (diagram B).

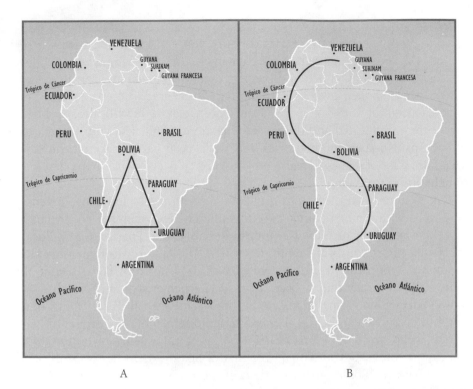

A   B

    To help you remember the order of the countries you could group them according to their first letters, VCE, PBP, UAC. Say the letter combinations out loud a few times, tapping your foot as you say them. Often, getting your whole body, or parts of it, involved with your learning process can be really helpful.

    Experiment with different learning strategies: acronyms, nonsense sentences, translations, visual patterns, etc., until you find one that suits you. You may need a combination of all of these. And share your strategies with someone else. He/She may have thought of something useful or amusing that could help you learn, and vice versa.

    Don't expect to memorize this information all at once and be able to retain it indefinitely. Once you have devised your system, split the information into chunks and try to learn one chunk at a time. You may decide to learn the names of the countries and cities in Central America first, or those of the northern part of South America. Keep going back to your acronyms or nonsense sentences at increasingly lengthier intervals until you are sure that you have memorized all of them. Test yourself by filling out blank maps. Your instructor may be able to provide you with these, or you can make your own by photocopying a map and whiting out the names of countries or cities you need to learn. Only knowledge which you use regularly will become committed to your long-term memory and this goes for all aspects of your language learning, so it's a good idea to start getting in the habit with something straightforward like map learning.

> SPEAKING SPANISH WITHOUT LEAVING HOME

Some people study a foreign language for years before they have the opportunity to visit a country where it is spoken; others never manage to go at all. While it is an extremely enriching experience to spend some time abroad, not just for linguistic reasons, students of Spanish in this country have an enormous advantage over students of other languages. Spanish is, without doubt, the second language in the United States and the number of Hispanics in this country is growing all the time. You may already be aware of this if you live in a part of the country with a large and well-defined Hispanic population.

There may be people in your class who come from a state or city where there are many Hispanics and the Hispanic influence is very obvious. Spend some time doing the following activity.

Å *Activity 2* ···

First take a few minutes to think about these questions and jot down notes on the following:

1. Did you have classmates with Hispanic names at high school?
2. If so, did you ever hear them speak Spanish at school? Do you know if they spoke Spanish at home with their parents?
3. Do you know from which area of the Spanish-speaking world their families originally came: Mexico, Puerto Rico, Cuba, etc.?
4. Did you ever notice Spanish last names in your phone book? Were there many or just a few? Can you remember any of these names?
5. Are there any Hispanic restaurants in your town? Have you been to them? Were all the people working there Hispanic? Write down the names of any of the Spanish dishes or foods that you ordered.
6. Can you think of any businesses or professional offices run by Hispanics in your town (shops, doctors, dentists, lawyers, etc.)? Write down any that you remember.
7. Are there any streets in your town that have Spanish names or are named after Hispanic people? How about churches, parks, libraries, etc.?

8. Are you used to seeing a lot of foodstuffs used in Hispanic dishes or products with labels in Spanish at your local supermarket? What sorts of products are they?
9. Are there any annual public festivities associated with the Hispanic community in your area? What are they like?
10. Have you seen notices or forms in Spanish at your local post office, library, or other public building? Do you know what they are about?
11. Are there any newspapers or magazines in Spanish published or sold in your community?
12. Do you know if there are any telephone messages available in Spanish in your area (for instance, information about local public services, help for filling out tax forms, etc.)?
13. Do you know of a Hispanic migrant community, for example Hispanics who spend a few months a year harvesting tomatoes, apples, grapes, or other produce? Do you know where and how they live when they are there? Where do they come from?
14. Are there any churches with services in Spanish? If so, what denomination are they—Catholic, Baptist, Methodist, etc.?
15. Are there any movie theaters that regularly show films in Spanish, or video stores that have a large selection of videos in Spanish?

Once you have answered these questions, mingle with your class and ask the same questions of at least five people. Write down their name by the number of the question and briefly jot down the information they give you. When you have finished your survey, share the results with your teacher and the rest of the class.

Now think of how these questions relate to your present community setting. There may indeed be ways for you to use Spanish without leaving home.

Å Activity 3 ··

Below is some information about a few well-known Hispanics in the United States as well as some facts about different Hispanic groups. Match the information in column A with the right answers in column B. ¡OJO! (this means *Watch out!*), not all the answers in B are used.

	A		B
1.	Gloria Estefan is from...	a.	middle class
2.	This area of the Spanish-speaking world has contributed several baseball players to the U.S. league:	b.	the Dominican Republic
		c.	Puerto Rican
		d.	Spain
3.	Anthony Quinn's mother was from this Spanish-speaking country:	e.	20 percent
		f.	New York, Chicago
		g.	New Mexico
4.	César Chávez was a...	h.	union leader
5.	Most Puerto Ricans live in...	i.	Miami
6.	Half a million Cubans live in...	j.	California and Texas
7.	Most Mexican Americans live in...	k.	Cuba
		l.	60 percent
8.	Mexican Americans form _____ of the Hispanic population.	m.	actor
		n.	the Caribbean
9.	Juan Luis Guerra is a singer from...	o.	working class
		p.	Mexico
10.	Julio Iglesias is a singer from...		
11.	Rita Moreno is...		
12.	Cubans who came to the United States after Castro's revolution were mostly from the...		

After completing this activity you should realize that Hispanics are present in many areas of U.S. life and that certain geographical locations are associated with Spanish speakers from specific countries.

Since Spanish is the first language of so many people in the United States, in many areas of the community there is an increasing need for people who can speak both Spanish and English fluently. Whatever you are majoring in, you may well find that having a practical knowledge of Spanish will be a great asset to you when you start looking for a job.

Å Activity 4

Look at the list of professional fields. With a partner, draw up a list of the occupations within each field that would or might require knowledge of Spanish. Discuss whether this would be true everywhere in the United States or only in certain regions, in the city or rural areas, etc., and whether you would need to be able to speak, read, or write Spanish, or all three, for each occupation. Then, write down five professions or occupations not mentioned where you think knowledge of Spanish would be very or moderately useful.

	Would require Spanish	Might require Spanish
1. Travel		
2. Medicine and health care		
3. Social work		
4. Law		
5. Immigration		
6. Journalism		
7. Publishing		
8. Real estate		
9. Hostelry		
10. Translator of commercial texts		
11. Education		
12. Agriculture		
13. Commerce		
14. Banking		

➤ MOTIVES AND EXPECTATIONS

You may have signed up for Spanish with a very clear idea of why you want to learn it and this may be just the opportunity you have been waiting for! On the other hand, a lot of people find themselves sitting in a Spanish class wondering why they are there.

So one of the first steps in getting yourself organized is to decide why you want to learn Spanish at all.

Å *Activity 5* ···

Read the following list and check those items that apply to you. If your reason does not appear, add it at the end where it says *Other*. Try to be as honest as possible. There are no right or wrong answers and your teacher is not going to penalize you in any way.

1. I have a Hispanic background, but I was not taught Spanish as a child.
2. I want to visit Mexico (or Spain, Peru, Puerto Rico, etc.) and would like to be able to talk with people and understand what's being said.
3. Learning a language sounds like fun. It will be different from my other classes.
4. I have a language requirement and everyone tells me Spanish is the easiest language to learn.
5. I think Spanish will be useful to me in my future career.
6. I have a Spanish-speaking boyfriend/girlfriend.
7. I'm very interested in the art/culture/history of Spanish-speaking countries.
8. I think it's the language of the future.
9. I like Spanish television programs and want to understand more of what's going on.
10. I love Hispanic music.
11. My parent(s) told me to choose it.
12. I tried to enroll in another language, but it was closed out.
13. I've already tried French and German and failed; perhaps I'll be luckier with Spanish.
14. I don't know.
15. Other: _____

When you have checked your reasons, share them with a classmate. See how many points you have in common and discuss your differences. Of the reasons mentioned in Activity 5, which one(s) are you definitely not interested in (e.g., visiting a Spanish-speaking country, Spanish art and culture, etc.)? How about number 3? Do you think studying a language could be fun, or does this sound like a contradiction in terms to you? Why? Talk about these points with two or three more people and see if you agree or differ. Do you think any of the reasons you or your classmates have for learning Spanish will still be valid in five years? Do you think you will be using Spanish in some way at that time, or do you think it more likely that you will forget it as soon as you stop studying it? What are the reasons? With the person next to you, draft a list of at least five more reasons for learning Spanish.

Just as people have different motives for learning a language, they also have different expectations. Not everybody wants or expects to use the language in the same way. You probably have a syllabus and a set number of things that you have to do in order to pass your course, but it is much more important for you to decide what your personal goals are as they may or may not coincide with what you are formally taught.

What do you expect to get out of your first two semesters of Spanish in the way of practical results? Check the items that apply to you. Try to be as honest as possible and add any other expectations that you may have.

1. A good grade so that my GPA won't be affected.
2. Some understanding of the Spanish-speaking world and its peoples.
3. To be able to read a newspaper or journal in Spanish.
4. To be able to hold a conversation with a Spanish-speaking person.
5. To exchange letters with a Spanish pen pal or write other correspondence.
6. To understand the lyrics of Spanish songs.
7. To be able to rent a Spanish video or watch a TV program and know what's going on.
8. To have a better understanding of the Hispanic people in my community.
9. To read short stories or poetry in Spanish.
10. Other: _____

Talk about your expectations with a classmate, then share them with the rest of the class. Tabulate the results on the chalkboard so that you know how many people are mainly interested in learning to read Spanish, to speak or write it, etc.

➢ GETTING ORGANIZED

Your success in Spanish, to a large extent, will be in direct proportion to the amount of organized effort that you put into studying. Notice that the operative word is organized. Some people spend long hours studying a language, yet never seem to get the hang of it, while others may spend less time and yet get better grades. This doesn't necessarily mean that some are more intelligent than others, though intelligence obviously plays a part. Nor does it mean that some have a knack for languages and you just don't have it. It does mean, however, that some people go about learning a language in a much more organized way, so they derive greater benefit from the time that they do spend studying.

These goals, or similar ones that you may have set yourself, cannot be accomplished in a short time. If you want to be able to exchange letters with a Spanish-speaking person, for example, and are learning Spanish for the first time, it would be unrealistic for you to expect to send your first letter by the end of your second week of the course. However, if being able to communicate in writing is important to you, you will be willing to work toward that goal even if it takes a long time. Decide now what your long-term goals are and write them down so that you can remind yourself of them from time to time. Learning a language can sometimes be frustrating, and there will be times when you feel you are not making as much progress as you would like, so it is helpful to keep in mind that you have your sights set on something tangible, but that will take a while for you to attain.

In the meantime, there are a number of short-term objectives that you can and should set yourself. These will help you focus better on your learning process and give you a sense of achievement when you reach them. You also will be able to monitor your own progress in Spanish. You can look at these as small hurdles that you set yourself, and every time you get over one of them you have taken a step toward achieving your long-term goal.

As part of your Spanish course you will no doubt be given tasks to do outside class and it is important that you do everything asked of you. But these tasks are not your only objectives. Only you can decide what they are and what your time frame is for achieving them. For instance, if you decide that it would be a worthwhile objective to learn the names of the Spanish-speaking countries and their capital cities, you can plan to learn the names of all the Central American countries and their cities by the middle of the first week of class, and the South American ones before the end of the week. If you think it would be a good idea to learn the Spanish phrases that figure in the next section as soon as possible, you could plan to set aside enough time the first evening you have available to learn them. Try to specify the exact date you will do this. For example: On Sunday afternoon, from 4:00 P.M. to 6:00 P.M. I will study the direct object pronouns.

You will also find it very useful to start a Spanish-language journal. Your teacher may ask you to do this and give you specific instructions about how to go about it; if not, you can start like this: Buy a simple loose-leaf notebook with dividers. Label each section: Class notes/Homework/Test Dates, etc.

Use one section to write down any notes you take in class, another for homework and another for dates of quizzes or tests that you are given. You can also have a section to write down any new vocabulary that comes up in class that either you are not sure of or that you want to organize later in a vocabulary notebook. Use the notes section to write down any questions you may not want to ask in class but will ask later, either of a classmate or your teacher. You can keep another section for more organized notes that you have rewritten from rough notes taken in class.

In one section write out your class and lab schedule and all the activities that you participate in throughout the week, including the weekend, as far as possible. You will, of course, need to adjust your weekend activities as many of these will change. This will give you an idea of what time you have available to organize your studies. Now you need to decide how many hours a week you can afford to devote to studying Spanish out of class. If Spanish is not your main priority, naturally you will not be able to spend as much time studying it as you do your major. However, you do need to take into account that your progress in Spanish will depend on the effort you put into it, both in and out of class. Try to aim at spending a minimum of two hours per week for every hour of class, so if you have four classes that means eight hours out of class. That may seem like a lot, but you will find that this really pays off, and if you are well organized it won't be impossible to achieve.

Whatever time you decide to allot to Spanish, it's not a good idea to try and concentrate it all in one or two extended time periods. For instance, if you only study on Friday night and Sunday afternoon, this is going to be of far less use to you than if you divide the same amount of time in small segments throughout the week. Twenty minutes of concentrated effort will be of more use to you than two hours during which your mind might wander. It can help to reserve the same time for your Spanish study every day, so you get into a routine and it becomes increasingly easier to keep to it. It doesn't matter what time of the day you choose. Some people may decide that half an hour after breakfast is when they are most receptive; others prefer late at night. There are many ways in which you can add additional minutes to your Spanish study time without it being painful. If you travel to school by car, you can play a tape that goes with your course work or listen to Spanish songs. If you jog or work out on an exercise bicycle, you can do the same. While you are in the kitchen getting your meals, you can review your vocabulary and say it out loud. If you really want to find the time, you will discover that it is there for you.

Keep one section of your journal for personal reflections about your language-learning process. At some time you may want to share some of these with your teacher or classmates, or you may feel that they are too personal to share with anyone. That is fine. Language learning is a very complex process not only because it is a question of acquiring new linguistic habits, but it also brings us into contact with a culture that may be totally different from our own. It can make us question our values or even ourselves. There will be days when you have very positive experiences with your new language and are proud of the way you have used it in class. There may be other days when your self-confidence is shaken and you think that perhaps you've made a fool of yourself. This happens to everyone and if you can accept it as part of the process it won't seem too important. Write about these experiences as you see fit, preferably either daily or two or three times a week. This will help you analyze the negative ones and see how you can do better in the future. At the same time you can read over the good experiences and realize that, on the whole, you are doing pretty well.

As your knowledge of Spanish increases, try some of your own sentences in your new language. Gradually you will find that you can keep a simple, running diary of your life and interests in Spanish, and by the end of the course you will be able to look back and see just how much you have progressed.

> NUTS AND BOLTS   *Phrases for the classroom*

Hola, ¿qué tal? From the very beginning of your first class there are a few phrases that you can use that will get you in the mood for Spanish and be useful when communicating with others. You want to be able to say hi to others and ask them informally how they are. You have just done that with **Hola, ¿qué tal?** You can ask this of whoever is sitting next to you, then go on to ask **¿Cómo te llamas?** because you probably don't know that person's name. If he/she asks you the same question just say, **Me llamo...** At the end of class make sure you say **Adiós** and add, **Hasta mañana** if your next class is the following day, or **Hasta pasado mañana** if it's in two days' time. Think of your classmates as being some of your best allies in your learning process; they are going to be doing the same work as you. Some of them may have studied Spanish before and know more than you, so instead of feeling intimidated, think of this as an advantage. These are resource people to whom you can go and consult at various times. You don't always have to go to your teacher or feel that you have to figure everything out on your own.

There are times when you will need to ask or express certain things to your teacher and it's a good idea to get in the habit of expressing yourself in Spanish. You may need the answer in English, but your teacher will realize this. In the meantime, you are practicing Spanish in a real context, so as one of your first objectives set aside some time to learn the following expressions:

Repita, por favor.	*Say that again, please.*
No entiendo.	*I don't understand.*
¿Cómo se dice...?	*How do you say...?*
¿Qué significa...?	*What does... mean?*
Más despacio, por favor.	*Slower, please.*
Necesito ir al servicio.	*I need to go to the bathroom.*
¿Qué tengo que hacer?	*What do I have to do?*
No tengo papel.	*I don't have any paper.*
No tengo pluma.	*I don't have a pen.*
Estoy confundido/a.	*I'm confused.*

Gender

If you look at the last example, you will see that there are two forms— **Estoy confundido** and **Estoy confundida**— depending on whether you are male or female. In English you can say *I'm confused,* whether you are a man or a woman because gender, that is, the classification of words into masculine, feminine, or neuter, is not such an important issue in English. English does distinguish gender in some cases, however. For example, we talk about *my uncle/my aunt,* or *my mother/my father,* using different nouns according to whether we are dealing with a man or a woman. Similarly, when talking about a male we might say *He studies law,* whereas for a female we would say *She studies engineering.* In this case the pronouns are different and tell whoever is listening to us that we are talking about male or female individuals.

We have other ways of dealing with gender in English. Certain animals have different names according to whether they are male or female— cow/bull, stallion/mare, ram/ewe, buck/doe. In general, however, gender is only important to us when dealing with people. Occasionally we may refer to inanimate objects that we are particularly attached to, like a car, as *she.* The feminine pronoun tends to be used also for ships and countries, but this is the exception rather than the rule. At times, gender can be flexible in English in a way that it never is in Spanish. For example, you may talk of a baby whose sex you don't know or whose sex is of no interest to you as *it.* You probably wouldn't want to do that when commenting to your neighbor on how sweet his/her baby looks!

In Spanish, absolutely all nouns, animate and inanimate, have gender. Gender should not be confused with sex. In Spanish **la silla** *(the chair)* is feminine, whereas **el techo** *(the roof)* is masculine. There is nothing in either of these words, or in any other for that matter, that makes them inherently masculine or feminine. The reasons are historical and you don't have to worry about them. What you do have to start getting used to is learning the gender of every new word you come across in Spanish. It's not enough to write down in your vocabulary book **ventana** *(window);* you must write **la ventana** because **la** is the feminine *definite article* in Spanish and goes before feminine nouns. In English we have only one written definite article: *the.* The phonetic distinction between *the* + vowel and *the* + consonant may not seem very important to the native English speaker, but to the foreigner it is almost like learning two different forms for the article. They are generally not interchangeable. The masculine article that goes before masculine nouns in Spanish is **el.** Most words fit into one category or another, although there is a neuter form, **lo,** that you will learn about later on.

It is helpful to remember that most feminine words in Spanish end in -a—**la ventana, la puerta** *(door),* **la cocina** *(kitchen)*— and that most masculine words end in -o—**el techo, el cuaderno** *(notebook),* **el libro** *(book).* Use this helpful mnemonic device (one that helps you remember something): in your journal draw a large **o** and a large **a** at the top of the first page that you have reserved for vocabulary and add some simple features to make them look masculine and feminine. In columns below the drawings, begin to order your vocabulary as you come across it, writing the article with each word and its translation. As a start, try doing the next activity.

Å *Activity 7* ··

Below is a list of Spanish nouns and their English meaning. Look at the ending of each word and decide whether it is masculine or feminine. Then write each one in your journal, placing **la** or **el** before it as the case might be.

cuaderno	*notebook*	**pluma**	*pen*
silla	*chair*	**ventana**	*window*
puerta	*door*	**mesa**	*table*
libro	*book*	**mochila**	*backpack*
muchacho	*boy*	**profesora**	*teacher*
casa	*house*	**hermano**	*brother*
amigo	*friend*	**perro**	*dog*
lámpara	*lamp*	**gato**	*cat*
hamburguesa	*hamburger*	**pescado**	*fish*

➤ SUMMARY

In this chapter you learned a number of things that will be useful to you as you start out on your Spanish studies. You thought about the areas in the world where Spanish is spoken and may have come across some of these names for the first time. You discussed the areas where Spanish is mostly spoken in the United States, and the origins of the people who speak it. It may have surprised you to realize how many Spanish speakers there are in the United States. You have thought about your home community and the possibility of any Spanish influence on it. You have also considered some of the professions in which knowing Spanish is an advantage. You clarified your goals in learning Spanish and thought about your expectations from this course. You also started to think about planning short-term objectives and getting yourself organized. Finally, you learned some useful Spanish phrases that will help you get along in class from the first day and have started to explore the notion of gender.

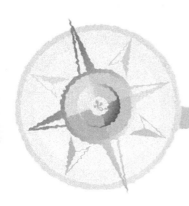

CHAPTER TWO

UNDERSTANDING A DIFFERENT CULTURE

"Why, Huck, doan' de French people talk de same way we does?"
"No, Jim; you couldn't understand a word they said—not a word."
"Well, now, I be ding-busted! How do dat come?"
"I don't know; but it's so. I got some jabber out of a book. Spose a man was to
come to you and say Polly-voo-franzy what would you think?"
"I wouldn't think nuff'n; I'd take en bust him over de head."

   Mark Twain, The Adventures of Huckleberry Finn

➤   BEFORE WE BEGIN

The mere fact that you are in a Spanish class means that it is highly unlikely that you would react to a Spanish speaker in the way that Jim did to Huck's hypothetical speaker of French. One benefit of studying a foreign language that is often cited is that it makes people more tolerant: it helps us recognize that our way of looking at the world and doing things is not the only one. It would indeed be wonderful if every single student of a foreign language came to understand others and to tolerate cultural and ethnic differences more easily. Unfortunately (and here perhaps instructors and textbook writers should take fair share of the blame), some first-semester or first-year Spanish courses do not cultivate this awareness. It is possible to study a language and finish a course with some understanding of the grammar and a certain degree of skill in reading, writing, and speaking, yet with very little real understanding of what belonging to that linguistic community means. Even worse, it is possible to speak a language and have very little empathy for those for whom it is their native language.

In this chapter we will examine some of the stereotypes associated with Spanish speakers. We will also try to make American culture "foreign" by looking at some aspects of it through a foreigner's eyes. We will try to decide what we mean by "culture," as well as consider some of the values that are

17

highly esteemed in American society and in Spanish-speaking communities. We will also see how our cultural outlook is intrinsically bound up with the language we use and how even common expressions and words can be very culturally specific.

Finally, we will continue with our examination of gender, and the concept of grammatical agreement of both gender and number.

> ## BECOMING THE "OTHER"

American TV programs are popular all over the world and are frequently dubbed in other languages. "Baywatch," purportedly the most popular of all exported American programs, is viewed in places as far away as Brazil, where it reaches even small villages on the edge of the Amazon jungle, and industrial cities in China, where its protagonist appears speaking fluent Mandarin. Viewers in Spanish-speaking countries are well acquainted with programs such as "Falcon Crest," "The Bill Cosby Show," "Dallas," "Oprah Winfrey," "Miami Vice," "Fresh Prince," and many others. The following titles reflect the popularity of American programs:

Los vigilantes de la playa
(Baywatch)
Las chicas de oro (Golden Girls)
Tiempo de conflictos (I'll Fly
Away)
Un mundo diferente (A Different
World)
Los Simpsons
Roseanne

Hospital (General Hospital)
Roc
Especial Wayne's World
Melrose Place
Canción triste de Hill Street (Hill
Street Blues)
La ley de Los Ángeles (LA Law)
Se ha escrito un crimen (Murder
She Wrote)

There are also Spanish versions of such popular programs as the following:

Misterios sin resolver (Unsolved Mysteries)
La rueda de la fortuna (The Wheel of Fortune)

The majority of Spanish-speaking viewers are never likely to visit the United States; nor do they speak English. Many, if not most of their concepts of American culture are formed from what they see in programs such as these and from American movies. Only those with an above average education are likely to have a more informed idea of American life. Taking this into account, do the following activity with a partner or in a small group.

A. Look at this Spanish television guide and locate all the programs that come from the United States.

TVE-1

(Del 4 al 11 de agosto)

JUEVES 4

07.35 ESTAMOS DE VACACIONES.
11.30 VACACIONES DE CINE.
13.05 McGYVER.
14.00 INFORMATIVO TERRITORIAL.
14.30 NO TE RIAS. QUE ES PEOR.
15.00 TELEDIARIO 1.
15.30 ALJANDRA.
16.25 MARIELENA.
17.15 HOMBRE RICO, HOMBRE POBRE.
18.10 NOTICIAS.
18.15 JUSTICIA CIEGA.
19.00 FUTBOL.
21.00 TELEDIARIO 2.
21.30 EL PRIMIJUEGO.
22.00 CINE: Película por determinar.
24.00 ADVINA QUIEN MIENTE ESTA
01.00 TELEDIARIO 3.
01.30 TENSION EN LA NOCHE.
03.00 DIGA 33.
03.25 TELEDIARIO-4.
03.55 DESPEDIDA Y CIERRE.

VIERNES 5

07.35 ESTAMOS DE VACACIONES.
11.25 NOTICIAS.
11.30 VACACIONES DE CINE: "Cabalgando hacia la muerte".
13.05 McGYVER.
14.00 INFORMATIVO TERRITORIAL
14.30 NO TE RIAS. QUE ES PEOR.
15.00 TELEDIARIO 1.
15.30 ALJANDRA.
16.25 MARIELENA.
17.13 HOMBRE RICO, HOMBRE POBRE.
18.10 NOTICIAS.
18.15 JUSTICIA CIEGA.
19.05 BLOSSOM.
19.35 ESTUDIANTES EN EL CARIBE.
21.00 TELEDIARIO 2.
21.30 MONTATELO.
22.30 FUTBOL
00.25 EL CINE MAS LARGO (I): "Mentiras".
02.25 EL CINE MAS LARGO (II): "Vida perra".
03.55 DESPEDIDA Y CIERRE.

SABADO 6

08.00 ESTAMOS DE VACACIONES.
11.15 CINE PARA TODOS: "El tigre y la llama"
13.00 BRINCOMANIA.
13.30 ¡NO ME LO PUEDO CREER!
14.30 NO TE RIAS. QUE ES PEOR.
15.00 TELEDIARIO 1.
15.30 PROGRAMA DOBLE:"Chicos made in USA" y "Aquí hay petróleo.
19.00 FUNCION DE TARDE
22.50 HUMOR
23.55 NINETTE Y UN SEÑOR DE MURCIA.
00.55 NOTICIAS.
00.25 CINE DE MEDIANOCHE (I): "Pureza de sangre".
02.25 CINE DE MEDIANOCHE (II): "Cuatro locos buscan manicomio".

03.55 DESPEDIDA Y CIERRE.

DOMINGO 7

08.30 ESTAMOS DE VACACIONES.
11.25 NOTICIAS.
11.30 VACACIONES DE CINE: "Tarzán y su compañera".
13.05 McGYVER.
14.00 INFORMATIVO TERRITORIAL
14.30 NO TE RIAS. QUE ES PEOR.
15.00 TELEDIARIO 1.
15.30 ALJANDRA.
16.25 MARIELENA.
17.30 HOMBRE RICO, HOMBRE POBRE.
18.20 NOTICIAS.
18.25 JUSTICIA CIEGA.
19.00 BLOSSOM.
19.30 FUTBOL.
21.15 TELEDIARIO 2.
21.45 COMO LO HACEN
22.15 LA DOCTORA QUINN
23.10 TRISTEZA DE AMOR
00.15 ¿Y QUIEN ES El?
01.00 TELEDIARIO 3.
01.30 TENSION EN LA NOCHE.
03.00 DIGA 33.
03.30 TELEDIARIO 4.
03.55 DESPEDIDA Y CIERRE.

LUNES 8

08.30 ESTAMOS DE VACACIONES.
11.25 NOTICIAS.
11.30 VACACIONES DE CINE: "Nicolasete y Nicolasón".
13.00 McGYVER.
14.00 INFORMATIVO TERRITORIAL
14.30 NO TE RIAS. QUE ES PEOR.
15.00 TELEDIARIO 1.
15.30 ALJANDRA.
16.25 MARIELENA.
17.30 HOMBRE RICO, HOMBRE POBRE.
18.20 NOTICIAS.
18.25 JUSTICIA CIEGA.
19.00 BLOSSOM.
19.35 ESTUDIANTES EN EL CARIBE.
20.30 VIDEO DE 1º.
21.00 TELEDIARIO 2.
21.30 PRET-A-POTER.
22.00 CODIGO UNO.
00.50 TELEDIARIO 3.
01.20 TENSION EN LA NOCHE.
02.50 TESTIMONIO
03.00 DIGA 33.
03.30 TELEDIARIO 4.
03.55 DESPEDIDA Y CIERRE.

MARTES 9

07.30 EURONEWS.
08.30 EPOCA DE CAMBIOS.
10.00 LA PELICULA DE LA MAÑANA: "La máscara de acero".
11.30 CLIP, CLIP ¡HURRA!.
13.00 PINNIC.

15.00 CIFRAS Y LETRAS JUNIOR.
16.30 POBLADORES DEL PLANETA.
17.30 LA PELICULA DE LA TARDE: "Un cazador siempre caza".
19.10 AL FILO DE LO IMPOSIBLE.
19.40 ALQUIBLA.
20.05 EURONEWS.
20.35 EL SUPERAGENTE 86.
21.00 LINGO.
21.30 MATRIMONIO CON HIJOS.
22.00 JUEVES DE CINE. "Sueño de reys".
23.45 DUDAS RAZONABLES.
00.35 SERIE ROSA: "La sonámbula".
03.50 DESPEDIDA Y CIERRE.

MIERCOLES 10

07.30 EURONEWS.
09.00 EPOCA DE CAMBIOS.
10.00 BALONCESTO
11.45 CLIP, CLIP ¡HURRA!.
13.00 PINNIC.
15.00 CIFRAS Y LETRAS JUNIOR.
15.30 GRANDES DOCUMENTALES.
17.00 TAHITI Y SUS ISLAS. EL ULTIMO PARAISO.
17.30 LA PELICULA DE LA TARDE: "Un caradura simpático".
19.00 AL FILO DE LO IMPOSIBLE.
19.30 AL GRANO.
20.35 EL SUPERAGENTE 86.
21.00 LINGO.
21.30 MATRIMONIO CON HIJOS.
22.00 LEER, VER... PATRICIA HIGHSMITH.
23.30 XL CERTAMEN INTERNACIONAL DE HABANERAS Y POLIFONIA.
01 20 CINE CLUB, SESION DE REPERTORIO, "Confidencias de mujer".
03.30 BALONCESTO.
05.35 DESPEDIDA Y CIERRE.

JUEVES 11

07.30 EURONEWS.,
09.00 EPOCA DE CAMBIOS.
10.00 LA PELICULA DE LA MAÑANA: "Fortunato".
11.30 CLIP, CLIP ¡HURRA!.
13.00 PINNIC.
15.00 CIFRAS Y LETRAS JUNIOR.
15.30 GRANDES DOCUMENTALES.
16.55 TAHITI Y SUS ISLAS. EL ULTIMO PARAISO.
17.25 LA PELICULA DE LA TARDE: "Su nombre es Carol Anne".
19.00 AL FILO DE LO IMPOSIBLE.
19.30 ALQUIBLA.
20.00 EURONEWS.
20.30 ALTETISMO.
21.00 TENDIDO CERO.
21.30 MATRIMONIO CON HIJOS.
22.00 LA ESTRELLA ES... EL CINE: "Cryano de bergerac".
00.30 DUDAS RAZONABLES.
01.10 CINE-CLUB, CINE JIRI TRNKA: "El príncipe bajaja".
02.30 DESPEDIDA Y CIERRE.

03.55 DESPEDIDA Y CIERRE.

B. Choose one of the American programs listed above, or any favorite program, and try to determine how it would influence a Spanish speaker's view of American society if this program were his/her only source of information about the United States. Consider the following points for discussion.

1. How are women portrayed?
2. What kinds of professions do people have?
3. Does violence play an important role, and if so, how is it depicted and by whom?
4. What evidence is there in the program of wealth? Are there signs of ostentation such as big cars, luxurious houses, expensive jewelry, and clothing, etc.?
5. Are there any minorities? If so, what kinds of roles do they play—main characters, (upper) middle class, working class, servants, etc.?
6. How are families portrayed? Are they close or are they plagued by divorce, illicit love affairs, problem or illegitimate children, drugs, violence, etc.? Are they nuclear families or extended families (uncles, aunts, cousins, grandparents)?
7. Does the program ever include weddings, baptisms, funerals, etc., and if so, are they generally realistic?

These are only a few of the questions you might like to consider. Draw up a list of inferences you think Spanish speakers would make about American society after being fed a diet of these shows; then discuss how realistic the shows actually are, or in what way you think they give a false view of American society and values.

➤ A TOUR THROUGH AN AMERICAN TOWN

If you are lucky enough to have visited a Spanish-speaking country, you probably noticed several things. Some would strike you as attractive or exciting, while others, if you felt they were unpleasantly different from what you are accustomed to, would seem weird or even disgusting. There are many features of your life and habitat which you accept as normal yet which for a foreigner might also appear peculiar, laughable, or unpleasant. Not every student of Spanish is able to visit a Spanish-speaking country, but everyone is able to look at his or her own town through the eyes of a stranger. Do the following activity in groups of three.

Ӽ *Activity 2* ....

You are hosting a middle-aged Spanish couple. Esteban, the husband, and his wife, Amparo, are visiting the United States for the first time and are having some difficulty understanding some American customs. Discuss the situation and make a list of the misunderstandings that occur. Explain how you would resolve them.

1. Esteban and Amparo return from their first trip alone downtown and they tell you that they saw the American flag flying outside all kinds of establishments: gas stations, liquor stores, private homes, grocery stores, even a dry cleaner. In Spain, they say, the national flag is usually restricted to government buildings. They want to know why the flag is used so much in this country and what it signifies for most people. Esteban tells you that in Spain there is both a national flag and a flag for each of the autonomous regions. On many occasions the flying of either one of these flags has signified discord.

   Esteban thinks the proliferation of U.S. flags demonstrates an excess of patriotism or national pride. He reminds you that flags and insignia were the hallmark of some extremist political doctrines in Europe such as Fascism. Amparo, for her part, considers it disrespectful to display the national flag outside of a liquor store. The host tries to justify to them this extensive use of the national flag.

   Now make a list of all the buildings in your town where the flag is flown. Visit your downtown area and check on this. Count the number of flags.

2. U.S. visitors to Mexico and other Spanish-speaking countries are sometimes surprised, perhaps unpleasantly, to find cakes or candy connected with death, such as the *huesos de santo* in Spain or the sweetmeats cooked for *El día de los muertos* in Mexico. However, Esteban is amused and his wife Amparo is shocked at finding a funeral parlor next to a fast-food establishment. The host tries to convince them that going straight from visiting a loved one who has passed away to getting a hamburger does not indicate a lack of respect for the dead (at least for the majority of Americans).

3. Your visitors have noticed and are intrigued by all the drive-through establishments they have seen. There are some drive-through banks in Spain, they explain, although they've never used one themselves, but this is the first time they have ever seen such a variety (fast-food places, bakeries, ice cream parlors, dry cleaners). They also were perplexed when walking downtown to find that the mailboxes had the slots for the letters on the wrong side: facing the street instead of the sidewalk. They cannot understand why Americans, who are so health-conscious, don't walk more. They think that so many drive-through establishments must be an indication that Americans are lazy. The host tries to explain the role of the car in American society.

4. The host decides to take Amparo and Esteban to a couple of garage sales, hoping that they will enjoy hunting for bargains. The host is surprised and rather offended to find that they are appalled by the experience, particularly since one of the sales is at the home of a friend of the host. You don't understand their attitude at all but Amparo explains that the idea of opening up one's home to complete strangers and putting on display all the junk one has been collecting for years is totally foreign to her. The mere thought not only of one's neighbors seeing all these things but of actually putting a price on them is horrible, and she feels acutely embarrassed for the organizers, who seem to be having a good time. She concludes that Americans have no sense of privacy, as well as no sense of the ridiculous. She finds it just as difficult to understand how the host could even buy some secondhand clothing at the other garage sale, particularly since he/she comes from an affluent family. Esteban, on the other hand, treats the whole thing as a joke and says that it is due to the American's sense of practicality. The host tries to explain this American pastime to the couple and what social values, if any, it reflects.

5. Esteban and Amparo are getting ready to continue their travels and are thinking of staying at a certain chain of low-priced motels. The host wants them to have a most favorable impression of the United States and tries to persuade them to stay elsewhere. They have already stayed at one of these motels and were quite satisfied, pointing out that the linen was clean, the room was carpeted and had a bathroom. It also had a telephone, color TV, and air-conditioning, symbols of luxury. In addition, the motel was cheap. The host tries to explain to them what, for him/her, constitutes a good motel.

6. For their final meal, the host takes the couple out to one of the local restaurants where you can eat all you want for $10.99. Esteban is intrigued to see people eating only with their fork in their right hand and keeping their left hand under the table. He wants to know what people are doing with their hand hidden and why they don't keep their knife in their right hand to cut their food. The host, who finds that the way Esteban and Amparo are eating leaves a lot to be desired (especially the way in which Esteban mops up his gravy with his bread), is offended that Esteban should question American eating habits.

   Meanwhile Amparo is obviously trying to hide her distaste at something. Eventually the host realizes that she is upset at seeing some people filling their plates to overflowing and even going back for more, while others, who have helped themselves to too much, are leaving large amounts of food on their plates. She expresses disgust. She has been brought up to serve herself only the amount she thinks she can eat and to not leave anything on her plate. Try to convince her that greediness is not a trait of most Americans and that many agree with her.

Now, as a group try to think of other aspects of daily life that you think may be interpreted differently by a Spanish speaker not familiar with American culture, and what kinds of erroneous conclusions he/she might come to about the "American way of life" and American values.

➤ EXAMINING OUR ATTITUDES

There were three lady flies who were friends and lived near Barcelona. They decided to go off on vacation and meet at the end of August to share their experiences. When they met up again, one said: "I had a wonderful time. I spent a month on the Costa Brava living it up. The night life's fantastic." The second one said, "Look at my tan! I hardly left the beach." The third one didn't look at all well; in fact she was very pale. The second fly asked the third one: "What's the matter? Have you been ill? You look as though you haven't seen the sun at all." And the third fly replied: "You can't imagine what bad luck I've had, girls. On the first day I went down to the beach. There was a man from Barcelona sitting in the sun opening his wallet and I flew in by mistake. I've only just been able to get out."

(Catalonian joke)

In all cultures there exist stereotypes of different nationalities or even different regions, as in this joke about Catalonians sometimes told by other Spaniards. Nobody really thinks that all Catalonians are stingy with money. In the same way, Irish people do not all have red hair and a terrible temper, all Asians aren't industrious, and not all Mexicans are lazy and put everything off until **mañana.** Whether we realize it or not, all our lives we have been absorbing these stereotypes propagated by our own culture about those who are different from us.

Sometimes stereotypes change over the years if there are social phenomena which are strong enough to bring about that change. A few years ago, in a survey done in Britain and Spain shortly before Elizabeth I paid her first official visit to Spain, people were asked about the qualities and defects of the Spanish and British. The same questions were asked of both nationalities. Surprisingly enough, both Spaniards and British seemed to agree that the British are very much more violent a race than the Spanish. Thirty years ago, most Spaniards would probably not have characterized the British as violent;

in fact, they would probably have described them as passive. Most likely, this changed image of the British is due to the violence at British soccer games and the presence of British hooligans at soccer games throughout Europe.

Whether you have studied Spanish at school before or not, you bring to your Spanish class a series of beliefs, conscious or not, of what being "Hispanic" means. The very term is a creation of American culture. Spanish-speaking people think of themselves as being Peruvian, Argentinian, Bolivian, Mexican, Venezuelan, and so on. Although all the Spanish-speaking countries have a language in common, their cultures can be very different and they would not dream of lumping themselves all together as Hispanic. In the same way, it is only in this country that the word "Spanish" has come to mean "anyone who speaks the Spanish language"; in the rest of the English-speaking world, the Spanish are those who come from Spain. Perhaps the fact that all Spanish-speaking people tend to be referred to by Americans as Hispanics harkens back to the days of the melting pot, the desire to level out all differences and produce a single culture.

You may think that the different American accents are very distinctive and that it is easy to distinguish someone from Montgomery, Alabama, from someone from Boston, for instance. Many British people, however, not only cannot distinguish a northerner from a southerner, but are capable of confusing someone from South Africa with someone from the United States. At the same time, most Americans are incapable of distinguishing an accent from Birmingham, England, from one from the west country. Think how you would feel if someone found your accent indistinguishable from all other English-speaking people and assumed that your life-styles must be very similar. For these people Americans, Australians, New Zealanders, South Africans, and Canadians would be one and the same. It is likely that your pride would be hurt and that you would be shocked at their ignorance. Consider then how someone from the Andes must feel if you confuse him or her with someone from Central America, or how a Cuban would react if you assumed that Cubans and Argentinians must have a great deal in common.

One of the most exciting features of learning Spanish is that it opens the door to knowledge about so many fascinating cultures and peoples. You will indeed find that Spanish-speaking people have many things in common, just as they do with your own culture, but there also are a great many differences and you should be prepared to find out about these as they contribute to the richness of the Hispanic world.

Like it or not, we all have prejudices and fixed ideas. That is why, when learning a language, it can be very healthy to bring these out into the open, to come to terms with them and begin to dispel the myths. With that in mind, do the next activity with a partner and compare your answers.

1. Share with your partner any jokes you know about Americans from different states or regions (Nebraska, Texas, the South, etc.). If you were
from any of those places, would you find the jokes offensive? Are there
any particular qualities that people associate with those who come from
certain states/regions (e.g., "southern hospitality")? How much truth do
you think there is in these generalizations?
2. When you think of Hispanic people, how do you imagine their physical
appearance? Try to find pictures of Hispanic people with fair hair and
blue eyes, or with red hair.
3. When you think of the kinds of houses that people have in Spanish-
speaking countries, which of these do you think of first: luxury villas;
apartment buildings; shanty towns; two-story houses with a back yard?
4. Which of the following do you immediately associate with Hispanics?

doctor	farmhand	lawyer
businessman	unskilled factory worker	engineer
politician	vendor	janitor
illegal immigrant		

5. When you think of "Hispanic" food which do you immediately think of:
tacos; tortillas; spicy sauces; fish?
6. What kind of climactic conditions do you associate with Hispanic countries: snow; cold, rainy weather; temperate climate; tropical climate?
7. Which of these adjectives do you consider refer particularly to Hispanics:

family-oriented	aggressive	fun-loving	ambitious
indolent	passionate	responsible	materialistic
hard-working	violent	respectful of elders	law-abiding
independent	rowdy	polite	demonstrative

8. Of the qualities listed in number 7, which do you consider are particularly respected in American society? Which ones do you think are often
quoted in stereotypes of Americans? Add any other values you think are
prized in your culture. Do you think the same values are esteemed in
Hispanic culture?

➤ WHAT IS CULTURE ANYWAY?

By the time students go to college, most have been exposed at school to
some kind of "culture" class, whether they have studied a foreign language or
not. At college you are probably obliged to take certain "culture" classes as

part of your core curriculum. If you have studied Spanish before, you are sure to remember some aspects that were presented to you as special lessons about culture. Before going any further, do the following activity with a partner.

Å Activity 4

In your Spanish classes at high school, which of the following "cultural" activities were you offered, and which did you most enjoy? Would you consider any of the activities more cultural than others? Why? Were there other activities not mentioned below? If you did not take Spanish in high school, think about the ones you think you would have enjoyed.

1. Learning how to cook certain Hispanic dishes.
2. Attending lectures, illustrated with slides or videos, on Hispanic art, architecture, history, geography, etc.
3. Going on class trips to theaters to see Hispanic dance groups or to Mexican restaurants for a meal.
4. Listening to songs in Spanish and learning the words.
5. Doing skits or plays that re-create certain features of Spanish life (for instance, staging a Spanish wedding, setting up a Mexican restaurant, going to a bank in Guatemala, etc.).
6. Reading Spanish-language newspapers and magazines.
7. Seeing feature films in Spanish.
8. Watching Hispanic television programs.
9. Interviewing native Spanish speakers in class or at the Spanish Club.
10. Reading plays or short stories in Spanish.
11. Preparing group or individual presentations on festivities such as *El día de los muertos, Los sanfermines, La Semana Santa,* etc.

While all the above activities embrace some cultural aspect, none of them on their own, or even together, can give you a complete vision of Hispanic culture. Everything in our society has some cultural value, and while it is relatively easy to learn about the works of great writers or artists, or get information about what people eat and when they eat it, or how they celebrate important festivities, what their countries or towns look like, etc., this only gives us a very superficial view of that culture.

Language and culture are intrinsically bound up, and as you learn about one you should be learning about the other. Even very ordinary words and expressions can have a specific cultural meaning. For instance, one of the first words you learn in Spanish is **adiós**, which you are taught means *good-bye*. This is true, yet Spanish speakers often say **adiós** to an acquaintance on the street whom they want to greet, but have no time to speak with. Here, then, what you have learned as the equivalent of *goodbye* now means *Hi.* Similarly, one of the first irregular verbs you learn is **ir,** and you translate **(yo) voy** as *I go/I'm going.* You also learn that **vengo** is *I come/I'm coming.* However, if someone rings your doorbell in a Spanish-speaking environment, you don't say **Vengo,** but **Voy.** This is not a peculiarity of Spanish, it is just as logical to see yourself mentally as going toward that person as to see the same act from the other side of the door.

Words in themselves don't have an intrinsic meaning. That is, there is nothing about a building, for instance, that makes the expression *my house* the most appropriate one for that object. It is just a linguistic convention that English-speaking societies have developed in order to function. **Mi casa** may be the linguistic equivalent in Spanish, but the reality may be very different. *My house* may, for some, be a two-story building with four bedrooms, three bathrooms, and a three-car garage; for others it may be a two-bedroom, one-bath, apartment. *Coffee* and **café,** depending on where one drinks them, may seem to be two totally different beverages, even if they are both made from coffee beans. Hispanic people, accustomed to a much more concentrated drink, may just call American coffee bad, whereas for many Americans the coffee drunk in a Spanish-speaking country may seem excessively strong and bitter. What's more, Hispanics may be amused to see Americans drinking coffee throughout their meal when everyone knows that the correct moment to drink coffee is at the end, after dessert!

Sometimes you will find that there is no exact translation for a word in English or Spanish because that concept does not exist in the other culture, or if it does it is not considered important enough to deserve a special term. If you look up the word **botijo** in the dictionary, you will find something like: "round earthen jar with a spout and a handle." If you have never seen a **botijo** and don't know what it is used for, the dictionary definition will be useless. If you were in the country on a hot summer's day, you might be glad to see a **botijo** in a Spanish-speaking country because it might contain the only cool drinking water for miles around. In a culture where you are used to a proliferation of drinking fountains and water-cooling devices, the humble **botijo** is certainly not a necessity.

On the other hand, if you are an avid tea drinker, you might have some difficulty trying to find a good Spanish equivalent in your dictionary for teakettle. You might come across terms such as **caldera** or **marmita,** but these are no use because they designate large stewing pots. You might also find **tetera,** but this is the teapot that you serve tea in, not the receptacle you boil water in. Tea drinking in many Spanish countries is not as commonplace as it is in the United States. In Spain, although there are many people who prefer tea to coffee, middle-aged Spanish people tend to think of tea, herbal or otherwise, as medicinal: something to drink for a stomachache. Any receptacle is seen as fitting for boiling water for the occasional cup of tea. In Argentinian Spanish, on the other hand, there is a term, **la pava,** that applies to a receptacle very similar to the teakettle because in Argentina there is a very high consumption of **mate,** an herbal tea which could be considered the national beverage.

You will come across many common sayings in Spanish that show a clear influence of the Roman Catholic Church. If you are not very keen on someone you could say, **No es santo de mi devoción** (*He is no saint I pray to*). Or if you get distracted and forget something you may say, **Se me fue el santo al cielo** (The saint left me and went to heaven). Of someone who robs Peter to pay Paul you say, **Desnuda un santo para vestir a otro** (*He/She undresses one saint's statue to dress another*), a reference to the special garments that are often used to clothe images of saints and the Virgin Mary. In some parts of the Spanish-speaking world, if there is a robbery and everything is taken, you can say, **Se fue con el santo y la limosna** (*He/She took off with the saint's image and the offering for the poor*).

Expressions such as ¡**Dios mío!** (*My God!*), ¡**Válgame Dios!** (*Good Lord!*), **Dios mediante** or **Si Dios quiere** (*God willing*), and ¡**María Santísima!** (*Holy Mary!*) are much more common in Spanish than in American English where, in some circles, they might even give offense. In the Spanish-speaking world, it is not considered blasphemy to mention God or the Virgin's name in the most profane of circumstances. This is not considered blasphemy; indeed, those who use these expressions may be devout churchgoers, but they use religious expressions profusely because they are so common that they have become devoid of any true religious meaning.

Å Activity 5

A. Look up the following words in a dictionary. Discuss the definition with a friend and then try to draw the object. Check your drawings with those in an illustrated Spanish dictionary. Do you use these things in your own culture?

el porrón   las acelgas
el almirez   las vinagreras
el mate (you will find two definitions for this)   el palillo
el chiripá

B. See how many expressions you can come up with in English that make reference in some way to religion or the church (e.g., *For heaven's sake!*). Compare your expressions with those of your classmates and compile a list. Poll the class to find out how many of those expressions would be acceptable to all, how many would be slightly offensive, and how many would be extremely offensive.

Culture is not just words but also gestures and movements. We tend to think that although languages differ, gestures must be universal. This is far from true. American children are taught to move their open right hand, palm outwards, from side to side to accompany the expression *goodbye* (figure A). Spanish children, in the same social situation, are taught to raise their right hand, palm outward, and quickly open and close their hand (figure B).

A   B

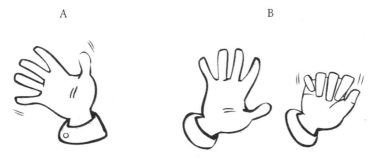

In American culture people are generally taught to look straight into the eyes of whoever is talking to them, supposedly to give an impression of honesty. However, in some Spanish cultures it is disrespectful for someone of humble origins to look into the eyes of someone considered socially superior, or for a youth to maintain eye contact with an elder. It is easy to see how this difference in nonverbal language could lead to misunderstandings even if all parties involved understood the actual words being said.

When you watch videos or if you have the opportunity to watch Spanish-speaking people in conversation, watch their body movements. You will notice that many of these are different from what you are accustomed to. Also watch the distance between people as they speak. Generally speaking, in Spanish-speaking cultures people tend to stand closer together when in conversation and frequently maintain some kind of body contact, such as laying a hand on someone's arm during conversation, when making a point. Embraces in public between men, either relatives or friends, are much more common than in American society, and a light kiss on one or both cheeks between women, even when they are not close friends, is normal. Americans, unused to such public displays of affection, may feel uncomfortable in such situations, whereas Hispanics may get the impression that Americans are cold and unfeeling.

As you learn Spanish, you don't necessarily have to use nonverbal language appropriate to Spanish culture, particularly if you feel uncomfortable with it. Spanish speakers will take into account the fact that you are foreign and will be pleased just to see that you are making the effort to learn their language. However, try to develop a sensitivity toward these aspects of Hispanic culture realizing all the time that learning Spanish is much more than translating ideas from English into Spanish.

Å Activity 6

With a partner make a list of as many kinds of gestures as possible that Americans use. Describe each one, and explain when each gesture might be appropriate or inappropriate and why. Also say whether you think the gestures would be used most or exclusively by adults, children, males, females, or by anyone.

Early on in your Spanish studies you will learn, or will have learned, about the two forms of address, **tú** and **usted.** Although this distinction may seem strange to you, it is a feature of many European languages: *tu* and *vous* in French, *du* and *Sie* in German, for instance. There are still some rural areas in England where the Old English form *thou,* the equivalent of **tú,** is used for family members; it is also used by the Amish in this country. Pay special attention to how **tú** and **usted** are used. Usage will depend largely on the Spanish-speaking area you are in.

Generally speaking, **tú** is used for relatives and close friends, and nowadays in most Spanish-speaking environments it is the normal form of address among young people even when they don't know one another. It is used by older people when talking to children, but children may address the older person as **usted,** particularly if he/she is not a relative. There still are families where children address their parents and, particularly, their grandparents, as **usted,** although the elders address the younger people as **tú.** In many Spanish-speaking areas it is customary to address professors and teachers as **usted** and it would be considered disrespectful to address them otherwise. American classrooms tend to be much more relaxed and informal than Spanish ones, so your teacher may allow you to address him/her as **tú.** Don't assume, however, that this is universal practice, and when in doubt address someone as **usted.** If that person wants to allow more familiarity he/she will soon suggest, **¿Por qué no nos tuteamos?** (*Why don't we treat each other as* **tú?**).

The existence of these two forms of address allows for many more nuances in personal relationships than in English with its one form *you.* If someone addresses you as **tú,** for example, and you reply using **usted,** you are sending a clear signal that you want to maintain a distance and don't consider that person as part of your inner circle of friends or even your equal. He/She will no doubt take the hint and then continue the conversation using **usted**, but your choice of familiarity may be considered offensive. Normally you should address someone in a socially inferior position as **usted**; treating them as **tú** would be offensive and awkward, for considering your respective social positions, he/she would be unable to address you as **tú**. There are households, though, where the lady of the house addresses her housekeepers as **tú**, and they reply to her as **usted**, without any offense meant or taken. In these cases, daily contact in the home has led to what might appear as an anomalous linguistic situation.

The plural of **tú** is **vosotros** in Spain, but in most of the Spanish-speaking world it is **ustedes**. Whether **ustedes** (the plural of **usted**) is meant to be formal or familiar (the plural of **tú**) will always be clear to you from the context. In some Spanish-speaking areas, notably the Río de la Plata region of Argentina and Uruguay, the form **vos** is used instead of **tú**. The plural of **vos** is **ustedes**. Because English has lost this distinction between a polite and familiar form of address, it is sometimes difficult for the English-speaking student of Spanish to be fully aware of the social significance of this distinction in Spanish. The choice of **tú** or **usted** will always give a particular slant to your conversation and say something about the relationship you have, or think you have, with the person to whom you are talking. And although Spanish speakers tend to make allowances if an English speaker of Spanish does not use the right verb tenses, they may not be so tolerant when it comes to the incorrect use of forms of address: this is one cultural aspect of which you must be aware.

By now, you are beginning to realize the complexity involved with learning another language and the emotional aspects attached to it. Studying Spanish is not merely an intellectual exercise, a matter of mastering your verb tenses and acquiring sufficient vocabulary. It should also open a window for you on a different world and help you to start looking at life through the eyes of another. You do need to bear in mind, however, that the similarities are often greater than the differences. Not everything in Spanish culture is exotic, strange, weird, or exciting. Young people in the Spanish-speaking world look mostly like young Americans: they wear similar clothes and often the same brand names, the kind of music they listen to may be the same or very similar, as well as the way they spend their leisure time. People may eat different kinds of food (although American fast-food chains seem to have reached practically everywhere on the planet by now) and at different hours, but basically they have a great deal in common.

Most of all you need to become aware of the immense cultural differences among the Spanish-speaking countries and even within countries themselves. Europeans tend to be impressed by the homogeneity of the United States—you can travel throughout the country and despite its varied geographical and climactic features, you will find the same or similar fast-food restaurants, the same hotels, and more or less the same life-style. This can be reassuring or downright boring, depending on how you look at it. On the other hand, just within Spain you will find four official languages, of which Castilian, the kind of Spanish you are learning, is but one, and an immense variety of local customs, cuisines, folklore, and so on. By learning Spanish, then, you are giving yourself the opportunity to widen your horizons in a way you may not have thought possible. By taking full advantage of this you will almost certainly start to look at your own culture in a very different light.

Å Activity 7

A. Try to find the Spanish terms for these American concepts. If you think the dictionary does not define them clearly, perhaps because of their cultural significance, how would you explain them to a Spanish speaker?

baseball   cookout   Thanksgiving   grits   fried chicken

B. With a partner, draw up a list of five words you consider particularly significant in English because of their cultural relevance and say how you would explain them to a speaker of Spanish.

C. Say whether you would use **Ud.**, **Uds.**, **tú**, or **vosotros** to address the following people:

1. Your neighbor's little girl.
2. Ana and Marcos, from Venezuela, who go to the same sociology class as you.
3. The doctor who has treated you for several years.
4. The cashier at your local grocery store.
5. Antonio and Manuela Díaz, a middle-aged couple from Spain, to whom you have just been introduced.

➤ NUTS AND BOLTS   *Masculine and feminine nouns*

We have said that the majority of masculine nouns in Spanish end in **-o** and the feminine ones in **-a**. However, this is not true for all nouns. Below are some guidelines that will help you determine the gender of nouns. Keep in mind that there are many exceptions and that not all endings are included.

-a	la mesa, la bota	*table, boot*
-triz	la cicatriz, la actriz	*scar, actress*
-dad	la ciudad, la bondad	*city, goodness*
-ez	la estupidez, la delgadez	*stupidity, thinness*
-ión, -ción	la opinión, la lección	*opinion, lesson*
-sión, -zón	la inversión, la razón	*investment, reason*
-tud	la juventud, la longitud	*youth, length*
-ie(s)	la serie, la caries	*series, tooth decay*
-tumbre	la costumbre	*habit*
-eza	la cerveza, la realeza	*beer, royalty*

MASCULINE ENDINGS

-o*	el vaso, el sombrero	*glass, hat*
-ete	el banquete, el sorbete	*banquet, sorbet*
-or	el tambor, el tractor	*drum, tractor*
-ón	el malecón, el sillón	*jetty, armchair*
-il	el candil, el atril	*oil lamp, lectern*
-el	el pincel, el redondel	*paintbrush, circle*
-s	el compás, el arnés	*compass, harness*
-ín	el motín, el jardín	*mutiny, garden*
-aje	el sabotaje, el brebaje	*sabotage, (unpleasant) drink or medicine*

*Exceptions include **la mano** (*hand*) and **la dínamo** (*dynamo*). There are other words that end in -o and which are feminine, but these are abbreviations of longer words: **la foto** (**la fotografía**, *photo*), **la moto** (**la motocicleta**, *motorbike*).

As you study the vocabulary that comes up in your text, classify it (on cards or in a vocabulary notebook) according to gender and try writing the ending in a different color from the rest of the word. Gradually you will become familiar with these endings and will find it easy to recognize and to remember whether they are masculine or feminine words. The following may also help you to remember the gender of certain groups of words:

• Rivers are generally masculine, even if the word ends in -a.
  el Sena, el Támesis, el Tajo, el Amazonas, el Misisipi
  the Seine, the Thames, the Tagus, the Amazon, the Mississippi

• Cities may be masculine or feminine. Generally if they end in -a they are feminine, and if they end in -o or in a consonant they are usually masculine.

| Londres es hermoso en verano. | London is beautiful in the summer. |
| Sevilla es espléndida en Semana Santa. | Seville is splendid during Holy Week. |

- Seas and oceans are usually masculine.

| el Atlántico, el Pacífico, el Mediterráneo | the Atlantic, the Pacific, the Mediterranean |

- Islands are feminine.

| las Bahamas, las Bermudas, las Canarias | the Bahamas, the Bermudas, the Canary Islands |

- Colors: Several colors that end in **-a** are masculine.

| el lila, el naranja, el rosa | lilac, orange, pink |

- Words ending in **-ma**.

Many words of Greek origin in Spanish are masculine although they end in **-a**.

| el tema, el drama, el poema | subject, drama, poem |

- Trees and fruit: Often the name of a tree ends in **-o** and is masculine, whereas fruit of that tree ends in **-a** and is feminine.

el manzano, la manzana	apple tree, apple
el naranjo, la naranja	orange tree, orange
el ciruelo, la ciruela	plum tree, plum
el cerezo, la cereza	cherry tree, cherry

- Days of the week and months of the year are masculine.

El jueves vamos a comer fuera.	On Thursday we're going to eat out.
un sábado soleado	a sunny Saturday
un noviembre muy frío	a very cold November

- The cardinal points are masculine.

| el norte, el sur, el este, el oeste | north, south, east, west |

Å Activity 8 ··

A. Look at the endings of the following words and decide whether they are masculine or feminine. Then put **el** or **la** in front of each one. Look up the meaning of the words you don't know in your dictionary.

1. _____ nación	6. _____ biblioteca
2. _____ papel	7. _____ interés
3. _____ poema	8. _____ dolor
4. _____ maldad	9. _____ fortaleza
5. _____ calvicie	10. _____ pasión

B. What gender would the following have if you needed to talk about them in Spanish?

the Potomac	the North Sea
Chicago	the Balearic Islands
Washington	

The Definite Articles

At the end of Chapter 1 we said that every time you come across a new word that you need to incorporate into your active vocabulary, you should write it down with its definite article, **la** or **el**, so that you remember the gender. The definite article in Spanish, as in English, always precedes the word it accompanies: **la manzana,** *the apple.* Unlike English, however, the Spanish definite article not only has a masculine and feminine form, depending on the gender of the noun, but singular and plural forms.

| el hombre, los hombres | *the man, the men* |
| la casa, las casas | *the house, the houses* |

The definite article has to agree both in gender (masculine or feminine) and number (singular or plural) with the noun it modifies. Practice writing both the singular and plural forms of the nouns you have met, together with the singular and plural of the definite article. The plural of nouns in Spanish is usually formed by adding **-s** to nouns that end in a vowel, and **-es** to those that end in a consonant.

la chica	las chicas	*girl, girls*
la mujer	las mujeres	*woman, women*
el jardín	los jardines	*garden, gardens*

This contrasts with English where the plural is often formed by adding *-s* to words that end both with vowel and consonant sounds: *book, books; window, windows,* and *-es* to those that end in *-s: bus, buses.* There are many words in English that have totally different forms in singular and plural, such as *mouse, mice; woman, women.*

The definite article defines or specifies the noun it refers to. If we say *Open the window,* we are referring to a particular window (or perhaps to the only one in the room), or if your instructor tells you to *Study the lesson,* you know exactly to which lesson he/she is referring. Although the definite article has this basic meaning in both languages, the use of the article varies in both languages and you will find that it is used much more in Spanish. You will need to study these differences as you come across them and as they are pointed out to you by your instructor. For the time being, you should try to assimilate the basic concept of agreement in gender and number which is so important in Spanish and will affect not only your use of the definite article, but other grammatical features as well.

The indefinite article

In English we have two forms of the indefinite article in the singular: *a,* used before singular nouns beginning with a consonant, *a man, a door,* and *an,* used before nouns beginning with a vowel, *an order, an orange.* These forms do not have the specifying force of the definite article. If we say, for example, *Open a window,* we mean any window that happens to be in the room, not a particular one. The plural form is *some: Buy me some apples.* In Spanish, the indefinite article has both singular and plural as well as masculine and feminine forms: **un perro, unos perros, una silla, unas sillas.**

Å *Activity 9* ....

1. Complete the following with the correct form of the definite article.

   a. _____ árboles   d. _____ estudiantes
   b. _____ manzanas   e. _____ plumas
   c. _____ mujeres

2. Complete the following with the correct form of the indefinite article.

   a. _____ libros   d. _____ hombre
   b. _____ peras   e. _____ pupitre
   c. _____ pizarras

➤ SUMMARY

In this chapter we thought about some of the cultural implications of learning Spanish. We examined the role of stereotypes and the way they can consciously or unconsciously affect the way we view people from other cultures. We have tried to put ourselves in the place of foreigners for whom American culture and society may be puzzling, strange, at times even offensive. We have examined prevalent attitudes, some positive and others negative, about Hispanics and thought a little about what that term "Hispanic" means. We have examined various interpretations of culture and seen how learning a language means far more than learning to write words in the correct order. Language and culture are intimately bound up, and we have seen some of the instances where this is true. In the *Nuts and bolts* section we continued our examination of gender in Spanish and took a look at definite and indefinite articles, as well as the concept of grammatical agreement in gender and number.

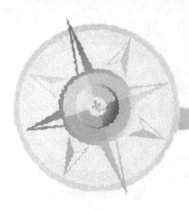

CHAPTER THREE

GRAMMAR, AND NONSENSE, AND LEARNING

Let schoolmasters puzzle their brain
With grammar, and nonsense, and learning,
Good liquor, I stoutly maintain,
Gives genius a better discerning.

> *Oliver Goldsmith,* She Stoops to Conquer, *Act I, Sc. 2*

La letra con sangre entra.
You have to suffer to learn.

> *Spanish proverb*

➤ BEFORE WE BEGIN

When people consider learning a foreign language, they almost inevitably think of mastering the grammar. This may provoke a number of reactions in them. Like Oliver Goldsmith, the idea of studying grammar may be so repugnant that they decide to leave learning a language if not to schoolmasters, at least to those who appear to have a "knack" for grammar rules. (Of course, they may or may not agree with Goldsmith's remark that "Good liquor... gives genius a better discerning.")

On the other hand, there are those who persevere, convinced that the study of grammar is an unpleasant medicine that is inevitable when studying a foreign language. And as the Spanish proverb suggests, they believe that one really has to suffer in order to learn. There are some people, though, who find grammar neither difficult nor boring; indeed, they actually enjoy learning it.

In this chapter, we will consider some past attitudes toward grammar. Then we will think about why grammar is still an important part of foreign language courses. We will try to define its role in your acquisition of Spanish and its place in your Spanish course. Most of all, we will try to demystify grammar and show that it need not be boring or frightening and, especially, that it is an aspect of learning Spanish that is within everyone's grasp.

> ## HOW DO WE FEEL ABOUT GRAMMAR?

Even if you have never studied a foreign language before, you have studied your own language, English, and almost certainly will have had formal instruction at some time or another in English grammar. You may also have attempted the study of a foreign language before, either Spanish or another, and found that you were unsuccessful. Possibly you attribute your lack of success to your inability to assimilate the countless grammar rules. Many students end up studying Spanish because various well-meaning people have advised them that "Spanish is easy," but once they come in contact with Spanish grammar, they discover that this is far from true. Before discussing the various approaches toward grammar and the role of grammar in language learning, it will be useful for you to air your feelings and possible anxieties regarding grammar. Take a few minutes to do the following activity. Be completely honest. In some cases, you may want to give more than one answer.

When you have finished, share and discuss your answers with your peers.

λ *Activity 1* ··

1. The word "grammar" suggests something:
   a. boring   b. difficult   c. exciting   d. interesting
2. The idea of studying Spanish grammar makes you:
   a. excited   b. very nervous   c. slightly anxious   d. indifferent
3. Studying grammar is good for you because:
   a. it helps discipline your mind.
   b. if you learn the grammar well enough, you can speak the language fluently.
   c. if you force yourself to study something that's boring and unpleasant, it's good for your spirit and mind.
   d. it will help you understand the underlying structure of the language and make progress in all language skills.
4. You think Spanish grammar:
   a. should be the main part of the lesson—after all, it's the most important part.
   b. should always be taught in English—we need to understand every word in order to understand the concepts.

c. Could be taught in Spanish as an integral part of the lesson, as long as there are enough examples to practice with and the language is of an appropriate difficulty.

d. Should not be taught at all—we should be able to infer the rules from the way the language is used.

5. Grammar A to Z! Underline the following concepts referring to English grammar that you could recognize in a sentence. Then place an asterisk by those that, without being given an example, you could explain to someone else and provide your own example for. Don't worry; you are not going to be asked to do this (although you might like to, just to find out whether you really could).

a. subject	i. reflexive pronoun	r. compound tense
b. direct object	j. preposition	s. simple past
c. indirect object	k. adverb	t. present perfect
d. possessive pronoun	l. adjective	u. past perfect
	m. definite article	v. future
e. subject pronoun	n. indefinite article	w. present progressive
f. object pronoun	o. demonstrative adjective	x. past progressive
g. direct object pronoun	p. demonstrative pronoun	y. modal auxiliary
h. indirect object pronoun	q. simple tense	z. conjunction

6. The last time you formally studied English grammar was in:
   a. college
   b. high school
   c. junior high
   d. elementary school
   e. you have never studied it

7. From the way you were taught grammar in the past (English grammar or that of a foreign language), you consider studying grammar as:
   a. an end in itself
   b. a means to an end, but you're not sure what end
   c. something totally irrelevant if you only want to speak the language
   d. a waste of time
   e. other (state your own impression)

8. Write a few lines recounting your past experience with grammar lessons, either in English or a foreign language, and explaining how you feel about approaching Spanish grammar.

_____

_____

_____

_____

_____

> WHY STUDY GRAMMAR?

Although methods of teaching a foreign language have changed radically over the years, a few concepts still linger that may influence our attitude toward studying grammar and our view of the role of grammar in acquiring a language. For centuries, language teachers have argued about the pros and cons of *deductive* versus *inductive* methods.

One school of thought has affirmed that students should not be given explanations about grammar, but should be left to figure out the rules for themselves by observing the ways in which the language works. Consequently, it is argued, they will reach a truer understanding of the grammar than if they were merely receiving grammar information. There is much to be said about this theory, which is *inductive;* unfortunately, if left entirely to themselves not all students would arrive at the right conclusions. In addition, class time is always limited so, although they might elaborate their own version of the grammar rules eventually, the course may be over by then. However, it is a valuable experience for students to reflect on language structures and to try to formulate some of the rules for themselves. Many teachers make some provision for this kind of activity in their course.

Those in favor of deductive methods argue that in order to master a language, grammar rules that account for usage should be explained explicitly. Students must then learn them in order to produce grammatically correct utterances. Deductive methods became popular in the eighteenth century, lasted through most of the nineteenth century, and survived into the twentieth. Here is an example from an early twentieth century text which follows a deductive method for teaching English to foreigners.

Lesson 1

The father, the mother, Charles, Louisa, Mary, Julia, Jane, Henry and Paul. This is the father. Is this Mary? No, this is the mother. Is this Julia? Yes, this is Julia. Is this Henry? No, this is not Henry; this is Paul.

Rule 1. "The" is the *definite article* for all three genders.

Rule 2. *Proper nouns* begin with a capital letter.

(Sophie Hamburger, *English Lessons after S. Alge's Method,* 13th ed., St. Gall: Fehr, 1919, p. 1)

Today both inductive and deductive attitudes toward grammar coexist, usually in modified forms. Your text and your instructor will probably lean more toward deductive methods. That is, you will not be expected to reason why different elements in Spanish grammar are as they are. Instead, you will be given a concise explanation, either in English or in Spanish, and will then practice these grammatical features, first through purely mechanical exercises—to make sure you know how to conjugate verbs, can make nouns and adjectives agree, etc.—to more creative, open-ended ones, which allow you to express yourself in the language, using both the concepts you have learned and your imagination.

There may be times, though, when you practice certain structures in class without being given any formal grammar rules. Then your instructor helps you arrive at conclusions about that structure. Both kinds of approaches can be useful for you and help you understand more fully how Spanish works. Before continuing, try the following activity. When you have completed it, discuss your answers with a friend.

Å *Activity 2*

1. Think of an example where you learned something inductively, that is, you worked out the rules for yourself just from experience and analysis (for example, how to play a certain game, figuring out, without a manual, the controls on a VCR, a microwave, etc.). How long did it take you to learn how to do this? Do you think you would have benefited by being given some explanation (for instance, an instruction manual)? Do you think that finding out by yourself how to do this helped you remember better than if someone had given you instructions? Was any prior experience with something similar useful?

2. Think of an example where you have learned something deductively, that is, you were given a set of rules (for example, how to play chess, poker,

etc., to interpret traffic signs and the highway code, etc.). Do you think you would have learned just as quickly if you had been left to your own devices? What advantages or disadvantages do you see in the way you were taught? For instance, if instead of taking a driver's education course and reading a manual you had been left to find out from experience and inference everything you know about the highway code, what might the results have been?

3. Read the following sentences and explain the grammar rule behind the italicized structures as clearly and briefly as you can. Can you remember ever having been *explicitly* taught these rules?

   a. When rabies *attacked* my Uncle Daniel,
      And he *had* fits of barking like a spaniel,
      The B.B.C. *relayed* him (from all stations)
      At Children's Hour in "Farmyard imitations."

(Harry Graham, "London Calling," in *More Ruthless Rhymes*).

   b. The aqueduct *was built by* the Romans. It *was constructed* out of stone.

Although the difference between inductive and deductive ways of learning grammar can have a considerable influence on how you actually learn and how successful you are at it, even more important is the question, why learn grammar in the first place? Grammar explanations and grammatical exercises still form a substantial part of most foreign language classes. If your goal is to learn how to speak Spanish, you may feel that this emphasis on grammar is unnecessary, and that grammar is necessary only for writing in the language. This is not true, however. We all know people who have great difficulty in communicating what they want to say because they lack a foundation in grammar. The "You Jane, I Tarzan" approach will not get you very far if the airline has lost your suitcase and you need to explain what it looks like, where it can be forwarded, and why you are so angry; or you want to invite someone out to a movie, tell them what time you are picking them up, and ask them where they would like to go to dinner afterwards. When we communicate orally, our main goal is to get our message across. We want to avoid ambiguity and misunderstandings. Usually we also want to avoid offending people and consequently need grammar in order to do all this. Consider the following:

You are walking toward your home one evening when a foreign neighbor of yours, in a great state of agitation, rushes up to you and says: "Hurry, father die. Call ambulance."

You may make any of the following hypotheses:

1. He is talking about your father.
2. He is talking about his father.
3. He is talking about someone else's father.
4. The father is dying.
5. The father has already died.
6. The neighbor has called an ambulance.
7. The neighbor wants you to call an ambulance.
8. Someone else has called an ambulance.

If, on the other hand, the neighbor says "Hurry, your father is dying. I have already called an ambulance," then there is no ambiguity.

The insertion of a possessive adjective (*your*), a present progressive tense (*is dying*), a subject pronoun (*I*), a present perfect (*have called*), and an adverb (*already*) has made all the difference. These are strictly grammatical elements yet they are essential for unambiguous oral communication. They are, of course, also necessary in written communication. It is true that in oral communication we also use other clues such as intonation and body language to help us interpret messages, but these alone are usually insufficient.

Ⲁ *Activity 3* ....

With a partner, come up with as many hypotheses as you can, along the lines of the preceding example, for the following statements. Then rewrite each statement, adding whatever grammatical elements are necessary to make it fit one of your hypotheses. Specify the grammatical features you have added (future tense, possessive adjective, subject pronoun, etc.).

1. Someone you don't know comes up to you when you are shopping in the mall and says: "Just steal wallet."
2. You get home one evening and find a message from your roommate: "Put dinner in oven."
3. Someone tells you: "Philip bumped into Mary while shopping."
4. A description of a police chase: "With the stolen car traveling at fifty miles an hour, the police again gave chase. Warning shots were fired and, after traveling several miles at high speed, a bullet pierced the car's rear tire."
5. Find a phrase in a newspaper article (or one that you have heard on television) that is ambiguous. What do you need to do grammatically to remove the ambiguity?

The goals of your Spanish course are, in all probability, communicative. That is, your instructor hopes that by the end of the course you will be able to understand a certain amount of spoken Spanish, express yourself orally in the language (however imperfectly), write messages and, finally, express some of your thoughts and feelings. It is hoped that you will also have some understanding of the culture and the way in which language works within that culture. In order to do all this, you will need a foundation in grammar.

Grammar, then, is a means to an end: it will help you to function more efficiently in the language, to get your message across with the least amount of ambiguity, and to understand both the content and register of the messages you hear (whether they are formal or informal). Grammar should never be an end in itself. Being able to reel off or write out with ease Spanish verb conjugations, or recite the rules for the use of the preterite and imperfect, for instance, may be a testimony to the time you have spent studying, to your perseverance, and to the capacity of your memory, but unfortunately it is no guarantee that you "know" Spanish.

> ## GETTING A FOOTHOLD ON SPANISH

Everything you learn about Spanish grammar has to be fully assimilated for it to be of any real use to you. You will go through several phases in your language learning. You will be introduced to new grammatical structures through dialogues and texts (probably both written and on tape or video). You may or may not be given a short grammatical explanation of the structure in class, depending on your instructor's methodology. You may be expected to read the explanation for yourself as part of your homework. You will no doubt practice new grammatical features in class through various kinds of exercises, some individual and some in groups or pairs.

As you progress you may discover that you understand your instructor's explanations about grammar and can follow them in your text. You know how to form a tense, for example, and are acquainted with the rules that tell you when you are supposed to use it. However, when it comes to practicing, you find that you make many mistakes and cannot understand why.

It is one thing to learn *about* a language and something quite different to be able to use it *actively* yourself. When you were learning how to drive, you probably understood immediately the theory behind parallel parking, but how long did it take you to do it and get it right? Understanding the concepts is an important stage, but it is only the beginning. You have to assimilate them gradually and make them your own in some way. This is why we emphasize many times throughout this book the importance of contextualizing your learning to make it meaningful *to you*. You cannot learn Spanish only in the abstract and expect to be able to function practically with that knowledge. Remember that learning a language is learning how to *use* that language.

Verb tenses, pronoun forms, vocabulary, and the like will mean nothing to you unless you can somehow relate them to your world. For this reason it is valuable to use the new grammatical features you are studying in sentences that are pertinent to you. For instance, if you learn the possessive adjectives **mi/mis, su/sus,** it will help you remember them better if you devise a sentence such as:

Mi hermano estudia en Chicago. Su amigo se llama Steve.

What was an abstract grammatical concept (possessive adjectives) has become something familiar. You have claimed it for yourself and because the sentences say something about *your* family, you are more likely to remember them than sentences from your textbook, which may have the same grammatical features but mean absolutely nothing to you. To be successful at learning Spanish, or any other foreign language, you have to constantly find ways to make that language your own.

You need to be aggressive in this sense: every time a new grammatical point is introduced and you understand it intellectually, you need to find ways of assimilating it emotionally. Look at the sample sentences in your text or given by your instructor and think, "How can I form a similar sentence which incorporates elements from my own life and is meaningful?" If you constantly do this, you will soon find that Spanish stops being a "foreign" language for you and instead becomes your own—a new way to communicate *your* thoughts and *your* interests.

À Activity 4

Look at the following sentences in English. Each features a particular grammar point. Write two similar sentences for each that have some reference to your world. The grammatical structure referred to is in italics. You will, of course, use your own vocabulary.

1. Passive voice. The country *was conquered by* the Romans.
2. Conditional. If it rains on Saturday, we *won't be* able to play croquet.
3. Conditional. Harold *would be* more attractive if he had a sense of humor.
4. Modal auxiliary. I really *must buy* some crumpets and strawberry jam for tea.
5. Negative command. My mother always used to say, *"Don't speak* with your mouth full."

If, instead of receiving formal instruction in Spanish, you were abandoned on your own in some remote town in a Spanish-speaking country where nobody spoke English, eventually you would learn how to speak the language. After a period in which you would be unable to understand or speak anything, you would start noticing and picking out certain things when people spoke to you, and gradually the amount of spoken language that you understood would increase. Eventually you would also learn how to speak, starting with a very rudimentary form of communication, but slowly bringing your speech into line with the standard language.

This slow acquisition would be helped by people asking you to rephrase your utterances when they didn't understand you or correcting your Spanish when you said something blatantly ungrammatical or inappropriate. You yourself would start correcting your own output based on hypotheses you would be forming from the constant input. If in addition to hearing the spoken language, you were exposed to large quantities of reading material, not only would your reading skills in that language become refined, but you would find that your writing skills, your vocabulary, and even your comprehension of the grammatical structures also would gradually improve.

In the classroom situation, unless you are living in the target-language culture, you do not have the benefit of being surrounded by people who speak that language all the time, but you do have the advantage of formal learning which helps you to cut some corners. Your speech and writing will also be far from "grammatical" to start with, and you can expect to study Spanish for many years before you are able to bring it in line with the language of a native speaker. It may be that you will never reach that point, but it doesn't matter. In the meantime, you will have learned enough to communicate for most purposes. Bear in mind that your instructor does not expect perfect output from you, either in spoken or written Spanish. Throughout your formal study of the language, there will be some concepts that you master thoroughly at a fairly early stage, but many that you only partially master. This is typical of the learning process.

You should expect to be exposed in your Spanish class to a level of oral and written Spanish that is slightly beyond your capability. This can be intimidating at first. You want to understand every single word that is being said to you and to know exactly what every written word means. However, this is neither necessary nor advisable. Current research shows that in order for you to advance linguistically, you need to be in contact with language that is slightly more advanced than your present level. If your instructor and your text only used language that was just at your level, you would not make any progress.

Do not worry, then, if you are exposed to some unfamiliar grammatical structures and vocabulary. You will understand enough in order to get the gist of things, and this experience with an unknown language will be very beneficial to your acquisition of Spanish. You need to accept ambiguity and uncertainty as part of the language-learning process and, as you advance in Spanish, your toleration of these factors will increase.

Å *Activity 5* ···

Answer the following questions. If necessary, look back over this chapter. Then discuss your answers with a classmate or in a small group.

1. If your instructor wanted to use an inductive approach to teaching gender and number agreement of nouns and adjectives in Spanish, how do you think this would be done? _____

   _____

2. You are an instructor who wants to teach the present tense conjugation of regular Spanish **-ar, -er,** and **-ir** verbs. How would you do this? _____

   _____

3. From what my instructor has done so far and the class textbook we are using, I think his/her approach is mainly _____

   _____

   This is substantiated by:
   a. _____
   b. _____

4. I now think that grammar is an important part of my Spanish course because _____

   _____

   _____

   _____

5. I think I will be able to cope with studying Spanish grammar if I
   a. _____
   b. _____
   c. _____

6. My instructor and the class textbook will be using Spanish that is rather more difficult than I can manage because _____

   _____

7. Now when I think of studying Spanish grammar I expect it to be
   a. boring   d. difficult   f. fun
   b. interesting   e. frightening   g. unpleasant
   c. a challenge

(You may check more than one option. It is all right to check *a, e,* and *g,* if that's what you feel. Your instructor will do his or her best to get you to change your mind before the end of the course).

➤ NUTS AND BOLTS   *Recognizing parts of speech*

In Activity 1, number 5, you were asked whether you could recognize certain grammatical concepts in English. In the next chapter we will be looking in more detail at some of these concepts in relation to both Spanish and English. In preparation, read the following passage and see if you can locate the parts of speech listed in the box below. Write each part in the appropriate box. In some cases, there will be several examples. Check your answers first with a partner and then with your instructor.

> "I am old. I cannot go anywhere else, even if I wanted."
> Even if Mtazi Mtsweni wanted, she could not go anywhere else even if she were young. She had been living for three years in Tweefontein E— hundreds of families scraped close together like a landfill of people on a shallow dusty rise nearly barren of trees. Mostly the families had made their homes of packing crates and corrugated sheet metal. They lacked plumbing, water, and electricity.... She wanted to go to a son in Witbank. The company had bought him a house, but the authorities would not let her move to Witbank.

> (*National Geographic,* vol. 169, no.2, February 1986, p. 262)

Subject (noun)	Direct object (noun)	Indirect object (noun)	Subject pronoun	Conjugated verb

➤ SUMMARY

In this chapter we explored some of the feelings you may have toward studying grammar, which may or may not be based on previous experience, either with English or with a foreign language. We have recognized that while grammar is almost certainly a feature of the Spanish course you are taking, it is not to be considered an end in itself. Grammar is necessary for communication, and without it both written and spoken messages may risk being ambiguous—and the result can be confusion. Grammar helps us be more precise.

We also saw how attitudes have changed over the centuries toward how grammar should be taught. Whereas some people may advocate an inductive method of studying, that is, leaving the student to work out the underlying grammar rules from examples and experience, others are in favor of a deductive approach, or stating the rules and showing how they are applied. We have seen advantages and disadvantages in both attitudes. Most importantly, we considered some of the emotional aspects of learning a foreign language and discussed the necessity of claiming that language for yourself by using every new grammar structure in sentences that are relevant to you.

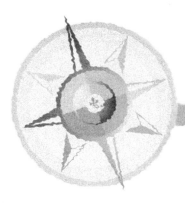

CHAPTER FOUR

HOMO GRAMMATICUS

> *(It) is grammar that makes language so essentially a human characteristic. For*
> *though other creatures can make meaningful sounds, the link between sound and*
> *meaning is for them of a far more primitive kind than it is for man, and the link*
> *for man is grammar. Man is not merely homo loquens; he is homo grammaticus.*
>
> Frank Palmer, Grammar

➤ BEFORE WE BEGIN

In the previous chapter we argued that grammar is essential when learning another language if we are aiming at meaningful communication.
However, one thing that makes many people nervous about learning a foreign language is that whenever you open a foreign language textbook it
seems to be filled with lots of grammar terms. You may be familiar with
these terms, but may not fully understand them all, even in English. It is also
possible that you have had very little or even no formal English grammar, or
you studied it so long ago that you have forgotten what *conditionals, passive
voice, non-finites,* and the like really mean.

It can be worrying to think that suddenly you are going to be asked to
recognize or, even worse, apply these terms to a language that you don't
even know! If grammar makes you nervous, remember what we said in the
previous chapter: learning a language is learning how to *use* it, not just talk
about it. Yet a certain amount of grammar terminology is inevitable when
learning a language. We have already discussed some very important terms:
grammatical gender, and *definite* and *indefinite articles.*

In this chapter, we will examine some other basic concepts to help you
understand how sentences work both in English and Spanish. Gradually, as
you see how all these elements work together, you will gain an insight into
the whole picture. Sometimes people are so intent on memorizing certain
forms or learning the uses of sentence parts, that they forget to stand back
and see how these fit together like a jigsaw puzzle.

> THE VERB

The verb is probably the most important part of a sentence. It may express:

1. an *action:* John *swims.* Sheila *is playing* tennis. Bob *walked* home.
2. a *state* or *process:* Mark *feels* ill. Mr. McDonald *died.* The baby *was born* yesterday. Terry *has grown* a lot lately. Kathy *has* the flu. The car *is* broken.
3. an *emotion* or *mental process:* I *think* you're wrong. She *wonders* if he'll come. They *want* to buy it.

Let us consider some of the verb forms in these sentences. The verb forms *swims, walked, feels, died, wonders* are conjugated; that is, their forms are different according to the subject that accompanies them.

To buy is an infinitive. This form is invariable and never changes.

Å Activity 1 ··

Read through the following text and write all *conjugated verbs* and all *infinitives* on the appropriate line. Compare your answers with that of a partner.

> The largest bird in North America, with a spectacular wingspread often exceeding nine feet, the California condor continues to decline rapidly and faces a very uncertain future. In the past year, the known wild population drastically decreased from 16 to 9. Scientists are continuing intensive research to determine the exact causes of mortality, and to learn more about the birds' requirements for survival.
>
> Nothing could bring back the California condor should it vanish completely.
>
> (Adapted from a Canon advertisement)

Conjugated verbs: _____

Infinitives: _____

One chapter in this book is devoted entirely to verbs because the Spanish verbal system is more complex than the English one. Here, however, we will look at the kinds of infinitives you will find in Spanish and at the conjugation of the present tense.

In Spanish, verbs are classified into three conjugations, depending on the ending of the infinitive.

ENDING

-ar	amar, trabajar, comprar
-er	comer, vender, coser
-ir	vivir, escribir, morir

Activity 2

Scan the following passage in Spanish and find all the infinitives. Then list them according to whether they belong to the **-ar, -er,** or **-ir** group. Notice that you do not have to understand the text in order to do this. However, by the end you will have an idea of the gist because there are a number of cognates (**plan, familiares, internacionales,** etc.), and you can see that this is an ad for MCI which you may have read in English, as it is mailed in English and Spanish to their subscribers.

Usted se subscribió a El Plan 24 Horas de Familiares Alrededor del Mundo porque quería ahorrar en todas sus llamadas internacionales. ¡Pues MCI quiere que ahorre aún más! Ahora podrá recibir descuentos en todas sus llamadas a los TRES números internacionales que seleccione.... Recuerde llamar a su número especial durante el Horario Preferido de El Plan 24 Horas de Familiares Alrededor del Mundo para poder recibir los máximos descuentos.

Vea cómo podrá ahorrar aún más con El Plan 24 Horas de Familiares Alrededor del Mundo.

(MCI)

| **-ar** verbs | **-er** verbs | **-ir** verbs |

Regular verbs in Spanish will always conform to a certain pattern, depending on the ending of the infinitive. Once you have learned the pattern you will be able to conjugate any regular verb in the present tense.

In English the verb pattern for the present tense is always the same in regular verbs and is simplicity itself. All forms are identical except for the third person singular which adds -s.

Let us look at a regular verb like *to walk*:

	SINGULAR	PLURAL
1st person	I walk	we walk
2nd person	you walk	you walk
3rd person	he/she/it walks	they walk

In Spanish there are six different forms for each verb, and these will vary depending on whether they are **-ar**, **-er**, or **-ir** verbs. This is why you may find mastering Spanish verbs frustrating and time-consuming. You will find the conjugations for the present tense of regular **-ar**, **-er**, and **-ir** verbs in your textbook. As you will see, **-ir** and **-er** verbs have a lot in common. Of the six verb forms, four are identical (**yo, tú, él, ellos**) so this should make them easier to learn.

	COMER	VIVIR
yo	como	vivo
tú	comes	vives
él/ella/Ud.	come	vive
ellos/ellas/Uds.	comen	viven

The **i** that appears in the infinitive of the **-ir** verbs also appears in the **nosotros** and **vosotros** forms.

	VIVIR	MORIR
nosotros	vivimos	morimos
vosotros	vivís	morís

In the case of **-er** verbs, the **e** that appears in the infinitive also appears in the **nosotros** and **vosotros** forms.

	COMER	BEBER
nosotros	comemos	bebemos
vosotros	coméis	bebéis

The dominant vowel of **-ar** verbs is **a**. It appears in all forms except that of the first-person singular. Look at **tomar:**

yo tomo	nosotros/nosotras tomamos
tú tomas	vosotros/vosotras tomáis
él/ella/Ud. toma	ellos/ellas/Uds. toman

Å Activity 3

Look at the following verb forms and decide whether to place them in the **-ar, -er,** or **-ir** boxes. In some cases, you may not know, unless you are acquainted with the infinitive. Why not?

1. vosotros invitáis (you invite)
2. tú compartes (you share)
3. ellos disfrutan (they enjoy)
4. nosotros asistimos (we attend)
5. yo discuto (I argue)
6. vosotros coséis (you sew)

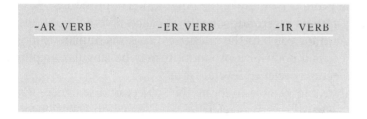

-AR VERB	-ER VERB	-IR VERB

Say the verb endings aloud several times, tapping your foot or your fingers on the desk as you say them so that you get a good rhythm. It should only take you five minutes to memorize the endings; then you need to practice conjugating different regular verbs to ensure that you know how the endings attach to the stem. It is worth spending time on your verbs. If they give you any trouble, it's not because they are particularly difficult but because they are different from English, and students of Spanish generally don't devote enough time to them.

Always learn your verbs as they appear in your text. Don't wait until you have a long list of them. Learn each verb tense thoroughly as it comes up. This will help you learn others. Learn the irregular verbs one-by-one as they are dealt with in your text. You can try writing them out in a verb section of your loose-leaf folder, writing the endings in a different color from the stem to help you remember. Make sure you always know to whom each part of the verb refers and what the verb means.

➤ THE SUBJECT

Look at the following passage:

> After months of delays, Channel Tunnel operators Monday *began* showing off "Le Shuttle"—the spartan boxcars that *will haul* vehicles underwater between France and England....
>
> The double-decker boxcars that *hold* eight average-size automobiles *offer* their passengers little in the way of amenities—just overhead lighting and a toilet. The passengers *can sit* in their vehicles, *walk* to the toilet or *mingle* with other passengers....
>
> "It's a fast, efficient, fun way of crossing the channel," Eurotunnel spokesman John Noulton *said*.... "At this stage of the game, there shouldn't be delays," *said* Tom Smith, from London.
>
> (*Indiana Daily Student,* October 4, 1994)

If we ask "what" or "who" of the italicized verbs, we will locate the subject, which may be a noun or a pronoun. It may come before or after the verb, although in English it usually comes before. If the subject is a pronoun, it may be a personal pronoun, or any of the other kinds of pronouns.

The subject may also be a gerund, sometimes called a verbal noun (as in "*Eating* spinach is good for you") or the infinitive: "*To err* is human, *to forgive* divine." If the subject is a noun or a pronoun, it may be singular or plural. Sometimes one subject may refer to several verbs.

It is important always to be able to locate the subject of a sentence. If you don't know who or what the verb is referring to, your comprehension of an oral or written text is likely to be very poor. One thing that you will notice is that in English the verb must always agree in number with the subject. This means that if the subject is singular, the verb is singular; if it is plural, the verb is plural. In English this often goes unnoticed because, as we discussed in the previous section, the English regular verb has only one different form in the present tense, that of the third person singular: *I/you* (sing.)/*we/you* (pl.)/*they say; he/she says*. In the past tense all forms are the same:

I/you/we
The Channel Tunnel operators }   said
John Noulton

Consequently, even though we know that the verb and subject must agree, in English we frequently don't have to worry about whether the subject is singular or plural, so we tend not be aware of this issue. In Spanish, you must *always* know whether the subject is singular or plural because, as we have seen, the parts of the verb are different.

À Activity 4 ··

Read the following passage and underline the subject for each of the italicized verbs. Decide whether the subject is a noun or a pronoun and, if possible, specify what kind of pronoun it is. Check your answers with a partner.

> Warning: Madrid *contains* a potentially addictive form of night life. Occasional visitors *can develop* a sudden reluctance to go to bed early. Much of the local population *shows* symptoms of advanced insomnia. Those young at heart—and with a body willing to follow—*are* especially vulnerable....
>
> The cultural calendar *is* crowded with concerts and plays. Small art galleries *are flourishing*. After midnight, the choice *is* between dancing rock, salsa or sevillanas and listening to jazz, flamenco or even poetry.
>
> ... The Teatro de la Zarzuela *has* a busy program of concerts, ballet, opera and even occasional zarzuelas, the traditional Spanish operetta....
>
> Eating *is* of course a Spanish pastime for all seasons.... The main problem about eating in Madrid *is* deciding where to go.
>
> (*The New York Times*, October 22, 1989)

➤ SUBJECT PRONOUNS

In both English and Spanish pronouns are used to substitute for nouns to avoid repetition.

Susan went to visit her grandmother. Susan took *her* some flowers.

Taking it further, the subject Susan (proper noun) could also be replaced by a pronoun.

Susan went to visit her grandmother. *She* took her some flowers.

Subject pronouns, as the name suggests, function as the subject of a sentence. In the first sentence above, *Susan* is the subject, and in the second sentence it is *she*.

The same substitution occurs in Spanish.

Susana fue a visitar a su abuela. **(Ella)** le llevó unas flores.

You will find the forms of the Spanish subject pronouns in your text. What you need to remember is that subject pronouns are used very much less in Spanish than in English. Most of the time they are not necessary because we know from the form of the verb to whom we are referring. You should be particularly careful about not overusing the **yo** form; it can sound very egotistical and too emphatic to the Spanish ear:

Yo asisto a la universidad y yo estudio ciencias políticas. Yo quiero trabajar en política. (*I attend the university and I study political science. I want to work in politics.*)

In English you can sometimes omit the pronoun if two verbs refer to the same subject; for example, *I attend the university and study political science.*

However, we could not say: *Want to study politics.* Although we sometimes do this in informal speech—*Want an ice cream?* (Do you want an ice cream?), we do not do it in writing or in formal speech.

In Spanish, however, since it is evident from the verb that in this case the first person is referred to, the insistence on **yo** gives a very bad impression. Only use the subject pronoun if there is a real reason to emphasize or clarify. Since all six forms are different, we always know to whom we are referring, except in the third person singular: **él/ ella/ Ud. estudia,** and the third person plural: **ellos/ ellas/ Uds. estudian.** Sometimes these need to be used to avoid ambiguity.

Both **nosotros** and **vosotros** have a feminine form **(nosotras, vosotras)** which is used if everyone involved is female. If there is a mix of male and female, the masculine form is used: **Nosotros (Juan y Luisa) vivimos en Guadalajara.** Similarly the third person plural form has a feminine form **(ellas)** to refer to a group which is all female, and a masculine form **(ellos)** which can refer to an all-male group, or a mixture of men and women.

Ń
Ă *Activity 5* ··

Locate and list the subject pronouns in the following text. Could any of the pronouns be omitted?

Perhaps we are all blind to the limitations of those we love. Doña Leonor (Luisina Brando), a proud widow in a South American town in the '30s, certainly loves her daughter Charlotte (Alejandra Podesta). She is beguiled by Charlotte's grace, her easy imperiousness, her ease with languages, her virtuosity at the piano. And she refuses to accept what is evident to all: that Charlotte, now on the cusp of womanhood, is a dwarf.

(From Richard Corliss, "Small Wonder," *Time,* October 10, 1994)

Now read the following passage in Spanish. It is taken from a leaflet on the safety system of the BART (Bay Area Rapid Transit, in San Fransisco). Some subject pronouns have been omitted. What are they?

La seguridad es esencial en BART. Por consiguiente,* contamos con un programa positivo y continuo que llega a cada nivel de planeamiento y operaciones en todo el Distrito.

Además, como norma, tenemos programas que detallan los procedimientos de emergencia y programas salvavidas.

*consequently

(¡Todo sobre la seguridad en BART!)

➤ THE PRONOUN *IT*

Students sometimes have a problem finding the equivalent in Spanish for the English *it: It is interesting. It is raining. It isn't like that,* etc.

Although they often accept that **él** and **ella** may be omitted, somehow the omission of **it** seems to cause more trouble, so they try to invent a subject pronoun to put in its place and usually end up with **lo**; for example, **(Lo) es interesante.**

Nothing should be used to express *it* when it is a subject pronoun.

Es interesante.	*It's interesting.*
Llueve.	*It's raining.*
No es así.	*It's not like that.*

Sometimes you can add emphasis with **ello: Ello es interesante** (*It is interesting.*)

Å *Activity 6* ....

Read the following passage about AIDS (**el SIDA**) and decide to whom each of the italicized verbs is referring. If the subject of the verb is a noun, write it down. If the verb has an omitted subject, write the pronoun that could serve as the subject.

1. Los niños seropositivos[1] en edad escolar **pueden** ir a la escuela.
2. El medio[2] en el que **vivimos** está lleno de microbios a menudo peligrosos.[3]

3. El virus del SIDA es temible.[4] **Ataca** el mismo centro de mando[5] del sistema inmunitario.
4. La destrucción del sistema inmunitario de defensa **expone**[6] el organismo a infecciones graves y a ciertos cánceres.
5. **¿Puede** el beso transmitir el virus?
6. Los animales domésticos— perros, gatos, pájaros, etc.— no **son** portadores[7] del virus del SIDA.
7. Ahora **existen** pruebas[8] rápidas del SIDA que **pueden** dar un resultado en algunos minutos. **Permiten** detectar de forma más precoz[9] la seroconversión (subida[10] de los anticuerpos).
8. El sarcoma de Kaposi **es** el cáncer más frecuente en el curso del SIDA. **Afecta** al 35% de los pacientes que presentan el SIDA.

(Extracted from *SIDA. Los hechos. La esperanza,* Barcelona: La Caixa, 1993)

[1]HIV positive [2]environment [3]dangerous [4]to be feared [5]control center [6]exposes [7]carriers [8]tests [9]earlier [10]rise

➤ THE DIRECT OBJECT

Finding the object of a sentence is a little more complicated than locating the subject because you have to decide whether you are dealing with a direct object or an indirect object. First let us look at the direct object.

Dorothy drank a bottle of vodka.
Grandfather swallowed a chicken bone.
We called the doctor.

The words in italics are the direct objects of these sentences. We can find them by asking the following:

—*What* did Dorothy drink? —A bottle of vodka.
—*What* did grandfather swallow? —A chicken bone.
—*Whom* did we call? —The doctor.

What or *whom,* then, are the two questions you need to ask in order to find the direct object in a sentence. In Spanish you find the direct object in the same way:

Felipe estudia **física.**
El señor González vende **periódicos.**
El gato bebe **leche.**

—¿**Qué** estudia Felipe? —Física.

—¿**Qué** vende el señor González? —Periódicos.

—¿**Qué** bebe el gato? —Leche.

In the above examples, we have asked only the question *what* because we are dealing with things (physics, newspapers, milk). Look what happens if the direct object in Spanish refers to a person:

Marta besa **a su madre.**	*Marta kisses her mother.*
Luis saluda **a sus amigos.**	*Luis greets his friends.*
El profesor ayuda **al alumno.**	*The instructor helps the student.*

In all these cases, the preposition **a** has been placed in front of the direct object which, in each example, refers to a person, either singular or plural. There is no equivalent to this in English, so it is not translated. You may find it difficult to remember to put in the personal **a,** as it is usually called, precisely because it is not a feature of English.

Ñ
Ä *Activity 7* ....

Read the following sentences and locate the direct object in each one. If you were writing these sentences in Spanish, which direct objects would need the personal **a** in front of them?

1. He walked into the office and gave the secretary a letter.
2. After looking at the menu, Bob ordered a large steak and fries.
3. Our neighbors say they are going to buy a new car next month.
4. Don't give that toy to the baby—he could choke.
5. I saw John and his brother at the movies yesterday.

Pronouns, like nouns, can also be the direct object of a sentence. Look at the following sentences:

They informed *me* yesterday.

I saw *them* last night.

We ate *it* when we were on holiday.

To find the direct object you ask *what* or *whom* of the verb; in the preceding examples the direct object is a pronoun *me, them, it.* Obviously, this only occurs in a context in which everyone knows who or what these pronouns refer to.

À *Activity 8* ···

Read these limericks and find the direct objects (noun or pronoun) of the verbs in italics.

1. An epicure dining at Crewe,
   Found quite a large mouse in the stew;
   Said the waiter, "Don't shout
   And *wave* it about
   Or the rest will be wanting one too."

2. There was a young fellow named Wier
   Who *hadn't* an atom of fear.
   He *indulged* a desire
   To touch a live wire.
   (Most any last line will do here!)

Notice that whereas some object pronouns in English are different from the subject pronouns, others are the same.

SUBJECT PRONOUNS	OBJECT PRONOUNS
I	me
you (singular)	**you**
he/she	him/her
it	**it**
we	us
you (plural)	**you**
they	them

The pronouns that are the same both when they function as subject and when they are object pronouns are in bold. You no doubt have no problem in recognizing when they are functioning as one or the other and, if you are not sure, you only have to ask the right questions of the verb. You also have no problem in accepting that English uses different forms for some pronouns depending on whether they function as the subject or the object of the verb. Notice that the third-person singular distinguishes gender in English: *he/she; him/her.*

Now look at the forms of the Spanish direct object pronouns in comparison with those of the subject pronouns.

SINGULAR	SUBJECT PRONOUNS	DIRECT OBJECT PRONOUNS
1st person	yo	me
2nd person	tú	te
3rd person	él, ella	lo, la
	Ud.	lo, la
PLURAL		
1st person	**nosotros/nosotras**	nos
2nd person	**vosotros/vosotras**	os
3rd person	ellos/ellas	los, las
	Uds.	los, las

As you can see Spanish, unlike English, has no pronouns with identical forms for both the subject and the direct object. Spanish distinguishes gender in the direct object not only for the third-person singular, but for the third-person plural, and for the **Ud./Uds.** forms. Learning the pronouns may be a bit more complicated, but if you pay special attention to the forms in bold face, it should not be too time-consuming. Notice that the direct object pronoun for **nosotros/nosotras** consists of the first three letters of the subject pronouns, whereas the direct object pronoun for the **vosotros/vosotras** forms is the same as the last two letters of the **vosotros** pronoun.

The direct object pronoun for the first-person singular (**me**) has the same written form as the corresponding English pronoun, although it is pronounced differently. With the third person forms (**lo, la, los, las**), it may help to remember that **-o** and **-a** are the common endings of masculine and feminine singular nouns, and **-os** and **-as** are those of masculine and feminine plural nouns.

Spanish direct object pronouns are placed *before* the conjugated verb and not afterwards, as in English.

La veo.	*I see her.*
Lo venden.	*They sell it.*

Later you will learn how to place direct object pronouns when they accompany a command, a gerund, or an infinitive.

Read these sentences and circle the direct objects. The direct object may be a noun or a pronoun. Remember that Spanish uses personal **a** with direct objects referring to people.

1. Luis, ¿me invitas a tu fiesta?
2. —¿Conoces a Juan? —Sí, lo conozco bien.
3. —Me gusta tu falda. —La compré en El Corte Inglés, gracias.
4. —¿Me dejas tu periódico? —Sí, aquí lo tienes.
5. —¡Qué buenos son estos espárragos! —Los cultivo yo.

➤ THE INDIRECT OBJECT

In English we can usually locate the indirect object by asking of the verb *to whom* or *for whom:*

  a. I bought *Pat* the shoes.
     For whom did I buy the shoes? —I bought them for *Pat.*
  b. I sent *Albert* the note.
     To whom did you send the note? I sent it to *Albert.*

In *a, I* is the subject, *the shoes* is the direct object, and *Pat* is the indirect object. In *b,* the subject again is *I,* the direct object is *the note,* and *Albert* is the indirect object. In English and Spanish indirect objects, like direct objects, may be pronouns: I bought *her* the shoes. I sent *him* the note.

In English, indirect and direct object pronouns are identical, which means that usually you don't have to analyze a sentence to figure out which is which. Eventually you may get to the point where you start to doubt your ability to distinguish them.

Circle the indirect objects in the following sentences. Remember that they may be nouns or pronouns.

1. Bill has sent us a postcard from Miami.
2. Did you give the dog some food when you got home?
3. You should tell me the truth.
4. The store sold him a VCR that doesn't work.
5. We want to save you money.
6. That firm's giving us a 60 percent discount.
7. She bought the child a hamburger.
8. He made her a cup of coffee.

In Spanish, not only are there more forms than in English for the direct object pronouns, but for the third person singular and plural you have totally different forms for the indirect object. It is vital, therefore, to recognize the forms and determine their function in a sentence.

Look at the following pronoun chart. Note that the indirect object pronouns that differ from the direct object pronouns are in bold face. Remember that *all* indirect object pronouns except **nos** and **os** have an **e** in them. **Le** is used for all singular third person pronouns, and **les** for all third person plural pronouns. Try to think of a phrase that will help you remember that the **e** is a feature of indirect object pronouns, for example:

I DO INDIRECTS WITH EASE (E's).

SUBJECT	DIRECT OBJECT PRONOUNS	INDIRECT OBJECT PRONOUNS
yo	me	me
tú	te	te
él, ella	lo, la	**le**
Ud.	lo, la	**le**
nosotros/as	nos	nos
vosotros/as	os	os
ellos, ellas	los, las	**les**
Uds.	los, las	**les**

The first- and second-person singular (**yo** and **tú**) of the indirect object pronouns are identical to the direct object pronouns **me, te:**

Direct object.
¿**Me** reconoces?   *Do you recognize me?*

Indirect object:
¿**Me** prestas tu libro?   *Could you lend me your book?*

The first and second person plural (forms **nosotros** and **vosotros**) are also the same for the direct and indirect object pronouns, **nos, os:**

Direct object:
Nuestros amigos **nos** visitan   *Our friends visit us every year.*
todos los años.

Indirect object:

¿**Nos** compras el vino para
la cena?

Will you buy us the wine for dinner?

Remember that **os** is used only in the parts of the Spanish-speaking world that use **vosotros.** In other areas the singular subject pronoun usually is **tú** and the plural is **ustedes.** Consequently the corresponding plural indirect object pronoun is **les.**

Since **le** or **les** can refer to both masculine and feminine, Spanish often adds **a** + *noun* or *pronoun* to clarify matters:

Pedro le compró unas flores a su
madre.

*Peter bought some flowers for his
mother.*

Le mandé un regalo a mi
hermano.

I sent a present to my brother.

We do not do this in English (it is the equivalent of *I sent him a present to my brother*) so you need to be careful. The phrase **a mi hermano** is optional and is meant to clarify the indirect object. If the context were clear, it could be omitted.

➤ VERBS THAT TAKE INDIRECT OBJECT PRONOUNS

In Spanish the indirect object is used with a number of verbs that do not require it in English. The first verb like this that you will probably meet is **gustar.**

Me **gusta** la comida.

This kind of structure means *The meal is pleasing to me.* The verb does not agree with the pronoun **me** but with the thing that is pleasing (**la comida**); thus it is conjugated in the third person singular. If what is pleasing is a plural noun, the verb will be plural.

A Juan le **gustan** las nueces.

John likes nuts. (Nuts are pleasing to Juan.)

Notice that this kind of verb does *not* use subject pronouns so try to avoid translating it with one (*I like, we like, etc.*) It is better to think of it in terms of an impersonal verb. Other verbs like **gustar** which you may meet are:

encantar:

Me encantan las rosas. *(Roses are
enchanting to me) I love roses.*

faltar:

Nos falta dinero. *(Money is lacking to
us) We're short of money.*

doler:	Me duelen los pies. *My feet are hurting me.*
interesar:	Las lenguas extranjeras le interesan. *Foreign languages interest him/her.*
quedar:	¿Te queda mucho por hacer? (*Is much else remaining for you to do?*) *Do you have much else to do?*
	Estos zapatos me quedan estrechos. (*These shoes are fitting me tight*) *These shoes are too tight.*
fastidiar:	Me fastidia levantarme pronto. (*Getting up early is annoying to me*) *It annoys me to get up early.*

Ȧ Activity 11

Underline the indirect object pronoun in each of the following sentences and decide how you would express it in English.

1. A Mari Paz le encanta la tortilla de patata.
2. Les fastidia estudiar matemáticas a Juan y a Enrique.
3. A Federico le quedan cien dólares en el banco.
4. Todos los años Pedro le da unas rosas a su madre para su cumpleaños.
5. ¿Te interesan esos libros?

➤ DOUBLE OBJECT PRONOUNS

A sentence can have both a direct object and an indirect object pronoun. In this case, there are some things that need to be remembered. Look at this sentence:

He gives it[1] to me.[2]

The direct object pronoun, *it*, comes before the indirect object pronoun, *me*. This is the normal word order in English. In Spanish, however, the order is reversed:

(Él) Me[2] lo[1] da.

Think of a phrase to help you remember this, such as:

Look now at this example: *He gives it to him.*

If you want to put this in Spanish, you know that the direct object in this case is **lo** and the indirect object is **le.** However, you can not say **Le lo da.** Try saying it out loud; it's not very easy to pronounce. Now say **Se lo da.** Isn't this easier to pronounce? When two objects, one indirect and one direct that both begin with **l** (the third person direct objects, remember, are **lo, la, los, las**), are placed one after the other, the indirect object, singular and plural **(le/les),** is changed to **se.** Therefore, *He gives it to him/her/them* will all be translated into Spanish as **Se lo da.** If the context is not clear you can tag on a subject pronoun or a proper noun.

Se lo da a María/a él/a los González.

To help you remember that two pronouns beginning with **l** can not be placed next to each other, you might say the phrase:

The following guidelines may help you to remember the right order:

- If one of the two pronouns is **se,** it will always come first:

  Se me olvida.   *I forget it.*
  Se lo regalo.   *I give it to him.*

Forming a word consisting of the pronoun combinations will help you remember the order: **seme** (se + me); **sete** (se + te); **sele** (se + le).

- If you have **te** and **me, te** always precedes **me.** Remember: **teme** (te + me).

  No te me enfades, ¿eh?   *Don't get cross on me, all right?*

- **Te** also comes before **nos.** Remember: **tenos** (te + nos).

  No te nos mueras de cansancio. *Don't die (of tiredness) on us.*

- **Os,** the pronoun corresponding to **vosotros,** always comes before **nos** (the one for **nosotros**). Remember: **osnos** (os + nos).

  Os nos casasteis sin decir   *You two got married (on us) without*
  palabra.   *saying a word.*

- **Os** also comes before **me**. Remember: **osme** (os + me).

- The pronouns that begin with **l** (**lo, la, los, las, le, les**) will always be placed after the pronouns mentioned above.

Me lo mandaron.	*They sent it to me.*
Te la presento.	*I introduce you to her.*
Os lo dije.	*I told you (pl.).*
Se le olvidó (a él).	*He forgot it.*

- Double object pronouns, like single object pronouns, are usually placed in front of the conjugated verb, but they can be tagged onto the end of an infinitive or a gerund.

Te lo regalo.	*I give it to you.*
Voy a regalártelo.	*I'm going to give it to you.*
Estoy enseñándotelo.	*I'm showing it to you.*

Ⓝ Activity 12

There is a sale going on at Almacenes Arias and the sales clerk is finding it very difficult to keep all the customers happy. What does she say to each one? Follow the example.

CLIENTE: ¿Me busca una falda gris de la talla 46?
DEPENDIENTA: Ahora mismo se la busco.

1. ¿Me da un juego de sábanas de color azul?
2. ¿Nos trae seis pares de calcetines blancos?
3. ¿Le busca a mi madre una blusa verde de tamaño grande?
4. ¿Me devuelve el cambio?
5. ¿Le reserva a mi amiga tres toallas de baño de oferta?

> NUTS AND BOLTS *Direct and indirect objects*

Here is some additional practice on some of the concepts in this chapter.

Ⓝ Activity 13

A. Write ten sentences in English that contain both a subject and a direct object. (The direct object may be a noun or a pronoun.) Exchange your sentences with those of a classmate and find the subjects and direct objects.

B. Write five sentences in English that begin with the subject pronoun *it* and exchange them with those of a classmate. Translate each other's sentences into Spanish.

C. List separately the direct and indirect objects in the following sentences.

  1. They told Mark the bad news.
  2. He sold his brother a bike.
  3. She bought her friend a present.
  4. Mrs. Green made her daughter a dress.
  5. Bill gave Jennifer some flowers.

D. Now replace all the direct and indirect objects in exercise *C* with pronouns. Then decide what pronouns you would need and in which order they would come if you were writing the sentences in Spanish. (You may need to look up some of the words in the dictionary to find out the gender.)

➤ SUMMARY

We have considered a number of concepts in this chapter that you need to understand in order to see how sentences fit together. You must be able to identify the subject, direct object, and indirect object. You also need to become familiar with the Spanish pronoun system. We have seen that it is more complicated than the English system and that the order of Spanish pronouns is different from that of English. In spite of this, the pronoun system is by no means an unsurmountable obstacle. We have looked at various ways in which you might try to understand the system and commit it to memory. As always, however, practice will be of far more use to you than trying to remember charts. When you read in Spanish, make a point of looking at the pronouns and asking yourself, "Does this verb have an omitted pronoun and, if so, what is it? Is this pronoun a direct or indirect object? How do I know? What order are the pronouns in?" By constantly making yourself aware of all these elements that make up a sentence you will be halfway toward assimilating the concepts.

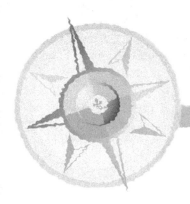

CHAPTER FIVE

LEARNING VOCABULARY

The word I forgot
Which once I wished to say
And voiceless thought
Returns to shadow's chamber.
    Osip Mandelstam, cited by L. Vygotskii

The meaning of a word represents such a close amalgam of thought and language
that it is hard to tell whether it is a phenomenon of speech or a phenomenon of
thought. A word without meaning is an empty sound; meaning, therefore, is a cri-
terion of "word", its indispensable component.
    Lev Vygotskii, Thought and Language

➤ BEFORE WE BEGIN

By the end of the first two of weeks of Spanish a number of students start feeling like Mandelstam, though for different reasons; that is, they become overwhelmed by the amount of vocabulary they are expected to memorize and find they are constantly groping for words. They also discover list upon list of vocabulary words which they suspect they eventually are going to have to learn. To make matters worse, they know for a fact that a lot of this vocabulary is going to turn up on quizzes and tests. When we think about the thousands of words we know in our own language, even at a very early age, the prospect of trying to master a similar amount, or even a few thousand in a foreign language can be daunting. In addition, this is only a small part of the language learning process; students also have to deal with grammatical concepts, verb conjugations, and many more features that at times seem to make the new language totally impenetrable.

Some students seem to have no problem with vocabulary. We have all met those who claim, "I have a photographic memory—I just have to look at a word and I can remember it," or others who don't say it but seem to have a special knack for remembering vocabulary and always coming up with the right word at the right time.

The first thing to bear in mind is that absolutely everyone is capable of learning the amount of vocabulary usually required in a first-year course. There can be no failures in this respect. Yet there are more or less efficient ways of using your time in order to reach your objective, so we are going to look at a few of these in this chapter.

➤ GETTING STARTED

In order to go about learning your Spanish vocabulary, think first about how you learn other things. This might give you ideas as to the best procedure. The following activity should reveal something about your own learning style.

Å Activity 1 ···

A. Discuss the following questions in groups of three or four.
  1. Do you normally study with background music because you find it helps you relax and memorize material, or do you find that music distracts you and that you need complete silence?
  2. When you need to memorize something, is it enough for you to look repeatedly at the page containing the material, or do you have to write things out (even more than once)?
  3. Do you frequently say things out loud to yourself if you need to remember them? Do you ever record them on cassette and then replay the cassette several times while you are exercising, driving to school, doing things around the home, etc.?
  4. Do you find it easier to remember things if you can relate them directly to some aspect of your own life?
  5. Do you make flashcards to help review material? If so, how do you organize them?
  6. Do you find subjects that demand some kind of physical activity (doing an experiment, constructing something, etc.) easier to grasp?
  7. At what times of the day do you concentrate best?
  8. Do visuals or three-dimensional objects facilitate your learning process, or is the written word sufficient for you?
  9. Do you always study for a test by yourself, or do you find it easier to learn in a group or with a partner?
  10. Write down any study habits that you think greatly enhance your learning process.

B. Do your study habits different substantially from those of your group? Share your findings with the whole class.

Are you surprised at the diversity of learning modes? Indeed, there is no one correct way of learning, and all you need to do is explore and find what works best for you by experimenting. It can be useful to start a Techniques Diary in a section of your loose-leaf folder. Here you would jot down what it was you needed to learn, approximately how long it took you to learn it, and what techniques you used to do so. Then note whether or not you think the techniques were particularly helpful. Vocabulary is a good area for you to start experimenting with. You may want to set a weekly goal of so many words that you need to incorporate into your active vocabulary. If you stick to approximately the same number of words per week but vary your techniques, it will give you an idea of what is successful for you and what is not.

> PRACTICAL AIDS

One learning aid that many students of languages use are flashcards, but this term can mean many different things. Someone once may have told you that making flashcards was the sure way to learn vocabulary; you have been doing it ever since but are not really sure whether it has helped you much. What you understand by flashcard may merely be an index card with the Spanish word on one side and the English translation on the other. You read the Spanish side first and then try to come up with the English word, looking on the back if you think you are wrong or can't remember. Then you do it the other way around. However this is not the only way to use flashcards.

Å Activity 2 ⋯⋯⋯⋯⋯⋯⋯⋯⋯⋯⋯⋯⋯⋯⋯⋯⋯⋯⋯⋯⋯⋯⋯⋯⋯⋯⋯⋯⋯⋯⋯⋯⋯⋯

Use index cards to make flashcards for the following words. Make them in any way you think will be helpful. They do not need to be done as described above.

> la tiza (chalk); las palomitas de maíz (popcorn);
> el jugo (juice); la pluma (pen)

Show your flashcards to at least five people and see whether any have made them in the same way.

Some ways you might have prepared the flashcard include the following:

• The Spanish word is on one side, the English on the other.
• The Spanish word is on one side, accompanied by a drawing, and the English word is on the other.

- A drawing is on one side and the Spanish word for it on the other.
- A drawing is on one side, and a short phrase or sentence in Spanish or English on the other helps you memorize the word even if it doesn't make much sense to others, such as **Paloma come palomitas de maíz.**

It can be very helpful to find an English word that sounds similar to the Spanish word, and then combine an image illustrating that concept with another that denotes the Spanish word. For instance, **tiza** may sound to you like *tea,* so you could draw a piece of chalk in a tea cup; **la pluma** sounds like *plume,* hence a pen made from a feather; **jugo** may remind you of Hugo; so a boy drinking a glass of juice could be accompanied by the phrase *Hugo likes jugo.*

A. La tiza

B. La pluma

In all these cases using color may help you to retain the information better. Try writing the Spanish word in one color and the English translation, if you use it, in another, so that you always associate red, for instance, with Spanish, and blue with English. You can also try drawing the item and making the letters of the Spanish word fit those drawings so that image and word are more closely linked. The letters of **la culebra** *(snake),* for instance, would wind around a snake, or **la farola** *(street lamp)* would be twisted around a street lamp. Your drawings don't have to be artistic, just good enough for you to recognize and identify them easily with the object they refer to. There are many excellent materials available to help young children read English. Look at some of them in bookstores; they may give you good ideas for learning vocabulary.

If you are fortunate enough to have access to a computer program that allows you to practice vocabulary or grammar, you should take full advantage of this. Not everyone enjoys working at the computer or finds it particularly helpful, but many students do find that it really helps them to review vocabulary in a way they are not able to do on their own. The computer gives you the advantage of getting immediate feedback, and you are not allowed to go on to the next question until you get each one right. This can be frustrating sometimes, but it lets you know right away whether you know your lesson or not. Computer exercises vary considerably, with some resembling flashcards. But others are much more imaginative and can be fun too. You may like to try comparing the time it takes you to learn a certain amount of vocabulary in traditional ways with the time it takes you on the computer to see whether it is worthwhile. You should also test yourself a few days after using both the computer exercises and the traditional methods to see whether your attrition rate, that is, the rate at which you forget the material, is greater in one or the other,.

The computer also allows you to do something physical while studying: combining the visual image or letters with the action of typing in the answer and, in the case of some computer programs, incorporating the pronunciation of the word as well. For someone who responds particularly well to kinesthetic modes of learning, this may be part of the solution for you.

Whichever method you choose to learn vocabulary, or anything else for that matter, it is important to set a time limit and a goal so that it will be easier for you to reach your objective without losing your concentration. There is a limit on how long we can concentrate on the task in hand; some people have a longer span of attention than others. If you think you have a short span of concentration, this need not be a handicap as long as you recognize it and take steps to make the most of the concentration you do have. Don't set yourself unrealistic goals. If you know that the maximum you can concentrate fully is fifteen minutes, don't expect to learn two hundred new Spanish words in that time. It may be that you can only learn ten, but once you have set that goal, try to keep to it.

Unfortunately, once we have learned something it doesn't necessarily mean that we have learned it forever. It may remain in our short-term memory for a while, but after a few days we might completely forget it. This happens particularly when we try to cram too much material into our mind in too short a time, especially under stress, as immediately before an exam. Even if you think you have learned your vocabulary, you will need to keep going over the words you have studied—using them in phrases and consciously bringing them to mind—if you want them to become part of your long-term memory.

➤ ORGANIZING WHAT WE HAVE TO LEARN

Half of the battle in learning vocabulary is organizing it in some kind of way that makes sense to you. Your textbook most likely presents it in a certain format designed to aid retention, but it may not be the best kind of organization for you. Look at the following words and decide how you could organize them in order to start learning them.

Divide these thirty words up into various groups in a way that you think would make them easy to learn. Compare the way in which you have classified the words with three other people. Have you all classified them in the same way? See how many of these words you can learn in five minutes, eliminating any of those that you already know.

> **la panadería** (*bread shop*); **el padre** (*father*); **el médico** (*doctor*); **la abuela** (*grandmother*); **bajo** (*short*); **la carnicería** (*butcher's*); **el abogado** (*attorney*); **alto** (*tall*); **vender** (*to sell*); **el tío** (*uncle*); **comprar** (*to buy*); **la farmacia** (*pharmacy*); **la enfermera** (*nurse*); **pálido** (*pale*); **la prima** (*cousin*); **hacer cola** (*to stand in line*); **la medicina** (*medicine*); **el panecillo** (*bread roll*); **triste** (*sad*); **el testamento** (*will*); **la oficina** (*office*); **el horno** (*oven*); **alegre** (*cheerful*); **el bolígrafo** (*ballpoint pen*); **la nuera** (*daughter-in-law*); **visitar** (*to visit*); **la tarta de manzana** (*apple pie*); **la chuleta de cordero** (*lamb chop*); **tener hambre** (*to be hungry*); **querer** (*to love*)

You might have chosen various ways to categorize these words. For example, a basic category would be the different parts of speech.

NOUNS
la panadería, el tío, el padre, la farmacia, el médico, la enfermera, la abuela, la medicina, la carnicería, el panecillo, el abogado, la prima, el testamento, la chuleta de cordero, la oficina, la tarta de manzana, el horno, la nuera, el bolígrafo

VERBS
vender, comprar, hacer cola, visitar, tener hambre, querer

ADJECTIVES
bajo, alto, pálido, triste, alegre

You would probably find this difficult to learn because there are so many nouns and relatively few verbs and adjectives. You could therefore regroup the nouns in the following way, to give them some kind of context:

FAMILY	SHOPS	PROFESSIONS
el padre	la panadería	el médico
la abuela	la carnicería	la enfermera
el tío	la farmacia	el abogado
la prima		
la nuera		

Of the nineteen nouns, you have now subclassified eleven, but you need to incorporate the other nouns in a meaningful context if you want to learn them easily and quickly. You also need to incorporate both the verbs and the adjectives. You could do the following:

FAMILY	SHOPS	PROFESSIONS
el padre — alto	**la panadería**	el médico — pálido
la abuela — alegre	el panecillo	la enfermera
el tío — bajo	el horno	
la prima — triste	la tarta de manzana	**el abogado**
la nuera	tener hambre	la oficina
visitar	**la carnicería**	el bolígrafo
querer	la chuleta de cordero	
	comprar	
	hacer cola	
	la farmacia	
	la medicina	

This provides you with the framework to invent a simple story that will help you remember the words. For instance, you go and visit the attorney in his office because you need to make a will and you fill out the necessary forms with a ballpoint pen. You feel hungry so you go to the baker's and buy a bread roll that has come straight from the oven, and an apple pie. Anything at all that will help you retain the information is valid and, generally speaking, the more meaningful the context you give your vocabulary, the easier it will be to remember.

You may have noticed that several of the adjectives listed are antonyms, or opposite in meaning: **alto—bajo; triste—alegre.** Even if you don't have to learn the antonym of a word, it may help you to remember it if you do. And it will certainly increase your vocabulary. Remembering synonyms, or words similar in meaning, can also help.

Ⓝ Activity 4

Some words in the following list are antonyms, while some are synonyms. Group the antonyms and the synonyms in pairs. If you don't know the meanings of some of the words, look them up in the dictionary.

enfadado	abierto	ancho	nacer
contento	lívido	estrecho	feliz
morir	levantarse	acostarse	pálido
rubio	lento	enojado	cerrado
despacio	moreno	líquido	sólido

Another way to help you learn vocabulary is to put each word in a simple sentence that has special relevance to you. Look at each new word you come across and think how it can relate to your life. For instance, if you have to learn **llamar por teléfono** you could write on a card: **Llamo por teléfono a mi novio Jeff** (supposing that you have a boyfriend called Jeff); or if it's the verb **querer, Quiero mucho a mi perro Pat.** You don't have to invent anything terribly original or witty, although if you can think of something humorous it might help jog your memory. All you need to do is make that word or expression your own by relating it to yourself.

If vocabulary refers to tangible objects, it can be a great help to label these objects with the Spanish name in your room or home. The kitchen yields many items which often come up in textbooks and if you label them, then while you are in the kitchen you can recite aloud **el frigorífico, el horno, la harina, la sartén, el microooondas,** etc., touching the objects at the same time to make the language real to you. If you have a weekend or evening job, you can also review your vocabulary in a discreet way, without pasting labels on things. For instance, if you work in a supermarket and have to arrange the fruit and vegetables, you can make the most of it by naming them to yourself: **la lechuga, el tomate, las manzanas,** etc. If you find this a helpful method, you will discover that there are many situations in your daily life in which you can review silently (or aloud) your Spanish vocabulary. Don't assume that vocabulary learning can only be done in a formal setting. The informal occasions are often both more fun and more productive.

À Activity 5

Make a list of all the informal situations in which you think you could review Spanish vocabulary, either aloud or silently. Compare your list with that of a partner. Are there any activities you could do together (sports, exercising, cooking) and go over your vocabulary too? Look at all the vocabulary you have come across so far in your textbook and see what kind of situations it lends itself to.

Sometimes it can be helpful to find English words that rhyme more or less with Spanish ones, or that sound similar even if they have different meanings. Look at the vocabulary you need to learn this week and see if you can come up with any examples. For instance, **a la moda** (*in fashion*): *She's in a good mood because she's **a la moda**.* Even though the vowel sounds of *mood* and **moda** are different, they are similar enough so that one word helps recall the other.

In all languages there are "families" of words, that is, words that are connected to others or are formed from others. In English, for instance, *father* is a noun while *fatherly* is an adjective, and *to father* is a verb. As long as you know what *father* means, you could guess the meanings of the other related words. When learning vocabulary it can be a big help to learn groups of related words. This will also help you with your reading skills. Look at the following groups of words and decide whether they are nouns, adjectives, or verbs, and what they mean.

blanco	**blando**	**el asesino**
blanquear	la blandura	asesinar
el blanqueador	blanduzco	el asesinato
blanquecino	emblandecer	
emblanquecer		

el azúcar	**la sangre**	**verde**
azucarado	sangriento	la verdura
azucarar	sangrar	verdoso
la azucarera	sangría	reverdecer

A dictionary can be a big help when learning another language, but it can also pose problems if used improperly. There are a few basic things that you need to be aware of when using a bilingual Spanish-English, English-Spanish dictionary. As you have probably realized, the Spanish alphabet is not exactly the same as the English one. There is a separate section for words beginning with **ñ**, although this is small. Dictionaries used to list words beginning with **ch** and **ll** separately, but as of 1994 these will be classified under **c** and **l** respectively, as in English dictionaries.

Dictionaries vary, but they all provide a set of symbols at the beginning that help you to interpret the offerings. It is very important to know whether you are dealing with a noun, a verb, an adjective, etc., since these parts of speech are not interchangeable.

In a Spanish dictionary if the word is a noun, it will probably be followed by *m.* or *f.* to indicate whether it is masculine or feminine. An adjective will probably be followed by *a.*, and an adverb by *adv*. Often one word in English can have various meanings, and to make sure you have chosen the correct one you will need to check with the Spanish-English section, not just the English-Spanish one. If, for example, you want to say that you have received a shot in the leg, you'll need to make sure that you are conveying that it was an injected medication (**una inyección**) rather than a gunshot wound (**un tiro**).

You should purchase as large and complete a dictionary as you can afford. In the United States dictionaries are comparatively cheap and this is an investment that will pay even if you study Spanish for only one or two years. If possible, you should also purchase a monolingual Spanish dictionary. You will find a multitude of examples of how to use words and in what context. Get in the habit of using your dictionary frequently. Look up words for fun and try to work them into your conversations or compositions.

➤ NUTS AND BOLTS   *More useful phrases*

In Chapter 1 we learned a few useful classroom expressions. Here are a few more for you to learn and use in your class.

¿Me prestas tu libro?	*Would you lend me your book?*
He olvidado los deberes/la tarea.	*I've forgotten my homework.*
Explíquelo otra vez, por favor.	*Explain it again, please.*
¿Cuándo es el examen?	*When's the test?*
¡Qué pase buen fin de semana!	*Have a good weekend!*

Å *Activity 6* ⋯⋯⋯⋯⋯⋯⋯⋯⋯⋯⋯⋯⋯⋯⋯⋯⋯⋯⋯⋯⋯⋯⋯⋯⋯⋯⋯⋯⋯⋯⋯⋯

In this chapter we talked about word families. See how many words you can find in the dictionary related to the following; then make a sentence for each one that has meaning for you. Specify whether the word in each case is a noun, a verb, an adjective, etc.

escritorio	expresivo
estudioso	extraño
azul	

➤ SUMMARY

The acquisition of vocabulary is a very important part of learning a new language and one that takes time. We have looked at some of the different ways that will help you learn the multitude of new words that you will come across. We saw that learning styles vary considerably, and that techniques that you use for mastering vocabulary may be very different from those of a classmate. In any case, you need to experiment until you find the technique or techniques that best suit you. It is also important for you to acquire good dictionary skills. Finally, we learned a few more expressions to use in class.

CHAPTER SIX

APPROACHING READING

Now who has acquired any facility in reading unless he has looked at the poets and conned over the historians and orators?

(*A.S. Piccolomini*, De Liberorum educatione, *ed. J.S. Nelson, Washington (1940).*

➤ BEFORE WE BEGIN

You may not have given much thought yet to which of the skills in Spanish—reading, writing, speaking, or listening—will be of most use to you in the future. Unless you intend to continue your studies in Spanish to an advanced level, you will probably study the language for only a couple of years. Your level of oral proficiency by that time is not likely to be very high, unless you are lucky enough to enjoy a prolonged stay in a Spanish-speaking country, or have the opportunity to practice frequently with Spanish-speaking friends. It is very likely that unless you continue to make an effort to practice your Spanish after you finish your classes, you will forget most of what you learned quicker than you may have thought possible.

If there is one skill that is both relatively easy for you to maintain and that is likely to be useful to you in the future, it is reading. Once you have acquired basic reading skills in the language, you can continue to improve on them even without instruction. You don't necessarily have to read the poets, historians, and orators, as Piccolomini suggests, but it is easy for you to pick up a newspaper or magazine in Spanish and read a few articles, or enjoy a short story with relatively little effort. Many Spanish-language newspapers and magazines from Argentina, México, Venezuela, Spain, etc. are sold in this country. You will also find newspapers in Spanish written and published in this country for the vast Hispanic population. Depending on the profession you choose, in the future you may find it useful to read professional articles or books in Spanish. Furthermore, studies have shown that reading helps improve writing skills.

Some people find speaking a foreign language rather an ordeal, although there is no need for it to be so. But reading should *always* be a pleasure. Many Nobel Prize winners for literature have been from Spanish-speaking countries: Gabriel García Márquez and Camilo José Cela are but two who have won it in recent years. You are studying a language that has one of the most important literary heritages in the world, both in peninsular and Latin American literature. And just after a couple of years of Spanish, this heritage is opened up to you. Of course, many famous Spanish works are translated into English, but think of the satisfaction you can get from reading them in the original.

Continued reading is also a way for you to maintain your language skills; it will increase your vocabulary and refresh your grammar. Even if you do cover the main grammatical points in your study of Spanish, this is not really long enough for you to assimilate these concepts fully. You need extensive contact with the language, and one way to get it is through reading. You will probably read short stories in Spanish, an excellent way to become acquainted with Spanish literature. The short story is a genre that has been cultivated by many Spanish writers and it is particularly accessible to the learner. Whatever you choose to read, make sure that it is truly a pleasurable experience as this, more than anything else, will ensure that reading in Spanish becomes a long-term habit with you.

➤ UNDERSTANDING WHAT WE READ

Before examining the strategies needed to read Spanish, perhaps we should examine our attitude toward reading in general, even in our own language. Do the following activity with a partner, and *be honest*—there is no right or wrong answer.

λ *Activity 1* ··

1. Do you keep a book on your bedside table to read just before going to sleep?
   a. always   b. sometimes   c. rarely   d. never
2. If you do have a book by your bed, what kind does it tend to be?
   a. textbook   c. science fiction   e. novel
   b. short stories   d. other   f. poetry
3. When was the last time you read something for pleasure?
   a. last week   c. last year
   b. last month   d. can't remember
4. When was the last time you bought a book because a friend recommended it to you?
   a. within the past month   c. last year
   b. within the past six months   d. can't remember

5. Before you went to college, did you read for pleasure?
   a. more than now
   b. less than now
   c. about the same as now
   d. I never read unless it was required
6. Approximately how many books would you say there are in your parent's home?
   a. less than a hundred
   b. 100–500
   c. 500–1000
   d. 1000–2000
   e. more than 2000
7. How often do you read the newspaper?
   a. every day
   b. on Sunday
   c. when there's something special in the news
   d. never
8. If you think you don't read much, what do you attribute this to?
   a. lack of time
   b. lack of interest
   c. difficult in reading
   d. your inability to select anything pleasurable

Sometimes people fear that reading in a foreign language will be too daunting a task, that their limited vocabulary will require them to exert too much effort to understand the text. When we read in our own language, however, we don't always understand every word, yet we make sense of the text. In fact, even if certain words are missing, we can still get the gist. Do the following activity. It is a cloze passage, that is, a text in which words are removed at regular intervals.

À Activity 2

First read the entire passage to get a general idea of what it is about. Then answer the questions that follow.

"Are we very sure _____ (1) we need a foreign _____ (2)?" Mr. Wentworth inquired. "Do _____ (3) think it desirable to _____ (4) a foreign house—in _____ (5) quiet place?"

"You speak," _____ (6) Acton, laughing, "as if _____ (7) were a question of _____ (8) poor Baroness opening a _____ (9) or a gaming-table."

"It _____ (10) be too lovely!" Gertrude _____ (11) again, laying her hand _____ (12) the back of her _____ (13) chair.

"That she should _____ (14) a gaming-table?" Charlotte asked, _____ (15) great gravity.

Gertrude looked _____ (16) her for a moment, and _____ (17), "Yes, Charlotte," she said _____ (18).

"Gertrude is growing pert," Clifford Wentworth _____ (19), with his humorous young _____ (20). "That comes of associating _____ (21) foreigners."

Mr. Wentworth looked _____ (22) at his daughter, who _____ (23) standing beside him; he _____ (24) her gently forward. "You _____ (25) be careful," he said. _____ (26) must keep watch. Indeed, _____ (27) must all be careful. _____ (28) is a great change; _____ (29) are to be exposed _____ (30) peculiar influences. I don't _____ (31) they are bad; I _____ (32) judge them in advance. _____ (33) they may per- haps make _____ (34) necessary that we should _____ (35) a great deal of _____ (36) and self-control. It will _____ (37) a different tone."

Gertrude _____ (38) silent a moment, in _____ (39) to her father's speech; _____ (40) she spoke in a _____ (41) that was not in _____ (42) least an answer to _____ (43). "I want to see _____ (44) they will live. I _____ (45) sure they will have _____ (46) hours. She will do _____ (47) kinds of little things _____ (48). When we go over _____ (49) it will be like _____ (50) to Europe. She will _____ (51) a boudoir. She will _____ (52) us to dinner—very _____ (53). She will have breakfast in _____ (54) room."

(Henry James, *The Europeans*)

1. The Baroness is thinking of moving near to the Wentworths and setting up:
   a. a house
   b. a casino
   c. some kind of establishment of ill repute
   d. none of these
2. The Baroness comes from
   a. the area near the Wentworths
   b. an unspecified American city
   c. Italy
   d. an unspecified European country
3. Mr. Wentworth is nervous about the having the Baroness nearby because:
   a. he thinks she's immoral
   b. she has no self-control
   c. he thinks she will bring gambling to the area
   d. he is wary of foreigners and their different life style
4. Gertrude is looking forward to the Baroness coming because:
   a. Gertrude's present life is too quiet
   b. she thinks the Baroness's life-style must be exciting
   c. neither *a* nor *b*
   d. both *a* and *b*
5. Mr. Wentworth is Gertrude's
   a. uncle
   b. father
   c. husband
   d. brother

Now go back and without looking at the answers that follow try to fill in the blanks. You will not be given a grade or points for this exercise; it is designed to help you reason about how you understand what you read. Often there are several possibilities, not just one right answer. As you do the activity, jot down why you chose one word or another.

For number 1, *that* is the only possibility, although the sentence would equally make sense without it. At first glance, number 2 could be practically anything, as long as it is a noun, since it is preceded by the indefinite article *a* and the adjective *foreign* which, in English, makes only a noun possible in this slot. If we read the second sentence, we find a reference to "a foreign house" and this is what tells us to go back and put *house* for number 2. For number 3 we need to complete a question: We have the auxiliary *do* and the bare infinitive (that is, an infinitive without *to*) *think*. English requires a subject pronoun in between to form an interrogative statement. *We* would be possible since Mr. Wentworth seems to be asking for the consensus of all present, but *you* makes more sense here as he appears to be asking for an opinion. Obviously, number 4 must be an infinitive since it is preceded by *to* and appears to refer to an action. Instead of *establish*, you may have used *have, set up, open,* or something equivalent since, as the text proceeds, it is evident that the Baroness is setting up house in the neighborhood.

As you see, in order to complete the text, you are making use of all kinds of knowledge about the English language. This is a difficult cloze because every fifth word is eliminated. If every eighth or tenth word had been omitted, it would have been much easier. Even without filling in the blanks, you were able to answer the questions because the context is sufficiently clear to give you a general idea about what is going on and, in some cases, a fairly precise one. In order to complete the text, sometimes you need to read the next few sentences before you are able to make a reasonable guess. One of the first decisions you make, consciously or unconsciously, before filling in the blank, is what *class* of word you need: verb, noun, pronoun, adjective, etc. You activate your knowledge of the English language in order to do this (as in the choice of an infinitive, word order in interrogative sentences, the use of adjectives and indefinite articles, etc.). Even if you don't always come up with the exact word, you should be able to make an approximation (for instance, for number 19, instead of *observed*, you could have used *declared, said, affirmed, muttered,* etc., and still have understood the context).

There may be words in an English text which you don't understand (for example, number 39, *in deference*). But you don't normally go straight to the dictionary to look them up because the context usually allows you to guess more or less what the word means. All you need to do is transfer to your reading in Spanish the reading skills that you use all the time in your own language. Let's look at the next activity.

In the text in Activity 2 the difficulty resides in guessing the words in the blank spaces. In the following poem, there are no blank spaces, but many of the words are nonsense words invented by the author, Lewis Carroll.

> 'Twas brillig, and the slithy toves
> Did gyre and gimble in the wabe;
> All mimsy were the borogoves,
> And the mome raths outgrabe
>
> "Beware the Jabberwock, my son!
> The jaws that bite, the claws that catch!
> Beware the Jumjub bird, and shun
> The frumious Bandersnatch!"
>
> He took his vorpal sword in hand:
> Long time the manxome foe he sought.
> So rested he by the Tumtum tree,
> And stood awhile in thought.
>
> And as in uffish thought he stood,
> The Jabberwock with eyes of flame,
> Came whiffling through the tulgey wood,
> And burbled as it came!
>
> One, two! One, two! And through and through
> The vorpal blade went snicker-snack!
> He left it dead, and with its head
> He went galumphing back.
>
> "And hast thou slain the Jabberwock?
> Come to my arms, my beamish boy!
> Oh, frabjous day! Calooh! Callay!
> He chortled in his joy.
>
> 'Twas brillig, and the slithy toves
> Did gyre and gimble in the wabe;
> All mismy were the borogoves
> And the mome raths outgrabe.

Locate the following words in the poem and suggest meanings for the words you choose.

1. Four nonsense verbs. Say whether they are infinitives or conjugated verbs. If conjugated, what tense are they?
2. Five nonsense nouns. Say whether they are singular or plural.
3. Five nonsense adjectives.

Carroll provides enough familiar context in this poem for us to get a general understanding of it even though there are numerous words we cannot know because they don't exist. Indeed, the term *jabberwocky* has passed into the English language as "nonsensical writing for comic effect" (*Concise Oxford Dictionary*). He presents us with a classic situation found in numerous myths and legends: an older man warns a younger one about a terrible predator that inhabits a dense wood and that needs to be slain in order to prevent it from continuing to kill anyone who crosses its path. The young man, like St. George setting out to kill the dragon, sallies forth on his horse, cuts off the creature's head with his trusty sword, and gallops back to the old man, who effusively congratulates him.

Once aware of the subtext, we are able to approach the Jabberwock poem with a certain confidence, for we know basically what happens. Only the details are missing, and we can provide many of these ourselves from the context and from what we know about English.

Here are some suggestions for the above questions although, since we are dealing with nonsense, obviously there are many possibilities.

1. Verbs: *gyre, gimble, outgrabe, whiffling, burbled, galumphing. Gyre* and *gimble* must be bare infinitives since they are preceded by the auxiliary *Did* (for example *Did you go? Yes, I did go.*). *Outgrabe* must be in the past tense since it seems to be a conjugated verb and the rest of the stanza is in the past. Humpty-Dumpty, one of the protagonists in *Alice Through the Looking-Glass* where this poem appears, later explains to Alice that *outgrabe* is the past of *outgribe*. *Apophony*, or a change of vowel in the past tense, is a common feature of English (*sing, sang, sung*). *Whiffling* and *galumphing* appear to be present participles, since *-ing* is characteristic of the present participle and gerund in English; and *burbled* must be the past tense of a regular verb since the *-ed* suffix is typical of regular past verbs. With regard to their meanings, this is open to interpretation. *Gyre* seems to be related to gyrate ("To gyre is to go round and round like a gyroscope," says Humpty-Dumpty) and *gimble* resembles *gambol*, a verb applied especially to young lambs. Both *burbled* and *whiffling* suggest noise and *galumphing* has actually passed into English ("to go prancing in triumph; move noisily or clumsily. Made by Lewis Carroll perhaps after gallop, triumphant," *Concise Oxford Dictionary*).

2. Nouns: *toves* (plural), *wabe, borogoves* (plural), *raths* (plural), *Jabberwock, Jubjub bird, Bandersnatch, Tumtum tree.* All the nouns appear to be connected with nature in some way—trees, birds, or other creatures (*toves, raths, borogoves*).

3. Adjectives: *brillig, slithy, mimsy, mome, frumious, vorpal, manxome, uffish, tulgey, beamish, frabjous*. Some of these seem to have a positive meaning (*frabjous*, for example, reminds us of *joyous; beamish* reminds us of *beaming*). *Slithy*, on the other hand, suggests *slither*, or *slimy*, and *manxome* and *frumious*, both from context and the way they sound, indicate something unpleasant or fearful.

In order to comprehend—at least in part—Carroll's nonsense poem, you have related the comprehensible parts of the poem to familiar stories or texts (a knight's fight against a fearful beast), worked out the part of speech of the words you don't understand, and tried to think of similar words that you do know and that might be related to them. You will apply these same techniques when dealing with texts entirely in Spanish. Perhaps the most important thing to realize is that even in your own language you don't always understand the whole text, but this does not prevent you from getting the gist of the text or even considerable details. If you can live with a little uncertainty and doubt when reading English without it making you nervous, you will be able to do the same in Spanish.

➤ LOOKING FOR CLUES   *Getting the most from the title*

Even before you start to read a text you can obtain a great deal of information from its title. It is worth spending some time just thinking about the title and deciding what the text is probably about. The title will suggest a certain kind of context to you (which may or may not turn out to be the right one), which triggers information in your mind about similar situations you may have read about or experienced.

Å *Activity 4* ....

Look at the following titles from articles or newspaper sections and decide what you think the texts that accompany them are about.

1. Ofertas de empleo
2. Anuncios breves
3. Buscan a los asesinos de una peluquera
4. Suplemento para toda la familia
5. Buscando amor
6. Los Oscar en directo
7. Nombran comité para estudiar racismo en sistema de justicia
8. Republicanos proponen duras leyes de inmigración

Skimming for gist

Once you have thought about the title of the article or story you are going to read, and what you expect from the text, skim through it quickly to try to get the gist. Don't worry at this stage about looking things up in the dictionary or about details; you are only trying to get a general idea. We frequently use this technique when we read the newspaper in our own language. Most of us don't have time to read the paper from cover to cover so we glance quickly at the headlines. Then if one in particular catches our eye, we may skim it rapidly to see if it is as interesting as we think it is. Sometimes we don't need to do more than this because we have extracted sufficient information for the time being, and we may go on to another article, perhaps intending to go back to the first one when we have more time. It may be, though, that after skimming we think that the information in the article is really important and worth spending more time on, so we reread it more attentively.

Newspapers in both English and Spanish frequently use short paragraphs, sometimes a single sentence, to sum up the content of the article. For instance, in an article entitled **Cáncer de próstata acabó con la vida de Fernando Rey** (*El Diario. La Prensa,* New York, March 10, 1994, p. 29) the following appears at the beginning in bold type:

> **Un cáncer de próstata, del que fue intervenido hace apenas un mes en una clínica madrileña, acabó ayer con la vida del destacado actor español Fernando Rey a los 76 años de edad.**

This introduction expands on the title. You now know that apart from dying of cancer of the prostate, Fernando Rey was a famous Spanish actor who had been operated on in a Madrid clinic just a month before, and died at the age of 76.

It is very good practice to write similar introductions of your own, after you have skimmed a text. By summing up the main ideas in one or two sentences, you can concentrate on the main points without worrying about the details. Now do the following activity.

Å Activity 5

Skim the following short texts in Spanish and then do the following activities. Some words are glossed for you in English. Don't bother to look up any more in the dictionary; you are sure to understand enough to grasp the main point, and that is all that is needed.

1. Provide a suitable title in Spanish if possible (or if necessary, in English), for each.
2. Write a couple of sentences in English that sum up the basic point(s).

3. Discuss with a partner whether the general ideas you have extracted from the texts seem familiar to you or not. That is, would you expect to see similar kinds of articles in American newspapers or magazines? If not, why not?

a. Nadie pone en duda que España es un país con raíces[1] religiosas profundas. Tampoco hay quien discrepe cuando se afirma que, durante siglos,[2] la Iglesia católica ha considerado a la mujer la guardiana de sus ritos y creencias, la instructora voluntaria de sus dogmas y la abanderada cristiana por definición. Pero sí nos atrevemos[3] a decir que, hoy por hoy, la mujer joven se ha apartado un gran trecho del camino religioso. En parte, porque los insistentes mensajes de Juan Pablo II no responden a los tiempos que vivimos; en parte, porque su vida ahora es mucho más compleja que la tradicional idea de casa-niños-misa[4]. Por eso empezamos a oír ásperas voces de protesta.

(*Cosmopolitan,* Madrid, December 1993, p. 16)
[1]*roots* [2]*centuries* [3]*we dare* [4]*mass*

b. Te estás esforzando por un futuro. Muchas noches. Muchos días. Ahora no se te pueden cerrar las puertas. Ven a Central Hispano 20.
Encontrarás todo un banco diseñado a tu medida.[1] Con productos concretos para tus necesidades. Un Crédito Personal que te financia la compra de tu ordenador,[2] tu moto, tu equipo de música o de deportes... lo que quieras. Un Crédito Joven para el pago de matrícula,[3] gastos de estudios, compra de libros...
Un Crédito Beca[4] que te adelanta[5] el importe de toda la beca concedida, que te permite realizar cursos en el extranjero... Un Master 20 que te financia los gastos y la estancia de todo tipo de master... Todo esto y mucho más lo tienes en el Banco de los Jóvenes. Aquí te comprendemos porque somos jóvenes como tú.
Estamos abiertos hasta las 19.00 horas.
Este es tu Banco. Ven con tu gente.

(*Central Hispano 20*)
[1]*to fit your needs* [2]*computer* [3]*enrollment* [4]*scholarship* [5]*advances you*

c. • **Si Ud.** quiere acabar con la inmoralidad y la violencia en la TV...
   • **Si Ud.** quiere defender a su familia contra la invasión de basura[1] que la TV nos arroja[2] diariamente en nuestros hogares[3]...
   • **Si Ud.** quiere defender el derecho a educar a sus hijos dentro de una atmósfera llena de respeto a las buenas costumbres...
   • **Si Ud.** quiere que los responsables por la programación en la TV respeten el principio de protección de la juventud y de la infancia...
   • **Si Ud.** quiere que los programas de TV respeten la moral, la religión y la Iglesia Católica...

SÚMESE[4] a la campaña que **S.O.S. Familia** está haciendo, en defensa de la juventud y de la infancia y contra la degradación moral en la televisión, rellenando[5] hoy mismo el cupón que publicamos a continuación.

Su participación en esta campaña nos es imprescindible[6] para asegurar el éxito de esta iniciativa.

Por favor, remítanos urgentemente su cupón-respuesta a la dirección indicada abajo...

[1]*trash* [2]*throws* [3]*homes* [4]*Join* [5]*filling out* [6]*vital*

d. Los Ángeles. —Croatas y musulmanes bosnios firmaron[1] ayer en Washington la creación de una federación territorial cuya superficie sólo alcanza el 30 por ciento de Bosnia-Herzegovina. De acuerdo[2] con el guión[3] del plan elaborado por la Administración Clinton, el siguiente paso es convencer a los serbios para que se integren en la nueva fórmula política que debe sacar a los bosnios del agujero[4] bélico.

"Espero que los serbios se unan a este esfuerzo por una paz amplia... Les invitamos y urgimos a ello", declaró el presidente Bill Clinton durante el acto protocolario.

(*La Vanguardia,* Barcelona, March 19, 1994)

[1]*signed* [2]*According to* [3]*outline* [4]*hole*

Ä Activity 6

Now that you have a general idea of what the texts are about, you are going to go back over them and look for specific information. This is called *scanning*. You don't have to read everything closely, just let your eyes run over the text until you locate the section where you think you have found the information you are looking for.

1. Scan Text *a* and write down the phrases that tell you that:
   a. for centuries the Catholic Church has considered women to be the depositary of its beliefs.
   b. Pope Juan Paul II doesn't know how to keep up with the times.
   c. life for women today is more complicated than it used to be.
2. Scan Text *b* and write down the phrases that tell you that:
   a. the Central Hispano 20 Bank will help finance your personal needs.
   b. the bank will help finance your post-graduate studies.
   c. the bank stays open late.
3. Scan Text *c* and write down the phrases that:
   a. ask if you want to end violence and immorality on TV.
   b. ask if you are in favor of TV programs concerning the teachings of the Catholic Church.
   c. tell you to fill out the coupon.

4. Scan Text *d* and write down the phrases that tell you that:
    a. the agreement between the Croats and Bosnian Muslims only affects part of the territory.
    b. Clinton wants the Serbs to sign an agreement too.
    c. an agreement with the Serbs would bring about widespread peace.

Look at the sentences/phrases you wrote down and think about what made you choose them. Is there a key word or words that told you that this phrase contained the information you were looking for? If so, what were they? Now write down the key word(s). Are there any words in these phrases that you consider superfluous when it comes to comprehending the specific information you are looking for? If so, what are they and can you specify what class of words they are (nouns, verbs, adjectives, etc.)?

Not all words in a text have the same value when transmitting a message. When we scan texts in our own language and in Spanish, we should pay particular attention to words that convey the most meaning (sometimes called *content words*). Usually these are nouns, verbs, and adjectives; many other words *(function words)* take second place (definite and indefinite articles, auxiliaries, prepositions, etc.).

The role of the reader

When we read a text, our interpretation very often depends on how we personally relate to it. With this in mind, do the next activity.

À *Activity 7* ....

1. Reread Text *a:*
    a. from the standpoint of a young woman.
    b. from the standpoint of an elderly man who thinks that "A woman's place is in the home."

What sort of reactions would the text produce in you in both cases?

2. Now reread Text *b:*
    a. from the standpoint of a student who may consider opening an account. What advantages do you see over conventional banks?
    b. from the standpoint of a parent who has a son or daughter at college. Do you see the same advantages? Are there any disadvantages?

3. Reread Text *c:*
   a. from the standpoint of someone who thinks that in a free country television should not be censored. Do you object to anything in the text?
   b. from the standpoint of a regular church-goer who agrees that a lot of what is shown on TV is immoral and can corrupt young people. Would you add any further arguments to the text?

➤ ORGANIZING WHAT WE KNOW   *Cognates*

One way in which you can increase your reading ability in Spanish is by being aware of cognates, words that look and mean something similar in both languages, and by making intelligent guesses about them. But not all words that look like cognates actually are. For instance, one word that often stumps students is **embarazado/a** which doesn't mean *embarrassed,* but *pregnant.* We call these words *false cognates* or **falsos amigos,** because although they look similar to one another they have in fact quite different meanings. Look at the texts in Activity 5 and find the cognates.

Here are some of the words that probably struck you in Text *a* as being similar to English:

religiosas, profundas, discrepe, se afirma, católica, guardiana, ritos, la instructora voluntaria, dogmas, cristiana, definición, en parte, insistentes mensajes, responden, compleja, la tradicional idea, ásperas, protesta

Religiosas immediately makes us think of *religious* and **profundas** of *profound.* **Discrepe** is a little more difficult; it brings to mind the noun *discrepancy* or the adjective *discrepant,* yet from context we see that it is a verb. This shouldn't be a problem; sometimes there are similar words in English and Spanish but they don't necessarily belong to the same word class. However, they can help us when trying to guess the meaning. If we know that discrepancy means *difference,* then we can guess that the verb **discrepar** must mean *to have differences* or *differ in opinion from.* In the same way, we see the adjective **ásperas** and are led to think of the English noun *asperity* which means *roughness* or *harshness.* This gives us a clue to the meaning of the Spanish word. Sometimes words in English and Spanish have identical or almost identical spellings (**dogma, insistentes**), whereas at other times you will have to use your imagination a little and think how the substitution of perhaps one or two letters can make all the difference: **mensajes/***messages,* **compleja/***complex.*

Now look at the cognates in the other three texts and try to guess their meanings.

Derivation and composition

By *derivation* we mean deriving or forming words from others by adding a prefix or a suffix to an existing one. For example, *preschool* is derived from *school; gangster* is derived from *gang. Composition,* on the other hand, consists of making new words by combining two or more that already exist. For example, *babysitter* is a combination of *baby* + *sitter*. When reading, try to recognize families of words, that is, words that may belong to a different word class from one you are familiar with, yet are connected in meaning.

In Text *a*, for example, you may not immediately know what **creencias** means, but if you can see the verb **creer** as connected with it, then this helps you understand. In the same way, **camino** will make you think of **caminar**, **duda** of **dudar**. You may think you don't know the meaning of **abanderada**, but if you can recognize the word **bandera** in the middle, this will help you guess the meaning. In Text *b* the verb **diseñado** may make you think of the noun **diseño**, or the noun **el pago** of the verb **pagar**. Text *c* includes the adverb **diariamente**, which you can relate to the adjective **diario**. All you need to do is apply the knowledge you have of how Spanish usually forms adverbs from adjectives, by adding the suffix **-mente**. You may not know immediately what the verb **asegurar** means in this same text, but you probably know the adjective **seguro**. If you constantly look for clues such as these, you will find that you know many more words than you thought you did, even without using a dictionary.

It helps to know the meaning of some common prefixes and how they change the meaning of a word. In English and Spanish for instance, *re-* often means *to do something again,* so **rehacer** is *to redo,* and **reconstruir**, *to reconstruct.* The prefix *des-* usually gives a negative slant to whatever word it is attached to so, if **teñir** is *to tint* or *dye,* **desteñir** is *to take the color out of something* or *to fade.* If **honesto** is *honest,* **deshonesto** is *dishonest.* A number of prefixes in Spanish are also used in English, for example:

PREFIX	MEANING	DERIVED SPANISH WORD
ante-	*before*	antepenúltimo
anti-	*against*	antisocial
auto-	*self*	autobiografía
ex-	*former*	ex marido
infra-	*under*	infravalorado
sub-	*under, less*	subnormal

Familiarity with Spanish suffixes will also help your reading skills. There are a number of suffixes, for example, that transform adjectives into nouns.

SUFFIX	ADJECTIVE	NOUN
-dad	bueno	la bon**dad**
	feliz	la felici**dad**
-ura	bravo	la brav**ura**
-eza	bello	la bell**eza**

The suffix **-ar** can change some adjectives into verbs.

ADJECTIVE	VERB	MEANING
azul	azul**ar**	*to make blue*
ágil	agiliz**ar**	*to make agile*
agrio	agri**ar**	*to make sour*

Spanish, like English, also combines nouns and adjectives to form a new word, as in **noche buena, Nochebuena;** or verbs and nouns, as in **abre latas, abrelatas** *(can opener),* **corta césped, cortacésped** *(lawn mower).* Some other examples are:

boca + calle	bocacalle	*entrance to street*
quitar + manchas	quitamanchas	*stain remover*
sordo + mudo	sordomudo	*deaf and dumb*
boca + abierto	boquiabierto	*open-mouthed*

By thinking about the meaning of the individual parts of a word you will probably guess the meaning of the whole word.

➤ LOOKING AT THE WHOLE FORMAT

We have looked at some of the individual aspects of a text that might help you to improve your reading skills, but there are other things that can help you understand the general meaning. Often texts are accompanied by some kind of illustration, which might well give you a clue as to what the text is about. Do the following activity.

The following illustrations are from ads in a Madrid newspaper. Match the illustration with the description of the kind of product or service being offered.

1. Ornamental plants, garden projects
2. Sailing lessons
3. A travel agent specialized in honeymoons
4. Buying, selling, and tuning of pianos
5. Fitted shelves for closets
6. Weight-loss center and medical esthetics

Even without knowing any Spanish at all, you can guess what these firms are advertising simply by looking at the illustrations. Some materials produced for native speakers with a low level of literacy often incorporate numerous illustrations, as well as simple language, to help them understand the message. Look at the following page taken from a leaflet widely distributed to help people find out about AIDS **(SIDA)**.

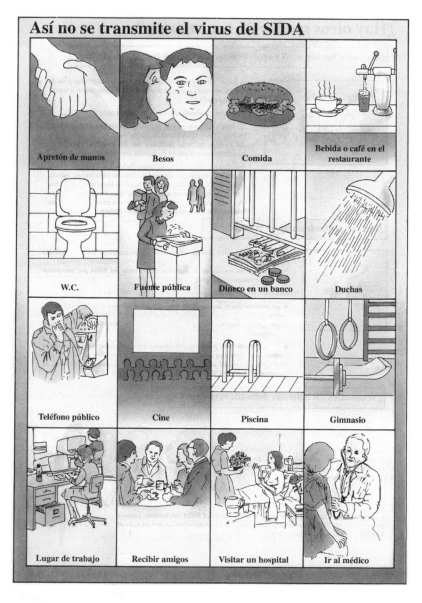

Así no se transmite el virus del SIDA

Apretón de manos	Besos	Comida	Bebida o café en el restaurante
W.C.	Fuente pública	Dinero en un banco	Duchas
Teléfono público	Cine	Piscina	Gimnasio
Lugar de trabajo	Recibir amigos	Visitar un hospital	Ir al médico

Apart from illustrations, you should take into account the different kinds of texts you read because you will often be able to call up all sorts of background knowledge from your own language and experience that will help you to interpret the text. For example, a photo of a dish of tomato soup and a text that starts off like this:

Ingredientes
un kilo y cuarto de tomates maduros
media cebolla
un pepino
dos cucharadas soperas de vinagre
una taza de aceite de oliva

You can guess that you are dealing with a recipe. You know that the standard form is to give you a list of ingredients and then a series of directions given as commands. This knowledge helps you focus on the text in hand, and even before reading it carefully you have some idea of what kind of language to expect. If, on the other hand, you come across signs of the zodiac, you can be fairly sure that you are dealing with a horoscope and have some idea of what to expect.

The following is the beginning of the Spanish Constitution of 1978. See how much of it you can understand without looking anything up in the dictionary.

Artículo 1.

1. España se constituye en un Estado social y democrático de Derecho, que propugna como valores superiores de su ordenamiento jurídico la libertad, la justicia, la igualdad y el pluralismo político.

2. La soberanía nacional reside en el pueblo español, del que emanan los poderes del Estado.

3. La forma política del Estado español es la Monarquía parlamentaria.

Now look at this extract from the American Declaration of Independence, in Spanish.

Sostenemos como evidentes estas verdades: que todos los hombres son creados iguales; que son dotados por su Creador de ciertos derechos inalienables; que entre éstos están la vida, la libertad y la búsqueda de la felicidad.

(Servicio Informativo y Cultural de los Estados Unidos de América).

The kind of language we are used to reading varies according to whether it's a doctor's prescription, a letter from an attorney, immigration forms, and so on.

You may not have read any of these kinds of texts in Spanish before, but from experience you know what kind of language you would expect in English, and this will help you when interpreting Spanish.

You especially need to lose any fear of guessing. Instead of rushing immediately to the dictionary, try to use some of the strategies mentioned above to figure out the meaning of a word. You may discover that even if you have no idea what it means, it really doesn't matter—for as long as you get the gist, you probably can do without looking it up.

> NUTS AND BOLTS

The linguist S.I. Hayakawa coined two terms: *snarlwords* and *purrwords*. *Snarlwords* are the epithets that exist in all languages which people use to hurl insults at one another. *Purrwords,* on the other hand, are the expressions we use to make people feel good about themselves. Learning a language can be a major effort, so at this point it might be a good idea to sit back and learn a few *purrwords* with which to commend yourself on the effort you have made so far and to encourage yourself to continue.

¡Bravo!	
¡Fantástico!	
¡Soy sensacional!	*I'm sensational!*
¡Genial!	*Brilliant!*
¡Formidable!	*Awesome!*
¡Olé!	
¡Qué gozada!	*What a joy!*
¡Ánimo y adelante!	*Keep right on!*

Practice saying these words aloud, and every time you learn new vocabulary or make some progress in your studies, say a couple of expressions to yourself with feeling!

Parts of speech

You will find it a great help when reading to be able to distinguish the different parts of speech (nouns, verbs, pronouns, adjectives, etc.). We discussed the Spanish subject and object pronouns in Chapter 4, as well as the verb endings of regular **-ar**, **-er**, and **-ir** verbs in the present tense. In Chapter 2 we discussed the most common endings for masculine and feminine nouns and looked at some of the groups of nouns that are usually one gender or another. In this chapter we looked at how we decide in a cloze passage what class of word we need to fill in the gaps and how, as with the Lewis Carroll poem, we can try to get the meaning of totally nonsensical words and determine what class of word they are. Now let us try and do this in Spanish.

Read the following cloze test in Spanish. Then decide what *kind* of word fits into each space (noun, verb, pronoun, adverb, etc.) and fill in the blanks.

El Sol, centro del sistema solar

El Sol es una enorme _____ (1) de fuego.

El Sol es _____ (2) grande, 740 veces mayor que todos los _____ (3) juntos y más de un millón de veces superior a _____ (4) Tierra.

Sin embargo, comparado _____ (5) otras estrellas , el Sol es _____ (6) estrella más bien pequeña. Si lo _____ (7) mayor que las otras estrellas es porque está más cerca de _____ (8).

(*Sociedad*, 5, Madrid: Santillana, 1982, p. 7)

The words that are missing are: **vemos, muy, planetas, esfera, nosotros, estrella, la, con, una.**

The following words are cognates. Without looking them up in the dictionary, what do you think they mean?

1. infiltrar
2. discretamente
3. discípulo
4. inflamatorio
5. nulo

6. responsabilizar
7. satisfactorio
8. carbonizar
9. desmoralizado
10. volcán

➤ SUMMARY

Reading, we have said, is one of the language skills that may be of most use to you after you have finished your formal study of Spanish. Moreover, you can continue to perfect your reading skills on your own without additional instruction, once you have grasped the basics of the language. Reading in Spanish can also bring you much pleasure. If only for this reason, it is worth putting some effort into it now.

We have examined some of the strategies we use when reading in our own language and seen how we can apply them when reading in Spanish. We have looked at the importance of titles and how they can help predict what it is we are going to read. We have discussed the difference between skimming a text for general meaning and scanning it for particular information. We have also seen how different people read texts in different ways, depending on such factors as age, sex, and social status.

Recognizing cognates can be a big help when trying to decipher a text in Spanish as can be understanding the way prefixes and suffixes work. Moreover, many prefixes have similar meanings in English. Understanding a text is not only understanding the written word. Drawings or illustrations that accompany a text also can be valuable in helping to decide what the text is about. We are accustomed to reading all kinds of texts in our own language—legal documents, recipes, prescriptions, etc.—and our background knowledge of these and the type of format they follow can be useful in helping us interpret Spanish texts of a similar nature.

And finally, in the *Nuts and Bolts* section we gave ourselves a linguistic pat on the back by learning a number of expressions of encouragement in Spanish with which to applaud our efforts.

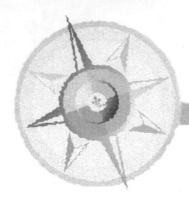

CHAPTER SEVEN

LISTENING WITH A PURPOSE

> *The steed bit his master;*
> *How came this to pass?*
> *He heard the good pastor*
> *Cry, "All flesh is grass."*
>
> *Anonymous*

➤ BEFORE WE BEGIN

One of the common complaints of beginning students of Spanish is that Hispanics speak far more rapidly than speakers of English. The more Spanish these same students learn, the slower it seems to them that Hispanics speak. If there is one language activity that makes students nervous, apart from speaking Spanish in front of their peers and the instructor, it is trying to comprehend what seems to be a totally incomprehensible language. Many students say, "I can read Spanish quite well and even write it, but I can't speak and I can't understand when a Spanish person talks to me." This may be due to a lack of exposure to the language—every skill takes its own time to develop—but it may also be because they have not been taught systematically how to understand spoken Spanish. This is the aspect of learning Spanish that we are going to concentrate on in this chapter.

➤ HOW DO WE LISTEN IN ENGLISH?

Presumably the horse in the limerick quoted above understood English, but that wasn't much help when he came to interpret the pastor's words because he heard, but didn't comprehend. One thing we need to realize early on in our language studies is that we don't always hear or understand absolutely everything in our own language, nor is this always necessary.

We have seen in the previous chapter how it is possible for us to read a text in English (or even in Spanish) in which certain words are missing, yet we can still get the general sense of it. Exactly the same thing happens with the spoken language. Think of an occasion when you may be trying to listen to something in English but have a hard time hearing the entire message. Such situations may include:

- Listening to a loudspeaker announcement at an airport or train station.
- Talking to someone on the phone from a public call box downtown where there is heavy traffic.
- Hearing what someone is shouting to you across a room or street.
- Listening to a radio station when there is interference.
- Having a conversation with someone in a discotheque with blaring music.

In circumstances such as these, we make use of strategies to compensate for not hearing the whole message; we may struggle particularly hard to listen for certain information (for instance, at the airport the gate number for our flight) or to hear key words (in a conversation from a public phone we may be talking to a friend about a visit and pay special attention to the directions to his house, or the time of the meal). Often large parts of oral messages can be safely disregarded without prejudicing our understanding. We can get the gist of a spoken message in the same way as we can get the gist of a written text, while not worrying too much about the rest of it unless we want to analyze it in detail.

We saw in the previous chapter that there are content words (verbs, nouns, adjectives) that contain most of the information we need, and often we can safely relegate function words (articles, prepositions, auxiliaries) to a backseat. The same applies to spoken messages. The content words are those that are going to relay the most important part of the message, with the function words helping to complete the picture.

One thing we have to deal with both in our own language and in Spanish is with what we call *fillers,* that is, words that have no specific meaning but gain time for the speaker while he/she tries to find the right expression. We also use exclamations with no intrinsic meaning.

"Have you heard the latest news about hm, hm, Stevens?"
"I sometimes have difficulty with uh hu finding the right word."
"Oh! I've cut my finger."

Basically, these are noises in the throat, coughs, or other kinds of acoustic signs that take the place of words. We also need to recognize these in Spanish. For example, when someone is in disagreement with another, he/she may say ¡**Bah...**, **bah...!** in Spanish. This has no particular meaning, but it voices disapproval. If you are hurt or have an unpleasant surprise, you might say ¡**Ay!** If you want to catch someone's attention, you'll hiss ¡**Chsss!** To make someone hurry up, if you know him/her well, you can say ¡**Hale, hale!**, whereas to express indifference you utter ¡**Psss...!** None of these are words in their own right. They are merely accoustic expressions of certain emotions. A foreign-language learner needs to realize that such sounds are not universal and have to be learned. Becoming acquainted with some of these will help you interpret some messages which might otherwise be incomprehensible. It can come as a shock, for example, to find out that Spanish roosters call out **kikiriquí**, Spanish dogs bark **wau wau**, and Spanish birds and chickens utter **pío, pío.** Now do the following activity.

Å Activity 1

A. Read the following passage from J. D. Salinger's *The Catcher in the Rye,* and write down all the words you consider have no real meaning but are used to intensify the meaning of other words, or to express emotion.

> She came over to me, with this funny look on her face, like as if she didn't believe me. "What'sa matter?" she said.
> "Nothing's the matter." Boy, was I getting nervous. "The thing is, I had an operation very recently."
> "Yeah? Where?" "On my wuddayacallit—my clavichord."
> "Yeah? Where the hell's that?" "The clavichord," I said. "Well, down in the spinal canal." "Yeah?" she said. "That's tough." Then she sat down on my goddam lap. "You're cute."

(J. D. Salinger, *The Catcher in the Rye,* Boston: Little, Brown and Co., 1991, pp. 95–97)

B. The following words represent certain sounds found in a Spanish comic strip. Match the sounds with the situations, then decide how the sound would be expressed in English.

1. ¡Flip Flap!	a. someone under water
2. ¡Riing!	b. a fight
3. ¡Cras! ¡Croc! ¡Plaf!	c. someone laughing
4. ¡Poing!	d. a telephone
5. Pluf, pluf	e. the wings of a bird
6. ¡Je, je!	f. someone jumping over a metal fence

In English we often use expressions which are merely social courtesies. For example, if we pass someone we know in the street, we may say "Hi, how are you doing?" or "Lovely day, isn't it?" We don't really expect an update on this person's health, unless we happen to know that he/she has recently been ill, nor do we really care about the weather. These are just social exchanges which make us feel good for having made some kind of contact. You need to recognize this kind of "contentless" language in Spanish, so that if you hear someone say to you **¿Qué tal?**, for instance, you don't bore them with a long account of your latest bout of arthritis or hay fever. Expressions that you might hear in casual social situations, or that might want to use yourself include:

¡Adiós, que le vaya bien!	*Goodbye, hope things go well!*
¡A pasarlo bien!	*Have a good time!*
Hasta la próxima...	*Till next time...*

Our knowledge of our own language sometimes allows us to organize and make sense of what may at first seem totally meaningless speech, just as we are able to make sense out of a nonsense text like that of Lewis Carroll. Try the next activity.

Ꭺ Activity 2

First read the following text silently and try to make sense of it. Then read it aloud. Hint: This is a fairy tale, so try to use the intonation you think is appropriate.

Wants pawn term dare worsted ladle gull hoe lift wetter murder inner ladle cordage honor itch offer lodge, dock, florist. Disk ladle gull orphan worry putty ladle rat cluck wetter ladle rat hut, an fur disk raisin pimple colder Ladle Rat Rotten Hut.

Wan moaning Ladle Rat Rotten Hut's murder colder inset, "Ladle Rat Rotten Hut, heresy ladle basking winsome burden barter an shirker cockles. Tick disk ladle basking tutor cordage offer groin-murder hoe lifts honor udder site offer florist. Shaker lake! Dun stopper laundry wrote! Dun stopper peck floors! Dun daily-doily inner florist, dun stopper torque wet strainers!"

"Hoe-cake, murder," resplendent Ladle Rat Rotten Hut, an tickle ladle basking an stuttered oft.

Honor wrote tutor cordage offer groin murder, Ladle Rat Rotten Hut mitten anomalous woof.

"Wail, wail, wail!" set disk wicket woof, "Evanescent Ladle Rat Rotten Hut! Wares are putty ladle gull goring wizard ladle basking?"

"Armor goring tumor groin-murder's" reprisal ladle gull. "Grammar's seeking bet. Armor ticking arson burden barter an shirker cockles."

"O hoe! Heifer gnats woke," setter wicket woof, butter taught tomb shelf. "Oil tickle shirt court tutor cordage offer groin-murder. Oil ketchup wetter letter, an den -O bore!"

(Howard L. Chace, *Anguish Languish,* 1953, cited by J. H. Hearndon, *A Survey of Modern Grammars,* New York: Holt, Rinehart and Winston, 1976, p. 86)

Just as we relate our own experiences and knowledge to an unfamiliar text to help us interpret it (as in the case of the Jabberwock), when trying to interpret a spoken message we also rely heavily on similar messages we may have heard. In the above text, the fact that we know this is a fairy tale gives us an important clue because we know what kind of structure to expect, however loosely; intonation is also vital. The cadence of the voice help us to interpret whether we are dealing with affirmations, questions, negations, and the like. And the tone of voice conveys the emotions of the speaker (anger, surprise, pleasure).

If you see a drawing like the following, or are told that the preceding passage is an original version of *Little Red Riding Hood*, you can see how Chace has very cleverly changed certain sounds in English for others and, by using words that actually exist in the English language *(anguish, languish)*, concocts a text that would be totally incomprehensible if we paid more attention to what the words mean than to how they sound.

Other important factors to take into account when interpreting spoken messages are the social class to which the speaker belongs, age, and the geographical area he/she comes from. Children do not speak the same kind of language as an adult, nor an adolescent the same as someone who is old. Some adults teach "baby language" to young children, so you hear them refer to ducks as "quack-quacks" and a scrape as a "boo-boo."

Similarly, in Spanish young children may refer to a cut or graze as **una pupa,** to meat as **chicha** (instead of **carne**), or to a grandfather or grandmother as **yayo** or **yaya** (instead of **abuelo, abuela**). Adolescents in both Spanish-speaking and English-speaking countries tend to have their own jargon which perhaps not even the older generation of that same culture may fully comprehend. Among the young people of Spain, for instance, it is common to hear the verb **currar** instead of **trabajar,** and in informal speech young people tend to call everyone **tío** (literally *uncle,* but with the meaning of *guy*), even their own father!

A member of the working class may not speak in the same way as someone who is upper middle class, an agricultural worker may use different language from an inner-city factory worker, and women often speak differently from men. For example, if you hear the expression ¡**Qué divino!** (How fantastic!) in Spanish, or ¡**Jolines!** (*Dear me!*), it will usually be a woman speaking since there are other expressions that would be favored by a man. We automatically take these factors into consideration when listening to our own language. We also usually know how to adjust to them. The problem is learning how to recognize such characteristics in a foreign language.

À Activity 3 ···

In pairs, take turns reading the following passages to each other. The person listening must not read the text. Try to decide what elements mark the regional or social aspects of each one. Are you able to understand the text fully without reading it? What words or expressions give you trouble?

1. In this text, Lee tries to reproduce the speech of country folk in Gloucestershire, England.

> "When lessons grew too tiresome, or too insoluble, we had our traditional ways of avoiding them."
> "Please, miss, I got to stay 'ome tomorrow, to 'elp with the washing—the pigs—me dad's sick."
> "I dunno, miss; you never learned us that."
> "I 'ad me book stole, miss. Carry Burdock pinched[1] it."
> "Please, miss, I got a gurt[2] 'eadache."
>
> (Laurie Lee, *Cider with Rosie,* Harmondsworth: Penguin, 1962, p. 56)
> [1]*stole* [2]*great*

2. This anonymous poem tries to reproduce the speech of the cockneys, a special form of London speech.

> *Biby's* Epitaph*
>
> A muvver was barfin' 'er biby one night,
> The youngest of ten and a tiny young mite,
> The muvver was poor and the biby was thin,
> Only a skelington covered in skin:
> The muvver turned rahnd for the soap off the rack,
> She was but a moment, but when she turned back,
> The biby was gorn; and in anguish she cried,
> "Oh, where is my biby?"—The angels replied:
> "Your biby 'as fell dahn the plug-'ole,
> Your biby 'as gorn dahn the plug;
> The poor little thing was so skinny and thin
> 'E oughter been barfed in a jug;
> Your biby is perfeckly 'appy,
> 'E won't need a barf any more,
> Your biby 'as fell dahn the plug-'ole,
> Not lorst, but gorn before."

* baby's

If you had never heard these varieties of English before, you might at first have some difficulty in understanding what they meant, but with a little more exposure and an understanding of the main differences between these kinds of speech and the one you are used to, you would probably be able to understand a great deal.

Now look at these examples of different kinds of Spanish.

- Güiraldes reproduces the speech of the Argentinian gauchos.

> —Güen día, Don Segundo.
> —Güen día, muchacho. Te estaba esperando pa hablarte.
> —Diga, Don.
> —¿Vah'a volver a ensillar tu potrillo?"

(Ricardo Güiraldes, *Don Segundo Sombra,* Madrid: Cátedra, 1982, p. 137)

> *"Good-day, Don Segundo."*
> *"Good-day, lad. I was waiting to talk to you."*
> *"Go ahead, Don."*
> *"Are you going to saddle your colt again?"*

Notice the use of **Güen** instead of **Buen** and the attempt to reproduce the aspirated **s**: ¿**Vah'a volver**... instead of ¿**Vas a volver**...."

- Mario Benedetti reproduces certain characteristics of the speech of Uruguay in this encounter between two men who haven't seen each for thirty years. The man who starts to talk is asking about the other's parents.

  "Me acuerdo hasta de la tortilla de alcauciles[1] que hacía tu vieja.[2] Sensacional. Yo iba siempre a las once y media, a ver si me invitaba a comer." Y lanzó una tremenda risotada. "¿Siempre?" le pregunté, todavía desconfiado. Entonces sufrió un acceso de vergüenza: "Bueno, fui unas tres o cuatro veces." Entonces, ¿cuál era la porción de verdad? "Y tu vieja, ¿está bien?" "Murió hace quince años."

  (Mario Benedetti, *La tregua,* Madrid: Cátedra, 1988, p. 89)

  "I remember the artichoke omelette that your Mom used to make. Fantastic. I always used to go at 11:30 to see if she'd invite me to lunch." And he burst out laughing. "Always?" I asked, still not trusting. Then he suddenly became embarrassed. "Well, I went three or four times." Then how much of that was true? "And how's your Mom, is she well?" "She died fifteen years ago."

  [1] In other parts of the Spanish-speaking world, this would be **alcachofas**.
  [2] **Vieja** (and **viejo**) in the *Río de la Plata* region are affectionate terms for one's mother and father, and even spouse. In other regions they might be considered disrespectful.

- The following is an attempt by the Mexican writer Laura Esquivel to imitate the speech of a Mexican servant girl.

  —¿Ay sí, no? ¡Su 'amá[1] habla d'estar preparada para el matrimoño,[2] como si juera[3] un plato de enchiladas! ¡Y ni ansina,[4] porque pos[5] no es lo mesmo[6] que lo mesmo! ¡Uno no puede cambiar unos tacos por unas enchiladas así como así!

  (Laura Esquivel, *Como agua para chocolate,* New York: Doubleday, 1993, p. 20)

  [1]mamá [2]matrimonio [3]fuera [4]así [5]pues [6]mismo

  "Oh yes, isn't that right? Your mother talks of being ready for marriage as if it were a plate of enchiladas. And even if it were, it's just not the same. You can't exchange tacos for enchiladas just like that!"

Spanish, because of the immense geographical area in which it is spoken, offers numerous varieties of speech, but just as you are able to understand different varieties of English, you will also find that you can adapt to different varieties of Spanish.

➤ LEARNING TO RELAX

When you just start learning Spanish you are not going to be asked to listen to and understand regional dialects, even though eventually you will be able to do this. Just trying to understand standard Spanish may be problem enough for you. One of the first lessons you need to learn is to relax. You should realize that at the beginning almost 100 percent of a conversation or spoken text will go over your head; at the very most you will be able to pick out a few words. Gradually this situation will improve, but progress will be relatively slow and in direct proportion to the amount of Spanish that you listen to. Just as extensive reading is the best thing you can do to improve not only your reading skills, but to increase your vocabulary and even your grasp of grammatical concepts, you need to listen extensively to spoken Spanish in order to improve your listening comprehension. Of course, there are specific things that you can do on your own to speed this process, plus others that your instructor will suggest, for in-class or in-lab exercises or at home. But even if you merely listened to a Spanish radio station every night, or tuned into a Spanish television channel, you would be contributing positively to raising your level of comprehension.

You must expect to listen to many grammatical structures and a vast amount of vocabulary that you have never heard before and do not understand. If all you listened to were recorded passages that contained familiar structures (possibly just the present tense, or little else) and only the vocabulary you had studied, you would be bored to tears and your listening comprehension would not improve. You need to listen to language which is more difficult than what you think you can cope with, and with a much richer vocabulary than your own active or passive vocabulary. Gradually much of this unfamiliar territory will start to sound familiar.

You need not panic, however. Your instructor knows perfectly well that your listening skills are very rudimentary. In the same way that you have learned the value of skimming and then scanning a reading text that may be too difficult for you to understand in its entirety, you will also learn how to listen to spoken Spanish and either just catch the gist of what is being said, or listen for very specific information that is relatively easy for you to pick out. You should recognize from the start that unless you continue with your Spanish studies well beyond the basic level you may never completely understand a spoken message, except in very simple cases, and even if you reach an advanced level, there will still be much that you don't understand. Think, however, as we have discussed above, how you are able to interpret messages in your own language even when you don't hear or understand every word. Gradually you will develop this capability in Spanish and will lose your fear of not understanding every word because you will know that it is not necessary to do so.

When you do listening comprehension exercises in class or in the lab, you will probably be given the opportunity to listen to the message more than once. In real life, this often doesn't happen. In conversations, however, we can always ask someone to repeat something, which is why, right from the start, you should learn and use the expression **Repita, por favor,** or something similar. When you listen to a taped conversation or text the first time, try not to translate it in your head; this would be simultaneous interpretation and you are a long way from being able to do that! Let the voice or voices go over your head, without becoming tense; otherwise your mind closes and you will understand even less.

The first time you hear a text, simply try to recognize how many speakers there are and, from their intonation and tone of voice, get some idea of their emotions or of the situation. Are they angry or happy, is someone asking questions? Does someone appear to be giving instructions? How about background noise? Is there anything that gives you a clue as to where they are or what kind of message this could be? Could it be a commercial on the radio or a weather forecast? Do you think it's someone reading the news or giving the time over the telephone? Does this appear to be an airport announcement, or a conversation among friends at a party? Do any of the voices sound as though they are children or old people? These are essential factors to listen for.

Go back and listen a second time. Now try to get the sense of what is being said. You may only be able to pick out a few words and some of these may be cognates. Listening to cognates in Spanish can be a lot harder than reading them because the stress often falls on a totally different syllable, making the word practically unrecognizable to you. For example (the stressed syllable in both languages is in italics):

English	Spanish
pro*fes*sor	profe*sor*
ca*the*dral	cate*dral*
*in*terest	inte*rés*
*di*alogue	di*á*logo

You will probably find that understanding at least some of the content words helps you get the gist of the message. You may not recognize a verb tense, but if you know what verb it comes from and what it means, this will help you. Similarly, understanding some of the nouns and adjectives will give you an idea of what is going on. We have seen that it often pays to make a guess when reading. You may not always be right, but sometimes you can approximate the meaning by taking context into account. This is also true of listening. Once you have established the context (the first time you listen to the message this is basically what you are trying to do) and have picked out some of the main ideas, you may be able to guess at many other things.

You will often be expected to listen to a big chunk of Spanish yet be asked only to pinpoint a few basic ideas. For example, you may listen to a fairly long announcement at a train station. Of all the data you are given, just decide whether the train you want to catch to a certain destination has been announced or not and at what time it leaves. If this is all you need to know, however long the announcement, all the rest of the information is irrelevant and you don't have to worry about it. You may be listening to a radio commercial for a furniture store sale, and the only thing that interests you is to know whether they are offering dining room tables and chairs, and if so, how much they cost.

➤ THE SPANISH AND ENGLISH SOUND SYSTEM

There are certain sounds in every language that are more important than others in helping to distinguish meaning. These are called *phonemes* and even though in European languages they frequently coincide, this doesn't always happen. Phonemes should not be confused with letters: they are units of sound and may be represented by one letter or by more. Consider si*t* and si*p*. The sounds that distinguish these two words are the sound of *t* and of *p*: they are enough to create two totally different words. Now consider si*t* and si*ck*. These two words are also distinguished by a difference in phonemes. In the first case it is the sound of *t* again, represented by the letter *t*, whereas in the second word it is a *k* sound represented by the letters *ck*. Spanish has some phonemes that English does not have, and vice versa. If it is any consolation to you, Spanish-speaking people find the English phoneme system extremely difficult to master, particularly because of the complexity of English vowels. We have some vowel sounds in our language that do not exist in Spanish and not only do Spanish-speaking people find these difficult to pronounce but, since they are not used to listening to these distinctions in Spanish, they often don't even hear the difference. For a Spanish-speaking person, the words *but* and *bat* may sound indistinguishable. This is a phenomenon that affects your listening comprehension too; because you are not used to listening for certain sound distinctions in English, you don't always hear them in Spanish. That is why it will help you improve your listening skills if you are aware of these differences and practice listening for them.

Let us look at some of the phonemes in particular.

- **r/rr:** You will have been struck by the sound of the Spanish **r** and will have probably noticed that there is more than one pronunciation, and that neither sounds like that of the English *r*. The **rr** is always strongly trilled: **perro**. The same pronunciation is also used when **r** starts a word: **raya, rey, rosa**. It is also trilled when it comes after **n** or **l**: **Conrado, alrededor**.

In other cases, **r** is pronounced by moving the tongue quickly against the gum area behind the upper teeth, the area known as the alveolar ridge. This is a quick tap or flap of the tongue in contrast to the English *r* which generally involves bending the tongue back to the roof of the mouth.

It is very important that you learn to distinguish between the two kinds of Spanish **r** otherwise you may confuse a number of words. Practice saying the following words with a partner, or get your partner to pronounce a word from one of the lists and try to guess to which it belongs.

pero	*but*	perro	*dog*
caro	*expensive*	carro	*car*
foro	*forum*	forro	*lining (of a coat)*
cero	*zero*	cerro	*hill*

- **n/ñ:** English does not have the phoneme represented by the letter **ñ**, even though a similar sound exists in words such as *onion*. You should not find it too difficult to hear the difference in these two phonemes. Practice reading the following aloud.

sonar	*to sound, ring*	soñar	*to dream*
mono	*monkey*	moño	*chignon*
cana	*grey hair*	caña	*fishing rod*
pena	*pain*	peña	*group of friends*
vano*	*vain*	baño	*bath*

* Remember that **b** and **v** are pronounced in the same way in Spanish—something else to bear in mind when listening.

- **l/ll:** There is much variety in the Spanish-speaking world with regard to the pronunciation of **ll**, but whatever the pronunciation, in all cases it will be clearly distinguished from the pronunciation of **l**. After following your instructor's indications for the pronunciation of **ll**, practice saying these pairs of words aloud to make sure you can hear the difference in pronunciation. Or say them aloud to a friend.

mala	bad (feminine)	malla	mesh
calar	to penetrate	callar	to be quiet
loro	parrot	lloro	I cry
lana	wool	llana	flat (feminine)
polo	pole	pollo	chicken
lama	slime	llama	he/she calls

- z and s: In many, but not all, Spanish-speaking areas, z and s are pronounced in the same way. In most of Spain, however, z (theta) is pronounced with a *th* sound, which is quite different from s. This is the same pronunciation given to c when followed by e or i. You need to hear this distinction clearly because there are many words distinguished in meaning in this way. Practice saying the following, pronouncing z as *th:*

cazar	to hunt	casar	to marry
loza	tableware	losa	flagstone
taza	cup	tasa	tax
maza	mace	masa	mass
cerrar	to close	serrar	to saw
cirio	candle	sirio	Syrian

- p, t, and k: You may have difficulty clearly hearing Spanish p, t, and k in certain words. In English, when these phonemes come at the beginning of a word they are pronounced with aspiration, that is, a little puff of air. Hold a small piece of paper in front of your mouth while you say words like *pea, tea,* and *key,* and notice how it gently moves. The aspiration is less if the phoneme *p* is preceded by an *s* (*speak, spear*), or is followed by an unaccented vowel (*upper, polite*). We are so used to hearing this aspiration in English, even if we don't realize that we do it ourselves, that when we don't hear it we may misinterpret what we do hear. The way in which the Spanish p, t, and k are pronounced often sounds like *b, d, g* to the English ear.

Word said	Word understood
peto	veto
pala	bala
tan	dan
cala	gala

- **b, d**, and **g**: These phonemes can also sound different in Spanish than in English. If they are found in initial position they are quite similar, but if they are in the middle of a word, then a variant is pronounced. Instead of the air passage being momentarily blocked completely, as in the pronunciation of English *b* and *p,* a small opening is left through which air passes. Sounds produced like this are called fricatives because friction is produced as air passes through the opening. Look at your lips in a mirror as you pronounce *cupboard, baby,* and *bubber.*

The Spanish fricative **b,** to an English ear, can sound like a *v;* the fricative **d** can sound like the *th* in *loathing.* This kind of **d** is heard in Spanish in words like **cocido** and **adverbio.** Fricative **g** is found in the middle of Spanish words when **g** is followed by **a** or **o,** or **gu** by **e** and **i.** For example: **llegar, algodón, hagamos.**

- And finally, Spanish vowels should not be difficult for you to hear and understand, for the Spanish vowel system is much less complex than the English one. There are five pure vowels.

  palo   pelo   polo   pino   puso

You should have little difficulty distinguishing these, even though they are not pronounced in exactly the same way as their English equivalents.

Linking

What people tend to find most confusing when they first start to study Spanish is deciding where one word ends and the next one begins. This is what contributes to the impression that Spanish people speak so fast: learners of Spanish find if difficult to recognize words because they all seem to run into one another. In a way this is true, mainly because Spanish practices a feature called *linking* that English does not. English, to Spanish ears, often sounds "choppy" or "clipped" because the divisions between words is much more marked than in Spanish. Some of the features that contribute to the smoothness of Spanish and, consequently, to the difficulty in understanding spoken Spanish are the following:

1. There are certain groups of words which, due to their grammatical features, are so closely linked that they form a single unit, and when they are pronounced have no pause between them. Among these groups are:

- A noun and its article: **la ventana** (*laventana*), **el aula** (*elaula*).
- An unstressed personal pronoun and whatever comes immediately after it: **Lo compró** (*Locompró*).
- Compound verbs: **¿Has dormido bastante?** (*hasdormido*).
- A preposition and whatever comes immediately afterwards: **la carta de Andrés** (*deandrés*).

2. When one word ends with a stressed vowel and the next word begins with the same stressed vowel, a single long vowel is pronounced.
He hecho (*heecho*) la tarea.
Mi hijo (*miijo*) estudia física.
Mamá ha llamado (*mamáa llamado*).
De pronto, habló Óscar (*hablóÓscar*).

3. If a word ends with an unstressed vowel and the next word begins with the same unstressed vowel, then again a single vowel is pronounced, but it is shorter than in the previous examples.
Nuestra amiga (*nuestraamiga*) Inés llega hoy.
¿Cuándo tienes tu clase de español (*deespañol*)?
Marisa accede a hablar (*Marisaccede*).
Este ejercicio (*esteejercicio*) es fácil.

4. If a word ends with the sound **s, n, d, r,** or **l,** and the next word begins with the same sound, only one of these consonants is heard, but with a longer duration. In the third example, the final **r** of **estudiar** would normally be pronounced as a single flap (see page 113) and the initial **r** of **ruso** as a trill. When they are combined you generally just hear the trill.
Las sillas (*lasillas*) están ahí.
El libro (*elibro*) es interesante.
Quiero estudiar ruso (*estudiarruso*).
Vino con Natalia (*conatalia*).

5. If a word ends with one vowel and the next word begins with a different vowel, the two vowels tend to be pronounced as though they formed a single syllable. This happens particularly with combinations of:
a)   e + a: Asiste a la universidad (*asistea launiversidad*).
b)   a + e: Esta escuela (*estaescuela*) es muy cara.
c)   o + e: Vivo en (*vivoen*) Chicago.
d)   e + o: ¿Me oyes (*meoyes*)?
e)   Stressed i or u + vowel: Tú hablas (*tuhablas*) muy rápido.

6. If a word ends with a consonant and the next word with which it is linked begins with a vowel, the consonant joins with the vowel.

el ET (the Steven Spielberg creature)   (*e lete*)
los hombres   (*lo sombres*)

These are not the only cases where linking occurs, but they are the main ones.

7. Sometimes when sounds are found in close proximity, they are influenced by one another so that they sound quite different from how they do when they are pronounced individually. This process is called assimilation and exists in both Spanish and English, but not always in the same way. It is one of the features that can make spoken Spanish difficult to understand. For example, an **n** which is followed by a word that begins with **b** is pronounced as **m** in Spanish. This is because when pronouncing the **n**, the lips are already closing together to pronounce the **b**, and this turns the **n** into an **m:**

un vaso (*um baso*)   un bebé (*um bebé*)

The same phenomenon occurs if **n** is followed by the sounds **p** or **m:**

un papel (*um papel*)   un martillo (*um martillo*)

If **n** is followed by the phonemes /k/ written with **c**, as in **banco** or **qu** as in **banqueta** or /g/ (**un gato, pongo**), it sounds like the pronunciation of the English *n* in words like *think, thing*. Try saying *thin* and *thing*. In spoken English, these two words are distinguishable only because of the difference in the pronunciation of the *n*. The second kind of *n* is the one you find in Spanish before /k/ or /g/.

8. When we discuss pronunciation in the next chapter, we will consider accentuation in Spanish and English in some detail. In addition to word stress (syllables within a word that receive more or less accentuation), there is also sentence stress both in English and Spanish. That is, some words in a sentence tend to receive more emphasis than others. It will help you when trying to understand spoken Spanish to be on the lookout for the kinds of words that receive the most stress in a sentence since these are usually the ones that carry most of the message. Some of the types of words that receive stress include:

adjectives: **viejo, delgado, gordo**
adverbs: **pronto, lentamente, tarde**
interrogatives: **¿qué? ¿cómo? ¿quién?**
nouns: **amigo, casa, perro**

numerals: **dos, primero, veinte**
personal pronouns: **tú, él, yo**
verbs: **compra, llegan, vamos**

The types of words that generally go unstressed are:

definite articles: **el, la, los, las**
prepositions: **con, por, para, debajo**
unstressed pronouns: **lo, la, se, le,** etc.

Due to their unstressed nature, you may have more difficulty in distinguishing them in speech.

Connecting images and sound

If you are lucky enough to have access to videos in Spanish, in addition to tapes, you will find that understanding spoken Spanish is not as difficult as you may have thought at first. While taking into account the questions we have considered above, you will also be able to watch the facial expressions and gestures of the people who are speaking—this helps considerably when trying to interpret a message. There are few things more difficult than trying to speak in a foreign language on the phone: we just have a disembodied voice to talk to and no visual clues whatsoever. This is basically what happens to you when you listen to a lab tape. When you can see the face and body of the people talking, however, things become much clearer. We use our body in more ways than we realize to convey our emotions and sentiments. Already you have probably noticed that Spanish speakers tend to use more gestures than Americans. Watching these will be a big help to you. If you are able to watch videos in Spanish on your own, try out the following. Run through the section you want to view without the sound, and concentrate on what you are seeing—the basic situation, age, sex, social condition of the people talking—anything in the background that gives you a clue as to what the conversation is about (an airport, bank, post office, etc.). How do the people look? Happy, angry, pleased, surprised? Are there any moments when they emphasize a point by tapping a foot, laying a hand on someone else's arm, shaking their head, etc? Then run the tape a second time trying to catch the gist of the conversation and fitting it in with the information you have already gleaned just from the gestures. You will be surprised at how much you can understand.

> SUMMARY

In this chapter we looked at some of the problems involved in understanding a spoken message in Spanish. We have seen that, as with reading, you will not be expected to understand everything. Making your objectives realistic is very important. This helps you to put things in perspective. You cannot expect to understand a large portion of what you will hear but, as we have seen, this does not matter because you will only be expected to pick out a few key words or ideas.

We have also seen that there are many contextual clues that will help you interpret a message. If you notice the age, sex, or social standing of the people who are talking, as well as the situation, it will help you focus and give you a great deal of information even before you start to think about the words themselves.

Understanding spoken Spanish poses some special problems for the English speaker because Spanish practices *linking*. That is, some words are joined in speech, whereas in English they may be pronounced with a slight pause in between. This is what makes it difficult sometimes for English speakers to understand where one word ends and another begins. The Spanish sound system is also different. There are certain sound units in Spanish that differentiate meaning, but which don't function as such in English. These special sound differences need to be recognized in order to help interpret messages. We have also mentioned the importance of watching body language and gestures as an aid to understanding the message.

CHAPTER EIGHT

SPEAKING OUR MIND

En boca cerrada, no entran moscas.   No flies enter a closed mouth.
Por la boca muere el pez.   It is through their mouths that fish die.
    Spanish proverb

I pointed to everything, and enquired the name of it, which I wrote down in my journalbook when I was alone, and corrected my bad accent, by desiring those of the family to pronounce it often.

    Jonathan Swift, Gulliver's Travels

➤ BEFORE WE BEGIN

These two Spanish proverbs seem to confirm some students' worst fears. Both caution against speaking too much. This, however, will never be the advice given to you by a language teacher, who is more likely to tell you to follow Gulliver's path—to ask questions, listen attentively to the way things are pronounced, and to take notes for future reference. Listen to this conversation between a French teacher and his student, a Spanish military officer, some two centuries ago:

    —Tengo miedo de decir disparates.
    —En los principios es menester resolverse a ello. Hable Vmd.* siempre sin temor.
    —Se burlarán de mí.
    —Déjese Vmd. de eso, que vendrá el tiempo que podrá Vmd. desquitarse.

    "I'm afraid of saying stupid things."
    "When you're beginning, you have to make up your mind to do it. Always speak without fear."
    "They'll laugh at me."
    "Don't worry about that, the time will come when you'll get your own back."

(P.N. Chantreau, *Arte de hablar bien francés, o Gramática completa*)

* This is an abbreviation for Vuestra Merced, an old form of address meaning "your honor" or "your worship." This gradually evolved into usted, which is sometimes abbreviated as Ud. and sometimes as Vd., precisely because of its origin.

This is probably the single most useful piece of advice you could get at this stage. Throw caution to the wind, don't worry about what other people think of you when you speak Spanish. In the end, you'll more than get your own back because you will have started to become fluent in one of the world's most extensively spoken languages, and that has already become the second language in this country.

➤ ATTITUDES TO ORAL EXPRESSION

Some people find speaking, particularly in public, much more of an ordeal than others. You may already be aware of having either a negative or a positive attitude toward speaking a foreign language. But in any event, go over these questions referring to oral activities in English with a partner and see if your attitudes coincide or differ. Then share your findings with the rest of the class.

Ä Activity 1 ....

1. At high school how many of these activities did you voluntarily participate in?
   a. speech contests
   b. public poetry or drama readings
   c. debate clubs
   d. theater
   e. public speeches
   f. class presentations

2. In which college courses have you had oral exams?

3. How do you usually do in oral exams (in English) compared with written exams?
   a. better
   b. worse
   c. much better
   d. much worse
   e. about the same

4. When you have to give an oral presentation in English in front of a class, do you ever get any of the following symptoms? Which ones?

   a. sweaty hands
   b. nervous twitch
   c. light-headiness
   d. trembling legs
   e. a blank mind from sheer panic
   f. headaches
   g. a stomachache
   h. desire to vomit
   i. sudden need to go to the bathroom
   j. others

5. Which of these adjectives best describes the state you are in just before you have to give a speech or presentation in English?
   a. petrified
   b. nervous
   c. calm
   d. elated
   e. embarrassed
   f. combination of the above

If you have never studied a foreign language before, you can skip the next activity; otherwise do it with a partner. *Be honest!* Whatever your answers, you will not be penalized. These questions are merely designed to help you come to terms with some of the negative feelings you may have about oral participation.

Å *Activity 2* ....

1. At what age did you start studying a foreign language (not necessarily Spanish)?

2. For how many years did you study a foreign language in high school?

3. Which of these activities were common when you studied a language before?
   a. individual presentations
   b. group presentations
   c. reading aloud
   d. skits
   e. dramatizations of stories or short plays
   f. answering oral questions in front of the class
   g. group oral activities
   h. class poetry readings
   i. recording individual tapes of free or structured conversation
   j. other oral activities

4. When you knew that there might be emphasis on oral participation in a foreign language class, did you usually:

   a. try to sit at the back of the class?
   b. sit in the front row so that you would hear better and be ready to answer more quickly?
   c. sit somewhere in the middle and try to go as unnoticed as possible?
   d. keep your eyes averted from the instructor in the hope that he/she wouldn't call on you?
   e. volunteer to answer the question immediately, even if you were not absolutely sure you were correct?
   f. volunteer only if you were 100 percent sure you were correct, so you wouldn't make a fool of yourself?
   g. mentally try to answer all the questions, whether you were called on or not?

Now go back and discuss with a partner the oral activities you participated in before you enrolled in this course and how you felt about them. Make a list of the oral activities that you most enjoyed and those that you hated. Then compare your lists. Share your findings with the rest of the class.

The previous activities have helped you recognize your general attitude toward oral activities with a particular focus on those in a foreign language. You have had the opportunity to bring your fears and anxiety into the open, and even your hostility to this aspect of language learning, if it exists. You should recognize that these feelings are quite natural and are shared by many of your peers. Indeed, there is nothing unusual about them. Learning a foreign language can be a threatening experience in many ways. We have seen in the chapter on culture that contact with a totally different culture can make you question your own and even your sense of identity. You have to look on this as a positive experience because it helps broaden your horizons in a way you may not have felt possible before.

In a similar way, learning to speak a foreign language and, in particular, to speak it in an unnatural classroom setting can be very worrying for some people because they fear sounding and looking ridiculous in the eyes of the instructor and, more importantly, before their peers. Our own self-image rarely coincides with what other people perceive. A sense of personal dignity is something shared by the majority, and thinking that we have made a fool of ourselves in front of others because of speech blunders can be a hard blow to our self-esteem.

When you are in a Spanish-speaking environment and you have no option but to use the language—to ask directions to the train station, to tell a taxi driver to take you to the airport, to reserve a hotel room, etc.—somehow you drag up the words and structures from within you. They may be far from perfect utterances, but you supplement your faulty Spanish with gestures, mime, facial expressions, the occasional English word, or even drawings on a piece of paper. You would also find that the Spanish-speaking people you were trying to communicate with would not only not laugh at you, but would be pleased that you were trying to learn their language and would do as much as they could to try and get your message. When speaking a language is a question of survival, people survive, and the fear of feeling foolish suddenly takes a backseat.

Be prepared to take risks if you want to learn to speak a language. You have to risk saying something that may not be understood, and need to rephrase it until it becomes intelligible. You have to risk guessing a word and being wrong. You have to risk grossly mispronouncing something and be willing to go back and resay it when you realize how it really should be pronounced. In the classroom, you have to risk saying things in front of your peers that some of them may be able to say much better than you and, yes, you might have to endure a few insensitive sneers if you say something that sounds really atrocious. By opening your mouth you always risk having a fly enter it, but unless you are willing to take that risk you cannot hope to improve your spoken Spanish. Ultimately, you are the one who will lose out.

You have to make up your mind that you are going to overcome your anxiety and take whatever steps are necessary to do so. If you have a positive attitude, there are many things that can help. Many famous people at one time in their life have had a fear, sometimes bordering on paranoia, with regard to public speaking. According to his widow, María Kodama, the Argentinian writer Jorge Luis Borges was one such person. As a young man he was so shy that he was incapable of standing up and addressing a crowd. As he became more well-known he found that he had to speak before large audiences. At first it was an ordeal for him, but he gradually overcame it so that nobody, in his later years, would have suspected that he had once had this problem.

Nobody is born speaking a language of any kind. Young children take about two years before they start producing much that is comprehensible, but in the preceding months they have been constantly absorbing language. When they do speak, they commit numerous mistakes and may continue to do so for years. If you think you have problems with Spanish irregular verbs, so do young Spanish-speaking children. It is not uncommon for them to say or write **(yo) sabo** instead of **sé** because they assume that the verb **saber** conjugates like a regular verb. They also may have trouble pronouncing certain phonemes, and it is only as they grow older and have extensive exposure to the language and more years of formal instruction that their speech gradually comes into line with that of standard Spanish.

If a student is starting to learn Spanish from scratch, nobody is going to expect that person to speak perfect or even near-perfect Spanish. However, take into account the following. Young children may not speak their native language perfectly, but this is no impediment for them to **hablar por los codos,** as is said in Spanish (literally, *speak through their elbows* or *talk the hind leg off a donkey*). Anyone who has had anything to do with young children knows that one of the characteristics of most of them is that they constantly ask questions and never seem to stop talking. Indeed, a nineteenth century Frenchman, Gouin, based a whole method for learning foreign languages on his observations of his young nephew and the way in which he asked questions.

Young children learning to speak their native language and adults learning to master a foreign language go through different processes, although there are many similarities. Undoubtedly, if you are not willing to practice the language, your oral skills will never improve. Some people adopt the attitude, "When I know enough of the language, then I will be willing to speak it." What they mean by "know enough" is "know enough grammatical rules." But while this may help you understand the language intellectually, it will be of little use to you when it comes to speaking. Like many other things in life, you need to practice speaking in order to acquire any fluency. It is like thinking you know how to drive a car just because you have read a driver's handbook. If you become extremely anxious when speaking Spanish there are several things you can do about it.

Strategy 1

Speak to your instructor during office hours or after class and let him/her know that you feel extremely nervous about answering questions in class or giving an individual oral presentation. Mention any specific situations in class in relation to oral activities that make you anxiety-stricken. Your instructor may have no idea at all of this problem and may have been attributing your hesitancy in such situations to a lack of preparation, or interest, or even personal hostility.

You cannot expect your instructor to excuse you from all such activities. If you are learning the language, you need to acquire proficiency in all four skills, and you cannot become proficient at speaking if you refuse to speak. There is also the question of grades. Most grades for foreign languages include an oral exam or exams and a course grade for participation. However, you may be able to reach some kind of agreement. Your instructor might be able to allow you a few weeks when he/she does not ask you to perform any oral activity in class in front of your peers, unless you specifically volunteer to do so. During that period you may need to meet with your instructor to show that you are doing the required work, even if you are not speaking up in class. Your instructor also may want to give you the opportunity at these meetings to do the oral activities on a one-to-one basis. Gradually, however, you will need to rejoin the class activities. But if you are allowed to do this at your own pace, within certain reasonable limits, you may feel more confident at it.

Strategy 2

Speak as much Spanish as you can outside class. This is obviously easier for those who live in areas with a large Spanish-speaking community than for those who don't, but it is still possible. You may have Hispanic friends who habitually speak to you in English, but who could be prevailed upon to speak to you regularly in Spanish. There may be Spanish-speaking international students at your college or university whose English needs improvement, and you can set up an exchange with them. You help them for an hour a couple of times a week with their spoken or written English and, in exchange, they spend a couple of hours speaking Spanish with you. There is probably an international office on your campus, or a Hispanic center where you can find out about such things. They may even have social activities that you could get involved with, giving you the opportunity to meet more Spanish-speaking people.

Strategy 3

Get together regularly with someone in your Spanish class and spend a couple of hours doing some kind of activity or sport you both enjoy, and only speak Spanish together. You could also hold a pizza party with other members of your class, where the only language allowed is Spanish.

You may think it won't help much to speak Spanish with someone whose Spanish is no better, even worse, than your own. That isn't the case. You may not learn a lot of vocabulary or new structures from your partner, you may not even learn how to improve your accent, but you will be forcing yourself to speak the language in a real context, as opposed to the classroom. For the time you are together, your mind will be in "Spanish gear" and this is always tremendously positive. Of course, if your partner happens to know more Spanish than you, the chances are that you will benefit from that.

Strategy 4

Make the most of any social gathering, particularly of an international nature, where you may have the opportunity to make new Hispanic friends. Actually knowing someone whose native language is Spanish can change your whole perspective on the language and will give you insights that are very difficult to transmit in a classroom setting.

Strategy 5

Watch Spanish-language films. Many video clubs have them and they may even be available on your campus. This is a pleasurable way to increase your listening skills and improve your speaking. Your vocabulary will increase as well as your overall understanding of how the language fits together.

Strategy 6

Speak Spanish aloud to yourself as you cook dinner, tidy up your room, do your wash, etc. You may not have anyone to correct you or answer you, but holding a running conversation with yourself in Spanish can really help you start thinking in the language. Imagine that you are describing to someone else just what you are doing at that moment, or think of a situation you may have come across in your text recently—for example, how to give directions. Pretend you are telling someone how to get to the post office in your town from a certain central point, or where the nearest bank is, etc. These are minutes that are well spent. Indeed, it can become addictive and you may find yourself thinking in Spanish and even speaking it aloud when you are out in public, so watch out!

Strategy 7

For those who feel physically ill at the thought of having to speak Spanish in front of others, how can you counteract the pit you feel in your stomach just before going to a Spanish class, or the headache that comes on mysteriously a half hour before Spanish class starts? Not everyone who is anxious about speaking the language, of course, suffers physical symptoms, but there are a surprising number of people who do. First you need to develop a positive attitude toward speaking Spanish, and the points outlined above should help you to do this. Make your instructor your best ally because between the two of you, a solution can be worked out. In fact, you will find that just by facing the problem and talking about it to your instructor, you will already have started to feel better.

Secondly, do your best to relax just before class. This may be difficult or almost impossible if you have another class immediately before, but even if you do, there are some simple things you can do like breathing exercises, a short brisk walk, or a cup of herbal tea. You may be able to put your headphones on in between classes and listen for a few minutes to whatever music relaxes you best. Try to prepare yourself mentally for the class and make sure you are well organized. If you are doing all your assignments and putting regular, daily effort into the class, you will be going to class in a positive frame of mind—this in itself should help your confidence.

Strategy 8

Don't allow your confidence to be shaken by classmates who seem to have a special gift for speaking Spanish and never appear bothered by performing in public. It is possible that they studied Spanish for several years at high school, or spent some time in a Spanish-speaking country, or have Spanish-speaking relatives. Indeed all of these may be true. As a beginner, you will not be expected to speak at any other level except at the one that corresponds to your level of instruction.

Å Activity 3 ··

Consider the suggestions made above for increasing your opportunities to speak Spanish. Think about your own circumstances and your campus. Which of these possibilities are feasible for you and how can you work them into your existing schedule? Write down your ideas and comment on them with a partner. Can you help each other? How?

➤ IT'S NOT WHAT YOU SAY, IT'S HOW YOU SAY IT

When you are speaking Spanish in a classroom setting, probably most of your energy goes into trying to produce grammatically correct utterances. While grammatical accuracy is important, it is by no means the only important factor in a real conversation. In your own language you not only know how to say things that are grammatically correct, you also know how to say things that are socially acceptable. Speech, after all, is a social skill.

Although we have been advocating practicing speech alone in the previous section, this is only a last resort, and should be combined with other ways of practicing Spanish. The whole purpose of speech is to carry out a social act: to express an opinion, to ask someone else to do something for you or to volunteer to do something for them, to express anger, irritation, excitement, and so on. Human beings use speech to get things done in society because they are essentially social animals.

Consider a few of the ways in which we may ask someone to do or not do something.

Close the door.
Please close the door.
Would you mind closing the door, please.
I'd appreciate it if you'd close the door.
Could you be awfully kind and do me the favor of closing the door?
I hate to be a nuisance and bother you, but do you think you could possibly close the door?

Don't smoke.
Please don't smoke.
Would you mind not smoking?
I'd appreciate it if you didn't smoke.
I'm terribly sorry, but would you mind not smoking?
I hope you won't object to my asking, but would you mind awfully not smoking... I suffer from bronchitis.

All these messages are intended to provoke an action from another person. That is, after listening to the message the other person is expected to close the door or stop smoking. Not all the messages, however, are appropriate for every circumstance and the native speaker knows intuitively which are socially acceptable and which aren't. For instance, if you sit next to an old woman you don't know on a bus and suddenly say to her, "Close the window," she may be so irritated by your "order" that she won't do it, or she may comply, but she will probably add some kind of remark about how rude young people are today. In either case, you will no doubt be embarrassed. Similarly, if someone offers to drive his boss somewhere and, as soon as he sees that she's about to light up in the car, declares, "Don't smoke," he may have ruined his chances of promotion in the near future. Again, the message, while grammatically correct, is inappropriate. On the other hand, if you said to your brother or mother, "Could you be awfully kind and do me the favor of closing the door," they would probably wonder what was wrong with you and think you were joking.

In Spanish, you also need to learn what is socially appropriate for every occasion. Unfortunately, as you can see from the two lists of expressions above, being polite is often linguistically more complicated than being rude. In Spanish, as in English, you need less command of the language to say **Cierre la puerta** than **Me hace el favor de cerrar la puerta,** or **No fume** than **¿Le importaría mucho no fumar? es que me afecta los bronquios.** However, even though you may use some complicated grammatical structures in more polite usage (the last one, for example, includes the conditional), you can learn some of these useful phrases as lexical items and sound quite authentic when you use them on the right occasion, even if you have no idea how to use the conditional in other situations or, indeed, don't even know what it is.

In Chapter 2, when dealing with culture, we discussed at some length the different modes of address in Spanish, particularly the nuances between **tú** and **usted.** It is very easy to give offense in a Spanish-speaking environment by mixing these forms. You should particularly remember that the fact that someone treats you as **tú** does not necessarily mean that you should treat them in a similar fashion. Age, gender, and social circumstances all play a role.

When you first start to study Spanish, you frequently learn how to ask lots of questions soliciting personal information. For example: **¿Cómo te llamas? ¿De dónde eres? ¿Qué estudias? ¿Dónde trabajas? ¿Tienes hermanos?,** etc. All these kinds of questions are very useful and, in a classroom setting among peers, quite inocuous. You should not assume, however, that it is socially correct to ask just anybody these very personal questions. If you were in an airplane sitting next to an elderly Spanish gentleman, it would be quite inappropriate for you to start badgering him with questions of this nature, however much you wanted to practice Spanish. You would need to have a repertoire of phrases more suitable for general conversation.

In the classroom, the kind of replies and reactions that you get from your peers are usually predictable. You ask them what they study and they tell you "Spanish and journalism," you ask them to give you a book and they give it to you. In real life, answers and reactions are not always predictable, particularly when dealing with a different culture. We have to learn, often by trial and error, to gauge whether what someone says is what they really mean and how we should react. For example, if someone says **Cuando vaya a Bogotá, visítenos,** they are not inviting you to their home for a meal, and even less, to spend a weekend. If you actually go, you may call them, then if they repeat the invitation it will probably be specific so you will know that they really do want to visit them: **Venga a cenar el jueves a las nueve.** You need therefore not just to learn the right formulas for the right situation, but to be able to react linguistically in one way or another depending on the answer you receive.

You are almost certain to find yourself at one time or another in circumstances when you are at a loss for words. You may start a sentence and then find that you can't find the right expression to end it. Or you may start to say something and forget, halfway through, what it was you were going to say because you were putting so much effort into trying to be correct. Part of the battle of learning to speak a foreign language is what we might call the art of deception. This does not mean that you are going to set out to deliberately deceive the person you are talking to, but that you are going to become successful at covering your tracks and "faking it" when you find yourself at a loss for words.

Early on in your study of Spanish you need to develop the habit of rephrasing things and finding alternatives. There have been numerous experiments with chimpanzees to find out whether they are capable of learning human language. In one such experiment a chimpanzee called Lucy, using a special sign language, aptly described a watermelon as "drink fruit." This kind of inventiveness is what you should strive to develop in Spanish, as well as circumlocution, that is, saying things in a roundabout way. If you don't know a specific word, think how you can explain it in simple terms in a way that gets the meaning across. If you don't know the verb **endulzar,** for example, but you remember **dulce,** you can say **hacer/poner dulce.** When learning words, learn synonyms and antonyms (as we have seen in the chapter on vocabulary), as this will help your expression. As a last resort, include something in English—there may be a similar Spanish word. All these are techniques that help your fluency, that is, your ability to keep talking in spite of adverse circumstances, to keep your speech flowing.

Not just any kind of speech is acceptable, of course. While a number of grammatical errors are to be expected when you start to learn a language, some may cause confusion and your message may not get across as you had intended. For example:

Estoy malo.	*I'm sick.*
Soy malo.	*I'm a bad person.*
Estoy violento.	*I feel ill at ease, worried.*
Soy violento.	*I'm violent.*
Fui al cine.	*I went to the movies.*
Fue al cine.	*He/She went to the movies.*

Speech is almost always accompanied by gestures and body movements, and even though nonverbal language differs considerably from one culture to another, using some sort of nonverbal language can often help you get your idea across as well as compensate for linguistic lapses. Watch Spanish-speaking people in conversation, either in real life or on video. Study their gestures and movements and try to incorporate some of these into your own conversations. Don't be afraid of using your body.

Å *Activity 4* ....

Do the following activity with a partner and take turns explaining. You need to buy the following products in a Spanish-speaking country but don't know all the vocabulary. How would you explain what you want? The person playing the shopkeeper can try to help the other out, but neither of you may use a dictionary.

1. You have to change a plug on a piece of electrical equipment and you need a screwdriver.
2. You want to write some letters home and need paper and airmail envelopes.
3. Something you ate at dinner has had a disastrous effect on you. You need some antidiarrhea tablets.
4. The airline has lost your suitcase and you need to replace your underwear.
5. Your feet hurt from walking, so you'd like to get some comfortable slippers.
6. It's very hot and you have only brought nylon socks, which make your feet smell. You need some cotton ones.
7. You have forgotten to bring your hairdryer, so you want to buy one.

➤ CONQUERING STRESS

You cannot expect to have perfect pronunciation when you are just starting Spanish, but there are some aspects of pronunciation that are more important than others because misunderstandings can arise if you are unaware of them. We will discuss how stress works both in Spanish and in English and talk more about the pronunciation of Spanish phonemes.

Stress—the accentuation of certain syllables within a word (word stress) and certain words within a sentence (sentence stress)—is a very important feature of the English language. Indeed, English is sometimes called a stress-timed language as opposed to Spanish which is a syllable-timed language. Stress does occur in Spanish, but only in fixed places, which we will discuss more at length in the next chapter. Even more important, whether a syllable is accented or not in Spanish does not have the same radical effect on vowels as it does in English. When we stress a syllable, we pronounce it with rather more energy than unstressed syllables and sometimes, although not always, this may even be accompanied by nonverbal language: a nod of the head, a tap of the foot.

In English stress is free, that is, it can fall on any syllable within a word. All words of two or more syllables in English tend to have one syllable that is more strongly stressed than the others. For example, in the verb *insult* the stress falls on the second syllable. In the noun *insult*, however, the stress falls on the first syllable. A word may have secondary stress; for example, *intellectual*. The main stress falls on *lect*, but there is a secondary stress on *in*. In certain polysyllabic words, there may also be tertiary stress. Some words in English have double stress, particularly if they are compound words: *boy scout, old-fashioned*.

It is important to realize what happens to vowels in English in unstressed syllables. Whereas in Spanish the quality of a vowel is approximately the same both in stressed and unstressed syllables (for example, in **amar** the first **a** is unstressed and the second is stressed, but they are pronounced the same), in English a phenomenon called *reduction* occurs. That is, we pronounce unstressed vowels in an extremely relaxed way, to the point that sometimes they practically disappear. The unstressed vowel may sound like a weak *i* or it may be the unstressed vowel that we call *schwa.* This is one of the most typical sounds of English and one of the most difficult ones for foreigners to reproduce. If a foreigner's speech in English sometimes sounds stilted and unnatural, it is often due to that person's inability to manage the English stress system and produce the unaccented vowels. Schwa does not correspond to any single letter. It is the sound of *a* in *cathedral,* the sound of *e* in *butter,* the sound of *o* in *convert* (verb), the sound of *u* in *circus,* and the sound of *i* in *terrible.*

English speakers are so used to reducing their vowels in unstressed positions that most of the time they are unaware of it. They then transfer this habit to Spanish where it does not exist, and reduce unstressed Spanish vowels also to schwa, particularly in words of several syllables. For instance: **oportunidad.** The last syllable **(dad)** is stressed, but English speakers frequently reduce the second **o** to schwa. The Spanish ear, trained to hear the full force of all vowels, gets confused, particularly since the vowel schwa does not exist in Spanish.

English stress is so free that a word can be stressed differently when pronounced alone from the way it is pronounced in a phrase. This happens particularly with certain words that can carry either single stress or double stress. For example, we talk about *the <u>Ber</u>lin wall* (with the stress on *Ber),* but when speaking of the city we say *Ber<u>lin</u>* (with the stress on *lin).* Stress is so important in English that it can change the class of a word (there are many words like *insult,* that are nouns if the first syllable is stressed and verbs if the second one is stressed), or even its meaning. Therein lies the humor of this sign seen outside an adult bookstore selling pornography in London: *All dirt cheap.*

If *cheap* is stressed, the meaning is *dirt cheap,* that is, extremely cheap. If both *dirt* and *cheap* are stressed, the meaning is all dirt (that is, pornographic literature) is cheap.

In Spanish, whether one syllable or another is stressed can also change the meaning and/or part of speech. Consider the following:

bebe	*he drinks*	bebé	*baby*
savia	*sap*	sabía	*he knew*
compro	*I buy*	compró	*he bought*

In English there are certain kinds of words that have both strong (stressed) and weak (unstressed) forms, depending on their use in a sentence. The auxiliary *to have*, for example, can be pronounced in several ways depending on the amount of emphasis we want to give it in a sentence.

He *has* done it. I say he has. (strong stress)
He has finished his work. (unstressed)

The Spanish auxiliary, **haber,** in contrast, does not have strong and weak forms, so you should avoid trying to reproduce the English system by trying to give it extra stress. This sounds unnatural in Spanish, particularly since there are other ways in which emphasis is given.

(Él) Sí que lo ha hecho.
Por supuesto/Desde luego que lo ha hecho.

English prepositions also have strong forms and weak forms. The former are often used if the preposition is in final position. On the other hand, prepositions in Spanish are unstressed and sound strange if stressed.

She put the hat *on.*
What are you looking *at?*

Pronouns and possessives in English have strong and weak forms. For example, *h* is not pronounced the same way in *He has his hat in his hand,* where the *h* of *his* tends to disappear, as it is in *It is his (not hers),* where it is stressed. Similarly, the *me* in *He gave me a book,* is pronounced differently from the *me* in *I said, give it to me.*
In Spanish, these words are not emphasized in the same way. Compare.

It's his book.   Es su libro. (unaccented)
                                  El libro **es de él.** (accented form)

Words that often give people trouble, with regards to stress, are those that are very similar in Spanish and English. Do the following activity.

Ȧ *Activity 5* ···

Say these words aloud. First pronounce the English words, then the Spanish cognate (necessary/necesario), taking care to place your stress in the correct place.

English	Spanish
necessary	necesario
interesting	interesante
university	universidad

television	televisión
microscope	microscopio
inspector	inspector
secretary	secretaria
urgent	urgente
professor	profesor
police	policía
geography	geografía
residence	residencia

➤ SAYING WHAT YOU MEAN

We have already said that nobody expects you to have perfect pronunciation in Spanish when you are just starting. In fact, you will probably never have perfect pronunciation, that is, you will never sound like a native. We all know someone who came to this country as a young adult, has lived here for perhaps thirty years, and yet speaks English with a (sometimes heavy) foreign accent. Some accents and intonation are so characteristic that we can often tell the person's origin: French, German, Italian, etc. On the other hand, children who come here at a very young age usually grow up not only speaking English perfectly, but sounding just as American as their neighbor.

Your ability to learn a foreign language does not necessarily diminish as you grow older. Indeed, there are some factors, such as intellectual ability to grasp linguistic concepts and strong motivation, that may make you more successful at mastering a language as an adult than when you were younger. However, there is no doubt that you will find it hard to attain the kind of perfect pronunciation that children seem to acquire without effort. But this is not necessarily a drawback. Many Spanish-speaking people find a slight foreign accent extremely attractive, just as we may find a slight French or Spanish accent attractive. The problems arise if your pronunciation of certain key Spanish sounds is so deficient that people misunderstand you. You will gradually be able to refine your pronunciation, but even in your first months of learning Spanish there are some sounds that you should concentrate on in order to avoid confusion.

In the previous chapter we dealt with some of these sounds, such as **r** and **rr, n** and **ñ, l** and **ll.** You should also practice words with **jota** since they may give you difficulty. Its pronunciation (**j**, and **g** before **i** and **e**) varies considerably in the Spanish-speaking world, from a sound that seems similar to the English *h*, to a very pronounced guttural sound in the throat. Whichever pronunciation you choose, it should be articulated clearly so that pairs like the following are distinguished.

mojo	moco
paja	paca
loja	loca
jurar	curar
jarro	carro

The sounds **d** and **t** can cause some problems since they are pronounced with the tongue pressed against the teeth, whereas in English the tongue presses against the alveolar ridge, that is, the ridge of the gums behind the upper front teeth. This shift of the tongue's position might not seem too important to you, but it alters the quality of the sound. The Spanish intervocalic *d* is particularly soft and an English *d* in this position not only sounds harsh, but can sound to the Spanish ear like an **r**, resulting in confusion.

You say	It sounds like
codo	coro
todo	toro
lodo	loro

The same occurs with the pronunciation of intervocalic **t**. If you pronounce it as an English *t*, it may also be interpreted as an **r**.

You say	It sounds like
coto	coro
pato	paro
meto	mero
foto	foro

You need to be careful with words that contain **b** and **v** as these two sounds are identical in modern Spanish. If you insist on distinguishing between them, it will sound strange and you may give the impression that you are trying too hard to be correct. Words like *tubo/tuvo* should be pronounced in exactly the same way.

Remember that the letter **h** is always silent in Spanish. If you pronounce it, it will be confused with the **jota** sound. For example, if you pronounce the **h** as in *Hugo*, it is heard as **jugo**.

The most common American mispronunciation of Spanish vowels is to diphthongize them rather than to pronounce them as pure vowels. For instance, the open Spanish **o** is frequently pronounced as the diphthong *o* in English words such as *rose, though*. This is not likely to cause confusion, but it may irritate the person you are speaking to as it sounds grating to the

Spanish ear. The **o**, perhaps more than anything else, immediately gives away an American speaker. Even though you can't expect your pronunciation to be perfect, you can strive to produce a Spanish that is pleasant to the ear, even if it has defects. Look on it as a courtesy on your part toward the Spanish people you hold a conversation with.

Try pronouncing the following words in which you contrast the English diphthong and the Spanish **o**, so that you can hear the difference clearly yourself.

English	Spanish
low	lo
toe	todo
no	no
doughnut	donut

Spanish **e**, which is similar to the sound of *e* in words such as *net* and *pest,* is frequently diphthongized by American speakers. This can cause confusion because Spanish has the contrast **e/ei**.

You pronounce with a diphthong	People hear
pena	peina
le	ley
ves	veis

➤ LEARNING FROM OUR ERRORS

Many people dread being corrected in front of everyone by the instructor. Some are able to take correction in good spirit and look on it as a way of helping them to improve. These are usually the people who have plenty of self-confidence. Not everyone is able to do this though. Some people feel deeply embarrassed at having their pronunciation or grammatical mistakes commented on by the instructor for everyone to hear, even if they know that half the class makes the same mistakes.

If you feel really uncomfortable at the way your instructor is correcting your pronunciation errors in class, you should have a word with him/her as soon as possible. You could say something like, "I know that it's really useful for you to correct my pronunciation because I learn a lot from your comments, but would it be possible for you to save them for when I come and see you in your office?" Your instructor shouldn't feel offended, or think that you think you are above correction. Instead, hopefully he/she will pick up on your sensitivity to being corrected in public and try to work something out.

Generally your instructor will probably only correct pronunciation errors that are so severe that they interfere with communication. We have dealt with a number of these above, so familiarize yourself thoroughly with these points; being aware of them is the first step toward overcoming them. Try not to take correction of your speech personally. Your instructor is not making a statement about you as a person when correcting your errors, but merely trying to help you perfect your oral skills.

You should expect to make far more mistakes in speech than you do in writing or grammar exercises. This is natural. Think of how you do your written homework: you may have a couple of days before you have to hand it in, you are able to do it alone in your room and, if you don't like what you've written, you can always tear up the paper and start over again. You may also have the benefit of consulting with peers who know more Spanish than you do, or even with native speakers . You may revise a composition several times before you present the final draft. When you are speaking, though, you are in a public situation, whether it is before a class or alone with the instructor. You cannot go back and eliminate what you have just said without anyone knowing; you have no time to sit and think about how to phrase things; you have to be concentrating on grammar (verb tenses, number and gender agreement, pronouns, etc.), pronunciation, vocabulary, and, in addition, worrying about whether what you are saying is socially acceptable—all at the same time! It is small wonder that errors in speech are so frequent, not merely when speaking a foreign language, but when speaking our native language too. The advantage, however, is that all except the very glaring errors tend to be quickly forgotten as we tend to concentrate mostly on the content of a message and do not worry too much if the person speaking to us makes an occasional mistake, as long as we can understand what they are saying.

You may be asked as part of your course work to tape certain personal information or specific grammatical structures. Here you do have the opportunity to think more carefully about what you are going to say before sitting down with the tape recorder. Moreover, you have the privilege of erasing a tape. Recording yourself, required or not, is a very good way for you to get an idea of your oral progress. If you periodically record a couple of minutes, perhaps once a week, and continue to do this on the same tape throughout a semester, then by the end of the period, when you go back and listen to your first recordings, you will be able to judge just how much your fluency, grammatical accuracy, and pronunciation have improved. We usually are aware of improvements in our writing because it is more tangible and easier to measure. We don't always know, though, if we are improving in our oral skills. A good way to judge your own improvement is to make a list of the main errors that your instructor points out when correcting you in or out of class. Keep this record in a special section of your loose-leaf folder and practice either on your own, or even better with a native speaker, to try and overcome those particular deficiencies.

However badly you may take correction, you can take heart from the following Biblical story. Things in your Spanish classroom could never be this bad!

> The Gileadites took the fords of the Jordan toward Ephraim. When any of the fleeing Ephraemites said, "Let me pass," the men of Gilead would say to him, "Are you an Ephraemite?" If he answered, "No!" they would ask him to say "Shibboleth." If he said, "Sibboleth," not being able to give the proper pronunciation, they would seize him and kill him at the fords of Jordan.
>
> (Judg. 12:5–7)

Above all, don't get discouraged; it can be very hard as an adult to realize that you have to start at a child's level of speech in your new language. There are so many things you want to talk about, and yet your tongue won't seem to obey. Take things slowly and work at speaking from many different angles, and gradually things will begin to fall into place.

➤ NUTS AND BOLTS

It's a good idea when learning a language to memorize a number of stock expressions which can help you out in many situations. They will also give you a hold on the language—the feeling that you have mastered something. You might like to learn the following expressions.

To ask for something in a polite way you might say:

¿Me deja Ud. su periódico/libro, por favor?	*Would you mind lending me your newspaper/book?*

To inquire whether something you intend to do will bother someone, you can say:

¿Le molesta a Ud. si le hablo?	*Do you mind if I talk to you?*

To express the fact that you have no strong feelings either way about something, you can say:

A mí me da igual.	*It's all the same to me.*
No me importa.	*I don't mind.*

To ask someone to do something you can say:

Me hace el favor de hacer...	*Do you mind doing...*
Al fin y al cabo...	*In the last resort...*

➤ SUMMARY

In this chapter we discussed people's general attitudes toward speaking in public and the more specific problem of speaking a foreign language in a classroom setting. Many students have secret fears about speaking a foreign language in front of their peers and instructor, and we have tried to bring some of these fears out into the open and deal with them.

We have seen that the act of speaking is extremely complex. One very important factor is that it is a social act, so speaking a foreign language can never be merely a matter of saying something grammatically correct: you have to learn how to say things that are also socially acceptable in Spanish.

We have looked at some of the difficulties involved in pronunciation and paid special attention to the role of stress in both English and Spanish. The importance of this aspect of language is not always adequately dealt with, and we have seen some of the dangers inherent in not paying enough attention. We also examined some of the misunderstandings that can arise if certain Spanish phonemes are pronounced as though they were English phonemes, and we have taken into account the fact that even if no misunderstanding occurs there may be certain errors of pronunciation that can irritate a native Spanish speaker. Finally, we looked at some of the attitudes people have about being corrected and how you can actually use error correction to your own advantage.

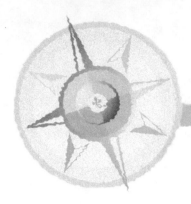

CHAPTER NINE

WRITING TO COMMUNICATE

> *His speech was like a tangled chain; nothing impaired, but all disordered.*
>
> *William Shakespeare,* A Midsummer Night's Dream

➤ BEFORE WE BEGIN

Many people feel more comfortable writing in Spanish than speaking it because they find it less stressful. Yet at the same time, as soon as they get away from filling in blanks and try to write something creative, they become disheartened because the amount of red ink on the work they get back seems to suggest that Shakespeare's words hold true for them too—that their writing is "like a tangled chain" and they despair of reaching any sort of reasonable level of written Spanish before they finish their courses. In this chapter we will examine the role of writing in general and your attitudes toward it. We will also try to develop reasonable expectations and objectives and look at some of the problems you face when trying to write in a foreign language.

➤ IS WRITING A PART OF OUR LIFE?

Before the telephone, knowing how to write well was a much-esteemed skill, since writing was the only way to communicate at a distance. Even now many families bring their children up to write a thank-you note every time they receive a gift or an invitation. Today many people hardly ever write at all, unless they have to write business letters or formal written reports for work or school. Do the following activity with a partner to see how much writing you do.

A. Look at this list of different kinds of written documents and check off those that you habitually or occasionally do in your native language. Add any other kinds of writing that come to mind.

Personal diary

Shopping lists

Telephone messages

Thank-you cards and letters

Letters to friends and relatives

Love letters

Letters of application for jobs

Legal documents

Official forms (for passports, driver's licenses, etc.)

Creative writing (poetry, short stories, etc.)

Letters to pen pals

Formal essays for college

Written exams

Telegrams

E-mail

Recipes

Instructions on how to use an appliance, CD player, etc.

Instructions on how to get to a friend's house, the post office, etc.

Newspaper reports

Other

B. Now answer the following questions. Afterwards, compare and discuss your answers with a partner.

1. Which of these documents do you find the easiest to write? Why?

2. Which of these documents do you find the hardest to write? Why?

3. What kinds of writing do you do for pleasure? If you never write for pleasure, to what do you attribute this?

4. Were you brought up to write frequently in your home, or was writing an activity largely restricted to school?

5. When you need to write a formal composition in English, which of these points give you the most trouble?

Ordering your thoughts

Grammar

Vocabulary

Word order

Style

Other

6. Which of the following do you tend to do when you write a long letter to a relative or a friend?

Sit down and write it straight off from start to finish

Reread paragraphs as you go along and go back and alter things

Look up words you don't know or aren't sure of in the dictionary, or just take a guess

7. Classify the kinds of written documents in the list above into formal and informal, together with any others that you may have added. What are the characteristics, in your opinion, of formal and informal writing?

Ӑ *Activity 2* ··

Some people have developed hobbies over the years that incorporate writing. Survey your class to find out how many people participate in the following activities.

1. Writing a pen pal, either in the United States or abroad
2. Doing crossword puzzles
3. Writing limericks or other nonsense poetry
4. Playing scrabble or similar games that test word invention, spelling, etc.
5. Using electronic bulletin boards
6. Other

Ӑ *Activity 3* ··

Now poll your class to find out how many people habitually use a word processor when they have to do any written work, and how they think this affects their attitude toward writing. The following are some questions you could ask. If you think of others, feel free to ask them.

1. If you use a word processor, do you think this makes you more prone to being adventurous with language because you know it is easy to go back and rectify any problems?
2. Are you more likely to write several drafts of a document on a word processor than if you were to write by hand or on a typewriter?
3. Do you think that the computer helps you order your thoughts better or, on the contrary, are you intimidated by computers and find that your mind goes blank when you are sitting at one?
4. Do you use e-mail frequently? If so, how do you feel about it?

> BEING REALISTIC: WHAT YOU CAN AND CAN'T DO

If you are just beginning Spanish it would not be realistic for you to expect to be able to write long involved essays on Spanish literature or history. Indeed, you will probably not be able to do that even after two or three years of instruction. There are, however, a number of things that you can learn to write at a very early stage. These are everyday things that we actually write and that have a true communication value.

Shopping lists

In the list of written documents in Activity 1, we see "shopping lists" and "telephone messages." In beginning Spanish you usually learn all kinds of words for food products and meals, as well as things that you might buy at a pharmacy (**aspirinas, termómetro,** etc.). Once you learn the appropriate vocabulary you will be capable of writing your own weekly shopping list in Spanish. If you are not asked to do this in class, you could try doing it yourself once a week.

> 1 kg[1] de patatas
> 1 bolsa de azúcar
> una caja de cereales
> un litro[2] de leche
> una lechuga
> dos chuletas de cerdo, etc.

[1]kilogram (2.2 lbs)
[2]liter (1.0567 liquid quarts). The decimal system is widely used in the Spanish-speaking world and you should become familiar with it.

In this country most products can be found in grocery stores throughout the year, because when fruit or vegetables are not in season they are either transported from the part of the country where they are, or they are imported. This is not always the case in Spanish-speaking countries, where what you find in the markets in the way of fresh fruit and vegetables may depend on what can be grown in that area at that time of year. With this in mind, do the following activity.

Å Activity 4

Here are some suggestions from a diary for Spanish housewives on what to buy in December and in July. Think about the area of the country you live in and the agricultural products produced there. If the fruit and vegetables you buy depended exclusively on what was grown in your area, could you draw up a winter and a summer shopping list in Spanish, similar to the one below?

Cesta de la compra

diciembre: Coliflor, lombarda, coles de Bruselas, escarola
              Besugo, rape, pavo
              Naranja, manzana, kiwi, piña, frutos secos

<table>
<tr><td>julio:</td><td>Pimientos verdes, judías verdes, pepinos
Boquerones, merluza, bonito, ternera
Ciruela, albaricoques, paraguayos, melón</td></tr>
</table>

(*Agenda familiar,* Madrid: Caja Madrid, 1989, pp.74 and 128)

If you don't know the Spanish words for the products that you habitually buy, or any of the ones in the above list, you can look them up in a dictionary. This gives you practice in writing something meaningful even if it is only a list. You will be practicing useful vocabulary, paying attention to spelling, and if you ever have the chance to go to a Spanish-speaking country, you will have a head start with your shopping! While walking around the grocery store, notice the number of products on the shelves that have labels in Spanish, that originate from Spanish-speaking countries, and perhaps have instructions in Spanish. You will be surprised at how many you find, even if you do not live in an area that has a large Hispanic population.

Schedules

Within the first few weeks of class you will learn words for different academic subjects and probably for different sports too, so you can write both a study schedule and one for your free time. If you need help with vocabulary, your instructor can provide it. Writing out a schedule is something you do every semester, so if you do it in Spanish, you are creating a meaningful document.

Telephone messages

Telephone messages are also within your capabilities at an early stage in your development. We know how we tend to write in a telegraphic way when we take down messages: *John, Philip called, 8:05 P.M. Return call before 10:00 P.M.* Keeping this in mind you can now jot down telephone messages of your own in Spanish.

Pepe, te llama Luis. Llamarlo nada más llegar a casa.
Ana, te llaman Rosa y Beatriz. Ir a su casa el sábado para gran fiesta.

Accounts

Something else you can write in Spanish is a record of your monthly accounts. It can go something like this:

Resumen del mes		
Ingresos normales (beca, préstamo, dinero de los padres, trabajo):		
Ingresos extraordinarios (dinero de la abuela, propinas, horas extra, etc.):		
Total ingresos:		
Gastos en efectivo:		
Transporte		
Gastos de supermercado		
Entradas cine, etc.		
Gastos cargados en cuenta (cheques):		
Alquiler de apartamento		
Equipo de música		
Ropa, etc.		
Total gastos:		
Diferencia:		
Ahorro mes:		
Pendientes de pago:		
Saldo en cuenta corriente:		
Saldo en cuenta de ahorros:		

Historical events

In English we often use the present tense to talk about the past in a more vivid way. We call this the *historic present*. Spanish also does this. If all you know in Spanish is the present tense, you can practice it by drawing up a list of famous events and after you have written them, quizzing a partner. The more bizarre the events you are able to describe, the more interesting it's likely to be. Here are some famous events:

16 de octubre, 1793: Muere en la guillotina la reina María Antonieta

12 de octubre, 1492: Cristóbal Colón descubre América

14 de diciembre, 1911: El explorador noruego Roald Amundsen descubre el Polo Sur

10 de junio, 1776: El Congreso de Filadelfia aprueba la Declaración de Independencia de los Estados de la Unión

Recipes and other instructions

One of the first verbal forms you learn in Spanish is the infinitive: **saber, tener, comer,** etc. In modern Spanish, the infinitive form is often used in recipes, so you could write up some of your favorite recipes and exchange them with others in your class. Here is a recipe for hard-boiled eggs with vegetables.

Huevos duros con verduras
Ingredientes: Huevos duros, 2; cebollas, 3; tomates maduros, 500 g[1]; pimientos, 500 g; jamón serrano, 200 g; dientes de ajo, 2.
Confección: Rehogar[2] primero los ajos enteros y las cebollas en rodajas, añadir los pimientos en juliana fina[3] y mantener a fuego lento hasta que estén blandos. Agregar[4] el jamón, partido en daditos[5] y darle unas vueltas[6]. Por último, incorporar los tomates pelados y en trozos. Cocer todo lentamente unos 30 minutos y sazonar.
Cortar los huevos duros por la mitad, introducir en este sofrito[6] y dejar cocer despacio unos minutos. Servir adornando la fuente con triángulos de pan frito.

(*Agenda familiar,* Madrid: Caja Madrid, 1989, p.80)

[1]*grams*   [2]*gently fry*   [3]*... cut in thin strips*   [4]*Add*   [5]*small cubes*   [6]*stir*   [7]*fried mixture*

The infinitive is also used for giving instructions. Try writing instructions for someone on how to use a dishwasher or washing machine. For example:

Para usar la lavadora:

1. Separar la ropa de color de la ropa blanca
2. Colocar la ropa en el fondo de la lavadora
3. Añadir el detergente en polvo
4. Elegir el programa apropiado
5. Apretar el botón

Poetry

Poetry is something else you can write when your knowledge of Spanish is very limited. Even if you never write poetry in English, you can try this. For example:

Primavera	*(1 noun)*
flores amarillas	*(noun + adjective)*
llover, brotar, renacer	*(3 verbs)*
corderitos blancos	*(noun + adjective)*
Primavera	*(1 noun)*

Diary

A diary is also something you can start writing almost from the start. It is a very good habit to start writing at least three or four sentences in Spanish every single day. Indeed, your instructor may ask you to keep such a diary and give you specific instructions about what kind of things to include. If not, you should do this for your own benefit. Free writing, that is, letting your mind run free and writing down your thoughts without worrying too much about how accurate your writing is, can be very beneficial.

We have discussed how important it is to take risks speaking. You need to practice constantly and make numerous mistakes if you are ever to improve. The same goes for writing. No one writes perfectly right from the start. Everybody needs practice, and a nonthreatening way of getting it is to keep a personal journal. In this way you make Spanish your own language, because you use it to record your thoughts and personal life, however imperfectly you do it. You will let your imagination take over and may be surprised to discover that writing in Spanish can actually be a pleasant experience. Here is what one student, Michelle, wrote about her diary in Spanish: **"Me gusta la idea del diario porque la gramática no es importante y puedo escribir más libre sin preocupación."** If you have never kept a journal in English, this experience could show you the value of taking time out from your daily life, if only for a few minutes, to record your thoughts.

If your instructor has asked you to keep a journal in Spanish, to avoid intimidating you he/she will probably not correct your errors. This will allow you to concentrate on getting your thoughts down in Spanish rather than writing something that is grammatically perfect. However, grammatical accuracy is also important, so you might want to elicit comments on your errors from your instructor from time to time. Nonetheless, you will also have formal occasions when you are concentrating specially on grammatical accuracy.

One frustrating aspect of learning a foreign language when you are adult is that you have adult thoughts and experiences and want to express them. But unfortunately the language you presently are able to use is more like that of a young child. However, once you realize that you can produce all types of documents with this very simple language, your knowledge of Spanish won't seem so elementary.

Å Activity 5 ....

Make a list of the types of simple documents you can write in Spanish. Include some that are not mentioned in the previous sections. Set yourself a date by which you can reasonably expect to have written at least one sample of each kind.

➤ DOING IT WITH STYLE

Whenever we commit our thoughts to paper, however simple the message, we always bear in mind to whom our written message is directed. Writing a letter to a friend is not at all the same as writing a job application letter. Content as well as style are very different. We may use colloquial language or even slang in our letters to friends and family, or regional expressions that we know these people understand and share but which we wouldn't use with people from other geographical areas. We are not so concerned about our grammar or spelling—friends are not likely to criticize us for adding an extra *s,* or leaving out a *p.* Just as our speech register changes according to the social situation in which we find ourselves, so does our writing style. This is something to keep in mind when you are writing in Spanish too.

Unfortunately, practically everything you will be writing in Spanish, unless you are lucky enough to have Spanish-speaking pen pals or relatives, will be directed toward your instructor. Knowing that your instructor is going to read everything and correct it may inhibit your style. Even so, it is possible for you to get a sense of different styles in written Spanish and to cultivate your own.

If you are used to using e-mail, it may be possible for you to communicate with your instructor by e-mail in Spanish. The style you choose will be fairly formal. You may find that you are unable to use Spanish accents, but don't worry, you will have plenty of opportunity to practice with accents on other occasions! Your letter to your instructor may look something like this:

Estimado Profesor Rodríguez:

Soy un/a alumno/a en su clase de Español 150. Perdone que le moleste[1], pero tengo un problema. Tenemos que entregar los ejercicios en clase el martes pero todavía no tengo el libro de texto. La librería no tiene bastantes libros. Voy a tener el libro el martes por la tarde. ¿Me permite entregar los ejercicios el miércoles por la mañana, por favor?

Se lo agradeceré. Reciba un cordial saludo de

Jami Smith

[1] *I'm sorry to trouble you*

Get in the habit of writing messages to your instructor, either to ask questions about class or just to relate something interesting that has happened to you lately. Your instructor will be pleased to communicate with you like this and you will be using your Spanish for a real purpose. Always communicate with your instructor in Spanish, even if you have to add an occasional phrase in English.

You could also communicate in Spanish by e-mail with a group of people in your class or even in another section or class. You could decide to exchange messages once a week about something that you all have an interest in. Your style, of course, will be different from the one you use with your instructor:

Oye, Pedro, ¿qué tal andas? ¿Sabes que hay fiesta en la residencia Rollins el sábado? Empieza a las 8 de la tarde y va toda la pandilla.[1] ¿Por qué no vienes?

[1] *gang, group*

Just as you need to use spoken Spanish at every opportunity, look for similar opportunities to use your written Spanish.

When you first start to learn a language, the kind of sentences you learn to write tend to be like this:

Mi padre es alto, moreno y delgado. Trabaja para una firma importante de computadoras. Mi padre se llama Richard Fox. Es de Chicago. Es muy simpático.

These are what we call *simple sentences*. They have only one clause, as opposed to complex sentences that have a main clause and one or more subordinate, dependent clauses. You need to practice writing simple sentences and descriptions, such as of your family and friends or of your room or home. You might also look at the language of advertising which, in its attempt to get a clear message across, sometimes uses simple sentences. Look at the following:

¿Te apetece ahora un Nestea? Nestea es té frío y al limón. Y además, no tiene gas. Está delicioso en cualquier época del año. No tienes que esperar al verano para disfrutar Nestea. ¿A qué esperas?

Å *Activity 6* ···

Try writing your own advertisement for a product you use frequently and exchange it with your partner. Is your language interesting enough to make your partner want to buy your product? How can you improve it? Look at advertisements in Spanish newspapers and magazines. Find ones that use a lot of simple sentences.

Writing simple sentences can get boring. There comes a time when you want to write something more interesting and, moreover, to combine concepts into more complicated structures. You might start off by learning to use the conjunctions **y** and **o** or **pero,** which allow you to combine two or more simple sentences quite easily.

Compre nuestro producto.
Ahorrará dinero.
Compre nuestro producto **y** ahorrará dinero.
Usa esta crema antiarrugas.
Parecerás más joven.
Usa esta crema antiarrugas **y** parecerás más joven.

Remember that if the word after **y** begins with **i** or **hi,** then you need to change the **y** into **e.**

El vestido está hecho de encaje **e** hilo.

O always establishes an alternative.
Puedes comer el pescado **o** la carne, pero no las dos cosas.

O is changed into **u** if the next word begins with **o**.
Tienes que hacer una cosa **u** otra.

Pero adds a certain reservation.
¡Mi padre trabaja mucho **pero** no gana mucho dinero.
Mi hermana está casada **pero** no tiene hijos.

There are a lot of adverbial expressions you can add to your sentences to make them more interesting. Some that may come in handy are:

en primer lugar	*in the first place*
para empezar	*to start with*
naturalmente	*naturally*
por supuesto	*of course*
sin lugar a duda	*without a doubt*
desgraciadamente	*unfortunately*
felizmente	*fortunately*
por eso	*because of that, on account of that*
por lo tanto	*consequently*
por fin	*in the end*
sin embargo	*however*
no obstante	*nevertheless*
a pesar de eso	*in spite of that*
para mi sorpresa	*to my surprise*
después de eso	*after that*
en resumen	*to sum up*

You will find lots of occasions when you can work these expressions, or similar ones, into your written Spanish.

Estudio dos horas de español todas las tardes, **naturalmente.**
Desgraciadamente, no puedo pasar estas vacaciones en Florida.
No estudié bastante para el examen y, **por lo tanto**, no saqué una A.

A lot of writing is concerned with complex sentences that have a main clause and one or more subordinate clauses. Often you will find in Spanish that you need to use the subjunctive in subordinate clauses, but this is not always true. Fairly early on you should be able to write some complex sentences. **Que** is used more than anything else in Spanish to connect clauses.

Creo que no debes ir a la fiesta el sábado porque tienes que estudiar más para el examen del lunes o no vas a aprobar.

We could divide this as follows:

> (yo) creo
> no debes ir a la fiesta el sábado
> tienes que estudiar más para el examen del lunes
> no vas a aprobar

Now do the following activity.

Ȧ *Activity 7* ···

You probably already know enough Spanish to write any of the individual phrases in the preceding example, but you may not have practiced linking them. Using the same formula, **Creo que... porque ... o** write two complex sentences related to your everyday experience.

In your first year of Spanish you may only write individual paragraphs, but sooner or later you will learn to connect paragraphs. Practice writing an introductory paragraph about something personal—your hobbies, your family, vacations, etc. Try to make it as interesting as you can by linking sentences with **y, pero, o,** or **porque.** Then think how you would continue your next paragraph. You may want to use some of the adverbial expressions quoted above to help you.

You will probably be using your dictionary quite a lot, even in your first year. As we said in Chapter 5, dictionaries can be a great help, but they can also let you down if you don't know how to use them. Even though you will probably want to use a bilingual dictionary to start with, you should gradually get used to checking things in a monolingual dictionary, that is, an all-Spanish dictionary that provides abundant examples of words within phrases. This helps you more than anything else to see how words really work in context. However, even if you only use a Spanish-English/English-Spanish dictionary, you should learn to use it correctly. The symbols used in dictionaries vary, so familiarize yourself with the ones in yours. You should buy the biggest dictionary you can afford. It will be of much more help to you and you will probably use it for a number of years. The symbols will tell you if the word you are looking up is a noun, a verb, an adjective, an adverb, etc. It will tell you whether your verb is transitive or intransitive, that is, whether it can take a direct object or not. The part of speech of a word is very important. Some people look up an English verb and, because they are in a hurry, don't notice that the Spanish word they have picked is a noun. They will need to look further before they find the equivalent verb.

A dictionary will also tell you whether a word is used in certain contexts (for example, in medical, legal, technological, nautical language, etc.). This is very important because often a word may mean one thing in a very specialized context and something quite different in another. Think about the word *hives:* a skin problem **(erupción cutánea)** is very different from (bee)hives **(colmenas)**. In English, even if you use the same word, you know from context which of the two you are referring to. You should not assume that words like this in Spanish are also used in both (or more) contexts, so don't accept the first word you come across.

Get in the habit of checking the word you choose with those offered in the other half of the dictionary. That is, if you look up an English word, after you have chosen what you think is the correct Spanish one, look it up in the Spanish-English section of the dictionary. Words can mean many very different things both in Spanish and English, so you need to check your context carefully. For example, *leg* is usually translated as **pierna** in Spanish, but only if you are dealing with human legs. A table leg or chair leg in Spanish would be **la pata**. English doesn't make this semantic distinction. Similarly, if you look up the word *corner,* you will find **rincón** or **esquina**, depending on whether you are referring to an angle from the inside or from the outside. Consequently, **rincón** is used for the inside corner of a room, and **esquina** for a street corner or the sharp corner or edge of a piece of furniture.

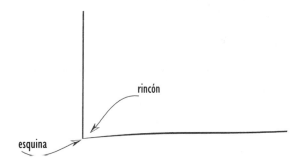

Again, English makes no lexical distinction here. Look at all the words offered when searching for something. It will make you realize that there is rarely one single word that has an exact equivalent in the other language.

Often words have totally different applications in each language. For instance, you often learn **gordo** as the equivalent of *fat,* and although this is true when referring to people who are overweight, there are some uses of

gordo in Spanish that can in no way be translated by *fat*. For example, coarse kitchen salt, as opposed to refined table salt, is **sal gorda; el gordo** is the first prize in the lottery; **Me cae gordo** means *I don't like him* or *He irritates me;* **Es un problema gordo** means *That's a difficult problem;* **leche gorda** is milk with a high-fat content; **hacer la vista gorda** is *to turn a blind eye,* and so on. This occurs time after time with the two languages and you should realize this from the start if you are to avoid a simplistic outlook towards learning Spanish. It does not mean that you have to learn absolutely every definition when you look up a word, but it will help you to realize the complexity of a language.

Samuel Johnson, the famous eighteenth-century English dictionary compiler, wrote under the word *oats* in his dictionary: "OATS n. A grain which in England is generally given to horses, but in Scotland supports the people." For fun you might like to try making up dictionary definitions of very common English words as though you were going to use these to explain something to a Spanish-speaking person. Finally, bear in mind that a dictionary can never give you the whole story. You may get a definition, but if it is of a concept you have never come across before, it may not be of much help to you and you will have to seek additional information. Look at the following: "Solid-hoofed herbivorous quadruped with flowing mane and tail, used as beast of burden and draught, and for riding on" *(Concise Oxford Dictionary).* If you came from a culture where you had never seen a horse before, this probably would not be of much use to you. A dictionary can be your best friend, but as with any friendship, it needs to be cultivated.

➤   MAKING THE MOST OF OUR ERRORS

We have seen in the previous chapter how we can learn from our errors in speech and how correction can have a positive effect on speech development. You should also be prepared to learn from your written errors, because an understanding of why your writing is incorrect can help you assimilate questions of grammar and style and help you improve in the future. If you are required to write short compositions, your instructor may ask you to do more than one draft. On the first draft he/she may not correct your errors but simply point them out and say what they are (lack of agreement, wrong verb tense, spelling, wrong lexical choice, etc.). Then it may be left to you to ponder these errors and to decide how best to rectify them. You will then do a second draft, which your instructor may decide is good enough to accept. Your final grade will of course depend on your instructor, so you should make sure you understand his/her grading system.

If you do learn to make several drafts of your work, you will find this a great help when trying to develop your writing skills. You also may be asked to critique rough drafts of your peers and should regard this as a good learning experience. You may think you don't know any more Spanish than your peers (indeed, you may know less than some), so how can your critique be of any value? However, an objective reader often catches errors that the author was unable to spot because he/she was too close to the text. When you have to examine someone else's writing and not only correct, but justify your corrections, you will find that it helps you considerably with your own writing. It is also a good idea, once you have completed a written assignment in Spanish, to set it aside for at least a day before turning it in. Then reread it. You will have put some distance between you and your text, and may find that you can read it almost through a different set of eyes.

Writing is definitely a craft; it does not come by magic or overnight. As such you will have to constantly work at it. You will find that your writing will improve with practice and with increased exposure to the language, particularly to the written language. So try to read as much as you can. Get in the habit of making a list of your most frequent errors, and when you check your work before handing it in, try to catch some of these errors yourself. One of the most frequent is lack of grammatical agreement: you may have a subject that is plural and a verb in the singular, or a plural feminine noun and a singular masculine adjective. You may have used stem-changing verbs and not changed the stem, or chosen the wrong tense. Some of these things are easier to catch than others, but if you constantly look for them, you are more likely to be successful. If you do not fully understand why you keep making the same mistakes, talk it over with your instructor. There may be additional explanations that you can read, or extra grammar exercises that will help you with particular structures. Remember, there are some errors that are more important than others. Spelling and accents are important, but these are things that you can refine, and generally people, will still understand you. On the other hand, if you use a third-person form for the verb when it should be a first-person form, the result may be total confusion for your reader. Check with your instructor to see what he/she considers to be your most glaring errors at this stage and the ones you should pay special attention to.

Here is what one student, Anne, wrote about learning to correct her own errors through frequent drafts.

> Ahora veo donde he mejorado porque tengo que escribir un ensayo larguísimo en mi clase de literatura y me acuerdo de los errores que cometía antes. Cuando estoy escribiendo mi composición de cinco páginas, unas veces cometo errores y de repente los veo. Una pequeña voz me dice: la Sra. Saz te ha dicho que eso está mal. ¡Se hace así!

You have to work toward developing your own "pequeña voz."

➤ NUTS AND BOLTS *Syllabification*

One of the things you will have found out at the beginning of your Spanish studies, and which affects both your spoken and written Spanish, is that in Spanish you do not divide up syllables in the same way as in English. Spanish syllables tend to begin with a consonant and end with a vowel.

1. **VCV** (V-vowel; C-consonant)

   If a consonant is found between two vowels, the consonant joins with the next vowel: **ca-sa, ca-fé, so-nar.**

2. **VCCV**

   If there are two consonants between two vowels they both join with the next vowel if they are the following:

bl	ha-blar	gl	i-glú
br	ca-bra	gr	a-gri-cul-tura
ch	bi-cho	ll	ca-lle
cl	e-clo-sión	pl	a-pli-car
cr	la-cre	pr	a-pris-co
dr	ma-dre	rr	pe-rro
fl	cha-flán	tr	li-tro
fr	o-fre-cer		

3. **VCCV**

   In other cases where there are two consonants between vowels, the word is divided between the consonants: **es-pa-ñol, Nor-ber-to, ar-cón, puer-ta, ven-ta-na**

4. **VCCCV**

When there are three or more consonants between vowels, if two of them belong to the groups listed in number 2, the division comes between this group and the other consonant.

bl	em-ble-ma	fl	in-flar
cr	es-cri-bir	tr	en-tre

If the two letters are **ns**, these are not divided: **cons-truir, cons-tan-te.**

5. **CVVC**

If two vowels are found between two consonants, the word is divided between the vowels **a, e,** or **o: co-rre-o, ve-as, co-lo-re-ar.**
If there is a combination of a strong vowel (**a, e, o**) and a weak one (**i, u**) then usually a diphthong is formed and both vowels are pronounced as one syllable: **plei-to, ai-re, bue-no.**

6. If there is a weak vowel next to a strong one, and the weak one receives stress, then instead of a diphthong, two separate syllables are pronounced and a written accent mark must be placed on the weak vowel: **con-ti-nú-o** (present tense), **ha-bí-a, Ra-úl.**

Dividing written Spanish

When you write Spanish, there are additional things you should keep in mind when dividing words at the end of a line:

1. Spanish-speaking people tend to leave less space at the end of a line (in a letter, for instance) than do English speakers, so you should write to the end of the line, dividing the final word if necessary.

> Querida Marta:
> Mil gracias por tu carta que recibí con cierto re-
> traso. Me alegro de que te encuentres bien...

Not:

> Querida Marta:
> Mil gracias por tu carta que recibí con cierto
> retraso. Me alegro de que te encuentres bien...

2. If a word has a recognizable prefix, it may be placed at the end of a line and the rest of the word at the beginning of the next, even if this goes against the rules above: **des-entender** or **de-sentender, in-acentuado** or **i-nacentuado.**

3. Do not divide a word if by doing so you would form another which is funny or sounds vulgar.

> ri-dículo *not* ridí-culo
> torpedo *not* tor-pedo
> computa-dora *not* com-puta-dora

4. Try to avoid dividing words of four letters (although we pronounce them as two distinct syllables) and two vowels (even if they form two syllables in speech.

> casa *not* ca-sa
> geografía *not* geografí-a
> aéreo *not* a-éreo

5. If a syllable begins with **r**, don't put it at the beginning of a line if it forms a separate word: **Alarico** not **Ala-rico.**

6. Don't separate abbreviations.

> EE.UU. *not* EE.-UU. *(the United States)*
> OTAN *not* O-TAN *(NATO)*
> SIDA *not* SI-DA *(AIDS)*

7. Don't put the conjunctions **y, e, o, u** at the end of a line.

8. Don't start a line with a syllable if the next word begins with the same one: **ca-la la lluvia.**

À *Activity 8* ....

How would you divide these words? (You may be able to divide them in several ways.)

a. barbaridad   d. mantequilla   g. antropología
b. bebé   e. historia   h. ordenador
c. correo   f. filósofo

Accent

Look at the following English words: *café, résumé*

These are words that have passed into English from French and have maintained their original written accent. However, we may or may not retain the original pronunciation. The accent mark is not necessarily associated in English with the syllable we stress. For instance, in some parts of the English-speaking world *café* carries the stress on the first syllable, and in others, on the second. Yet in all places the accent mark is used.

In Spanish, the written accent is *never* a matter of choice: it is an integral part of the linguistic system and extremely meaningful. We are not used to having written accents in English that are closely linked to the way we pronounce words, which is why it is sometimes difficult for English students of Spanish to realize the importance of accents.

Stress in Spanish works as follows:

1. If words end with a vowel, **n**, or **s**, the next-to-last syllable is normally stressed: *be*-so, *ca*-sas, *ha*-blan, Ma-*ri*-sa, ven-*ta*-nas, i-*nun*-dan. These words do *not* require a accent mark.

2. Words that end in a vowel, **n**, or **s**, and are stressed on the last syllable, *do* require an accent mark: **com-po-si-ción, mar-cha-rán, An-drés, can-tó**. Note that the Spanish accent always slants **á, é, í, ó, ú**. Some other European languages have accents that slant the opposite way, but not Spanish.

3. Words that end in any other consonant except **n** or **s**, naturally receive the stress on the last syllable: **pin-*tor*, ciu-*dad*, ci-ca-*triz***. These do not require an accent mark.

4. If a word ends in any consonant other than **n** or **s**, and the stress does not fall on the last syllable, then it will require an accent: **cés-ped, Héc-tor**.

5. Words that have stress on the third syllable from the end always have an accent mark: *pá*-ja-ro, *cón*-ca-vo, *há*-bi-to, es-*drú*-ju-la, ma-*rí*-ti-mo.

6. An accent mark is used sometimes in Spanish to distinguish two words that are spelled the same but have different meanings. The following are some very common ones.

de	*of* (preposition)	dé	subjunctive of **dar**
tu	*your* (poss. adj.)	tú	*you* (subject pronoun)
el	*the* (def. article)	él	*he* (subject pronoun)
este	*this* (poss. adj.)	éste	*this one* (poss. pronoun)
si	*if*	sí	*yes*
mi	*my* (poss. adj.)	mí	*me* (stressed form of poss. pronoun: **Dámelo a mí**)

7. All interrogative words have an accent mark: **¿Cuándo vienes? ¿Dónde estás? ¿Qué haces?**

Decide why these words have an accent mark. How would they be pronounced if the accent were not there?

1. bailó   2. ímpetu   3. geográfico   4. Belén   5. compás

Punctuation

You have probably noticed some differences in Spanish punctuation, such as: **¡Dámelo inmediatamente! ¿Qué dices?**

The inverted exclamation mark and question mark are perhaps the most characteristic elements of Spanish punctuation. You will find the inverted question mark, in particular, very useful when reading Spanish aloud because it tells you exactly when to start changing your intonation to that of a question, as in **Si quieres pasar una noche divertida, ¿adónde vas?** The inverted question mark just before **adónde** tells you that this is the moment to begin a rising intonation.

Here are some more idiosyncratic aspects of Spanish punctuation.

1. Generally only the first letter of a book or article title is capitalized: *Alicia en el país de las maravillas* (Alice in Wonderland).
2. Names of countries and cities are capitalized: **Perú, Madrid.** Names of the natives of those cities and countries are not: **peruano, madrileño.**
3. Days of the week and months of the year are not capitalized: **enero, lunes.**
4. Names or synonyms for God are capitalized: **Dios; el Altísimo.**
5. Languages are not capitalized: **inglés, español.**
6. Religious and political associations are not capitalized: **católico, republicano, demócrata, socialista, judío.**
7. The forms of address **don** and **doña** are not usually capitalized: **don Andrés, doña María de las Mercedes,** but they are often capitalized in Spain when referring to the king and queen: **Don Juan Carlos y Doña Sofía.**
8. **Ud.** and **Uds.** (or **Vd.** and **Vds.**), abbreviations of **usted(es)**, have a capitalized first letter, but not **yo** (I).

9. Direct quotes are normally preceded by a dash instead of quotation marks:

> Me recibió una muchacha con sonrisa fija:
> —Lo siento, todas las mesas están ocupadas.
> —¿Espero?

10. Decimals are often written with a comma and thousands with a period: 7,2 and 15.038.

Å Activity 10

As you read the following passage, add the accents and the correct punctuation.

> por que hiciste esto pedro? quedamos en ridiculo aceptando la boda con Rosaura. donde quedo pues el amor que le juraste a tita? que no tienes palabra?
>
> claro que la tengo pero si a usted le negaran de una manera rotunda casarse con la mujer que ama y la unica salida que le dejaran para estar cerca de ella fuera la de casarse con la hermana no tomaria la misma decision que yo?
>
> nacha no alcanzo a escuchar la respuesta porque el pulque el perro del rancho salio corriendo ladrandole a un conejo al que confundio con un gato.

(Laura Esquivel, *Como agua para chocolate,* New York: Doubleday, 1993, p. 21)

➤ SUMMARY

In this chapter we considered the role that written messages play in our lives and the different ways we write. We have seen how writing can be formal or informal, and how the person to whom we are writing can affect our style. We have seen that, as in the case of oral Spanish, it is best to be realistic and recognize what a beginner can and cannot do in the written language. However, even a beginner can use Spanish for a variety of activities that are similar to ones that Spanish-speakers actually use. We have seen how style varies from one kind of document to another, and about connecting sentences and clauses to make our writing more interesting. We also took into account the role of errors while learning to write. In *Nuts and bolts* we examined syllabification in Spanish, the written accent, how to divide words at the end of a line, and finally the differences between English and Spanish punctuation

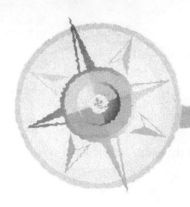

CHAPTER TEN

VERBS WITH A TEMPER

Alice was too much puzzled to say anything, so after a minute Humpty-Dumpty
began again.
"They've a temper, some of them—particularly verbs, they're the proudest—adjectives
you can do anything with, but not verbs—however, I can manage the whole lot!
Impenetrability! That's what I say!"

  Lewis Carroll, Through the Looking-Glass

➤ BEFORE WE BEGIN

Many students who have been mistakenly informed by others that
Spanish is an easy language become indignant and frustrated when they start
to become familiar with the Spanish verb system. The peak of frustration
often comes in the second semester when they seem to be confronted with a
different verb tense practically every week. Like Humpty-Dumpty, they may
feel that Spanish verbs, with their seemingly endless stem changes and
impossible endings for every person, do indeed have a temper, but when
they utter his comment, "Impenetrability!" it is certainly not with his confident affirmation, "I can manage the whole lot!"

In this chapter we will examine some problems English speakers have
when faced with a verb system that is so complex and different, in many
ways, from our own. We will see that there are certain basic concepts in our
own verb system which will help you understand Spanish verbs.

It may help to remember that Spanish-speaking children also have a hard
time mastering their verbs and take many years to do so. You cannot expect
to master them fully in a couple of years, but you will be able to learn
enough to express your basic needs in Spanish, and one day you may indeed
be able to say like Humpty-Dumpty, "I can manage the whole lot!"

162

In Spanish we talk about **tiempos verbales,** and this may be confusing because **tiempo** is also the word used for talking about real, historic time. English makes a lexical distinction here that Spanish does not. We use *time* to refer to real time, but when we are dealing with **tiempos verbales** we use the word *tense.* We will see how this distinction is very important in English and how you also need to take it into account in Spanish, even if there is not a separate word for it.

Part of the problem with the Spanish verb system is the way in which Spanish and English have developed historically. Spanish is a Romance language like French, Italian, Portuguese, Romanian, Catalán (spoken in Catalonia), Provençal (spoken in parts of France), and Romansh (spoken in parts of Switzerland). These languages have all evolved from Latin. English, on the other hand, is a Germanic language and even though there is considerable influence from Latin, the English tense system is Germanic in origin. Originally, there were only two tenses: the present and the past. The whole English tense system has evolved around these two tenses.

In early Old English, the simple past and simple present were used to express every kind of past, present, and future situation. The past tense was used to express all kinds of past situations. The context was made clear by adding adverbs. Compound tenses (those with two forms like the present perfect, *has come,* or past perfect, *had done*) were not introduced until the end of the Old English period.

Even today there are remains of this system: on occasions we still use the present tense to express future time.

He *leaves* for Washington tomorrow.
She *finishes* her studies next year.
The concert *starts* at six o'clock.

The adverbs of time—*tomorrow, next year, tonight*—let us know that even though this is a present tense we are talking about the future, not the present. Similarly:

a. I was talking to Mary last night and suddenly along *comes* her husband.
b. In 1953, Elizabeth II *is crowned* queen of England.
c. I *hear* that you've been given a scholarship.

As with the previous examples, the adverbial expressions in *a* and *b* give us the clue: *last night, In 1953.* Example *c* has no adverb, but this is a typical use of the present tense with verbs like *to hear, to tell, to say, to learn,* etc. It uses the present tense to make past events more vivid and dramatic and is called the historic present.

Spanish coincides with English usage in both these circumstances. The present tense may be used to talk about future events:

Sale para Washington mañana.
Termina sus estudios el año que viene.
El concierto empieza a las seis.

It can also be used to refer to the past.

Hablaba con María anoche y de pronto aparece su marido.
En 1953, Isabel II es coronada reina de Inglaterra.
Me dicen que te han dado una beca.

Whether one chooses the present to talk about the future or the past will depend on one's point of view. The speaker may want to state a fact, or add a certain slant to the message.

Ṅ Activity 1

Decide whether the verb tense in the following sentences coincides or not with real time. If it does not, say which tense is used and to what time it refers. List any adverbial expressions that indicate what kind of time is being referred to.

1. Marcos y Antonio van a las Bermudas en junio.
2. Los juegos olímpicos se celebran en Barcelona en 1992.
3. Nos informan que el avión sale con una hora de retraso.
4. Empiezo las vacaciones la semana que viene.
5. Enrique trabaja en una gasolinera.

You may also encounter some difficulty with Spanish verbs because of the way in which they are classified, which may or may not coincide with English. Traditionally we think of a verb as being a word that denotes action.

He *runs*. She *plays* tennis. They *do* their homework.

There are others that express processes.

The carrots *are growing* well.
We're *slowing down* now that we're older.
People *change* as they grow up.

Other verbs express sensations.

I *feel* sick.
His leg *hurts*.

These verbs can and often do take the progressive form: I *am feeling* sick. His leg *is hurting*. There are other verbs, though, that express how we view or understand things.

I *think* that you're right.
They *love* Florida.
I *suppose* it's true.

Verbs may or may not be classified in a similar way in Spanish. In English, for instance, we can use the verb *to grow* as both an activity verb and a process verb. If it is an activity verb, it is *transitive,* that is, it can take a direct object.

We *are growing* eggplant this year.

If it is a process verb, it is *intransitive* and cannot take a direct object.

Peter *is growing* so tall!

Spanish cannot use the same lexical verb in both cases. If we are dealing with an activity, we use **cultivar.**

Estamos cultivando berenjenas este año.   *We're growing eggplant this year.*

And if we are dealing with a process, we use **crecer.**

¡Pedro está creciendo tanto!   *Peter is growing so much!*

Another verb like this is *to run.* We use the verb intransitively in phrases such as:

Paul *ran* to the bathroom.

but we can also use it transitively as in:

Jane *runs* her own business.

In Spanish, we have to use **correr** to express the intransitive verb.

Pablo corrió al cuarto de baño.   *Paul ran to the bathroom.*

But we use a different verb (in this case **dirigir)** for the transitive sense.

Juana dirige su propio negocio.   *Jane runs her own business.*

Do not assume, then, that once you have learned one meaning for a verb that it has the same semantic and syntactic range in both languages. Check to see whether the same verb may be used transitively and intransitively, or whether you may need a different one.

The verb *to look* is another frequently misused verb.

Miraron el cuadro.	*They <u>looked</u> at the picture.*

When dealing with perception (that is, an intransitive verb) in Spanish, you need different verbs.

Susana tiene mal aspecto.	*Susan doesn't <u>look</u> well.*
Eduardo se parece a su padre.	*Ed <u>looks</u> like his father.*

^N Å *Activity 2* ···

One verb that is sometimes difficult to express in Spanish is *to have*. It is used idiomatically in all kinds of expressions (*to have a bath, to have a good time, to have a baby,* etc.). Write down as many idiomatic uses in English for the verb *to have* as you can. Then, with the help of a dictionary, try to find the Spanish equivalents.

➤ THE WAY WE LOOK AT THINGS: ASPECT

In spite of many similarities, Spanish and English do not always coincide in their use of verb tenses. There are two notions which further complicate matters: *aspect* and *mood*. Aspect is concerned with viewpoint—the way in which an action is seen by the speaker.

He *cleans* his car on Saturdays.
He's *cleaning* his car now.

In the first example the simple present tense refers to an event that occurs habitually. The adverbial expression *on Saturdays* makes this clear. In the second example, however, we want to draw attention to the fact that the event is taking place as we speak, so we use the present progressive: *He is cleaning*. The adverb, *now,* is optional because the progressive indicates that the event is happening at this moment.

Where's John?	He's *cleaning* his car.

The contrast of progressive with nonprogressive is one of aspect, not tense, in both English and in Spanish. We may conjugate the progressive in any tense.

He *was studying* last night. (past progressive)
This time next week we *will be lying* on the beach. (future progressive)

➤ EXPRESSING PRESENT AND FUTURE TIME

We have already seen how the present tense can be used in English and Spanish to express both future and past time. It also expresses present time in both languages, but the usage does not entirely coincide.

The simple present tense is mostly used in English to express habitual actions.

She goes to the gym on Tuesdays.
They spend their vacations on the coast.

There may be an adverbial phrase such as *on Tuesdays,* but in both cases, there is a sense of repeated action. We are not referring to real present time, that is, an action that is currently going on. Spanish also has this use for the present tense.

Va al gimnasio los martes.
Pasan sus vacaciones en la costa.

The present tense is also used in both languages to talk about things that are always true and, as such, are timeless.

Los tulipanes florecen en primavera.	*Tulips flower in the spring.*
Los inviernos son fríos en Michigan.	*The winters are cold in Michigan.*

The present is also used in English and Spanish in certain contexts such as sports commentaries, stage directions, or demonstrations, when we are describing things as they happen for someone else who may or may not see what we are doing.

Wilson intercepta y, ¡gol!	*Wilson intercepts and it's a goal!*
Primero elijo el programa y a continuación coloco la ropa en la lavadora.	*First I set the program and then I place the clothes in the machine.*

| Sale la criada, llevando la bandeja. | *The maid exits, carrying the tray.* |

Both English and Spanish also use the simple present for exclamations.

| ¡Por fin llegan! | *Here they come at last!* |

Where Spanish and English do differ in the use of the simple present is that English does not use this tense to talk about things that are going on just at this moment. Instead, the present progressive is used. Yet Spanish, even though it has a present progressive, often resorts to the simple present.

| ¿Qué haces? | *What are you doing?* |
| Preparo la comida. | *I'm fixing lunch.* |

It is not that Spanish cannot use the present progressive in these cases; in fact, it frequently does. We can say:

| ¿Qué estás haciendo? | Estoy preparando la comida. |

You should realize, though, that there is a slight nuance in meaning here. If you use the progressive in Spanish in these contexts, you are deliberately putting a stronger emphasis than normal on the process that is going on (doing, fixing), whereas in English you are merely stating a fact. You have no choice of another construction because if you say, *I fix lunch,* it makes a statement about what you do habitually, not what you are doing at the moment.

The Spanish present progressive is formed with the present tense of the verb **estar** and the present participle (**-ando** for **-ar** verbs, **-iendo** for **-er** and **-ir** verbs). Remember that the present participle *never* agrees with the subject of the verb, so forms like the following are ungrammatical: **Elena está cantanda.**

If Spanish has a use for the simple present that does not exist in English, English has a use for the present progressive that does not exist in Spanish. Note that we often say things like:

I'm going abroad next summer.
We're going to the movies on Saturday.

Here we use a present form, in this case a progressive one, to express future time. You cannot do this in Spanish: you would need the simple present.

Voy al extranjero el próximo verano.
Vamos al cine el sábado.

We generally use the present tense in English to express *habitual* actions: *We go to the movies on Saturday.* In more formal sentences, however, we may use it to refer to a single event: *Charles leaves for Paris tomorrow.*

With regard to expressing the future, English does not have a simple (that is, one word) future tense like many languages. Instead, it makes use of various auxiliary constructions or other tenses in a fairly complex manner to express different degrees of the future. For example:

a. I will do it tomorrow. (auxiliary *will* + infinitive)
b. He is leaving later. (present progressive)
c. The boat arrives on Monday. (present tense)

Spanish, on the other hand, has a future tense, although it too has other ways of expressing future time. Unlike the simple present that has different forms for **-ar, -er,** and **-ir** verbs, the future tense endings are the same for all regular verbs. (You will find these in your text.) This makes it a very easy tense for you to learn. Notice that there is a written accent in every form of the verb except for **nosotros.**

Iremos a Grecia el año que viene.	*We're going to Greece next year.*
Vivirán en México después de casarse.	*They'll live in Mexico after they get married.*

When the future is near, however, Spanish prefers to use either the simple present tense, as we have seen above, or the construction **ir a** + *infinitive.* This is probably the construction you will use the most, particularly in conversation.

Vamos a cenar en un restaurante argentino.	*We're going to have dinner in an Argentinian restaurant.*
¿Vas a estudiar medicina?	*Are you going to study medicine?*

For expressions of imminent future, we can use *to be about to* in English and **estar a punto de** in Spanish.

Estoy a punto de salir para el aeropuerto.	*I'm about to leave for the airport.*

If the future action involves intention on the part of the speaker, we can use the constructions **pensar** + *infinitive* or **tener intención de** + *infinitive.*

Pienso matricularme en física.   *I intend to enroll in physics.*

Tiene la intención de pasar un   *He intends to spend a year in Japan.*
año en el Japón.

The most common construction in English to express future time is with the modal auxiliary *will*. Consequently, this construction sometimes conveys the sense of *(not) to be willing*. This is particularly true when it is used in negative sentences.

Will you lend me a hand? (=would you mind lending me a hand)
He won't come. (=he doesn't want to)

In this context, you cannot just use the simple future tense in Spanish, but need to resort to certain expressions.

¿Te importaría echarme una mano?
¿Quieres echarme una mano?
No quiere venir.
No le da la gana de venir.

There is a use of the future tense in Spanish that exists in English but which is used far less. It is used to express a supposition or something that seems probable.

—Allí está Rosa con un hombre.   *"There's Rosa with a man."*
—Ah, será su hermano.   *"Oh, it must be her brother."*

À Activity 3

All the following sentences express future events, but in different ways. Look at the tenses of the verbs or verb structures and decide how you would express them in English.

1. Estefanía de Mónaco: "Espero mi segundo hijo para el mes de mayo".
2. Robert Redford se pondrá a las órdenes de Bob Reiner para protagonizar "The President elopes".
3. Ahora, por la compra de Fruition, recibirá gratis, en tamaño de viaje, *Advanced Night Repair.*
4. Larry Fortensky, marido de Liz Taylor, va a ser abuelo.
5. La Reina Isabel de Inglaterra piensa pasar sus vacaciones veraniegas en Windsor.

À *Activity 4* ··

We have talked about the use of the future to express suppositions. Form suppositions using the future, following this example.

Juan tiene el brazo escayolado *(in plaster)*. (tener una fractura)
Tendrá una fractura.

1. Pepe ha comprado aspirinas. (tener dolor de cabeza)
2. Mariana no me saluda. (estar enfadada conmigo)
3. Antonio está con una señora mayor. (ser su madre)
4. No encuentro el teléfono del fontanero. (estar en las páginas amarillas)
5. La princesa Diana no quiere aparecer en público. (estar cansada de la prensa)

➤ GETTING PEOPLE TO DO THINGS FOR US

From your first day of class you might need to ask someone to do something for you. Whether you actually manage to get people to do what you want, or whether you offend them in the process, depends to a large extent on what sorts of constructions you choose. We discussed some of the options in Chapter 8. The simplest way to ask someone to do something is with the *imperative,* or *command* form, adding **por favor** to soften its effect. You have met some of these in the **Ud.** form to talk to your instructor.

Repítalo, por favor.
Hable más despacio, por favor.

Your text will show you how to form the polite and the informal imperative. It is not always appropriate, however, to use the imperative. As we said in Chapter 8, it can sound brusque and even impolite. Other easy ways of asking in a more polite form are:

a. ¿Me presta su periódico?   *Would you lend me your newspaper?*
b. ¿Puede Ud. ayudarme, por favor?   *Can you help me, please?*
c. ¿Podría Ud. bajarme la maleta?   *Could you get my suitcase down for me?*
d. ¿Me hace el favor de abrir   *Would you do me the favor of opening*
   la ventana?   *the window?*
e. ¿Tendría inconveniente en   *Would you mind repeating that?*
   repetir eso?

You can also use these structures with the **tú** forms, and you will sound friendlier than if you use the **tú** imperative. Notice the use of the simple present tense in example *a*. In this case the person is *expecting* an affirmative reply, otherwise a tense that expresses a greater sense of doubt would be used (**¿Le importaría dejarme su periódico?**).

Examples *c* and *e* use the conditional (**podría**), and this always adds an additional degree of formality or politeness, tinged with a certain sense that the request may not be granted.

When making a familiar request in English, we often tag something onto the end of the request. Something similar is done in Spanish. These forms are only used when we are sure of an affirmative answer since nobody deliberately risks being snubbed.

Hazme un favor, ¿quieres?	*Do me a favor, would you?*
No olvides el pan, ¿de acuerdo?	*Don't forget the bread, will you?*

When we make a request in either language obviously our intention is that the request be granted, so it is very important to pay attention to the wording of our request. It is sometimes difficult in a foreign language to gauge whether we are expressing the same kind of nuances that we intuitively handle in our own language. This is why it pays for you to master some of these formulas and use them as frequently as you can.

À Activity 5 ....

Form suitable requests for the following, using as wide a variety of expressions as possible. Make sure that your request is socially appropriate. Check your answers with those of another classmate.

1. Ask an old gentleman you don't know to tell you the time.
2. Ask someone in your class to lend you his/her Spanish notes **(apuntes).**
3. Ask your friend's mother if she could serve you some more fried chicken.
4. Ask your younger brother to turn the radio down.
5. Tell your neighbor's dog to get off your lawn.

➤ MEMORIZING VERB FORMS

People often find the sheer quantity of Spanish verb forms and endings daunting. Verb forms are simplicity itself in English. For example, there are only four forms for regular verbs.

Stem	-S Form (3rd- person singular)	-ED (past tense and past participle)	-ING Form (gerund and present participle)
walk	walks	walked	walking
cook	cooks	cooked	cooking
like	likes	liked	liking

Irregular verbs may have several forms (*be: am, are, is, been; go: went, bring brought; sing: sang, sung,* etc.) but the effort needed to learn the forms of English verbs is nothing compared with that needed to learn even the regular Spanish verb forms, never mind the stem-changing ones. Moreover, English has no future tense, no imperfect aspect, and the subjunctive is rarely used. Small wonder that speakers of Spanish frequently claim that English "has no grammar," meaning few verb forms. At the same time, they tend to find it an extremely difficult language to master because of the difference in word order and pronunciation. The following are a few basics that need to be remembered when considering how to master the Spanish verb system.

1. At the elementary and intermediate level (or at the advanced, for that matter), nobody expects you to know everything.

2. Everything you learn in connection with verb tenses will be recycled time and again while you are studying Spanish.

3. Set aside a regular time to study verbs. Even if you don't have homework, a short, regular period of time—every day if possible—will help immensely.

4. You need to understand the *uses* of the verb tenses you are trying to learn. This may seem obvious, but there are a surprising number of people who learn the verb forms and then don't know how to use them.

5. Don't try to learn every single irregular or stem-changing verb. Make a selection of the ones most useful to you at this particular time. Your instructor can help you here.

6. Learn thoroughly whatever verb tense you are studying: if you don't do this, you are sure to have to come back to it again. For instance, when you get to the formation of the present subjunctive, you need to know what the first-person singular is of the present tense, and when you deal with the imperfect subjunctive, you need to know the third-person plural form of the preterite, and so on. You will be at a disadvantage if you didn't learn these things properly the first time.

There are many ways in which you can memorize verbs. It is not likely to be very productive if you just sit and stare at a list of conjugations, trying to commit them to memory. There are a number of computer programs that give you practice in verb forms and many people find these useful. Normally, you will have to do something active to commit these forms to memory. Review Chapter 5 on vocabulary because some of these techniques will help when learning verbs.

Notice any patterns that emerge. Frequently there will be a "boot" shape to the verb, as we saw with the present tense. That is, the **nosotros** and **vosotros** forms will stand out as being different. Look at the stem-changing verbs and notice which parts of the verb stem change. Again, this will produce the boot form.

puedo	podéis
podemos	**puede**
puedes	**pueden**

Write down the kind of stem changes that occur. For example, for stem-changing in the present tense:

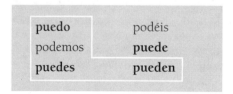

o → ue	poder	puedo
u → ue	jugar	juego
i → ie	querer	quiero
e → i	pedir	pido

Make sure you can conjugate the whole verb in these cases. Try to remember one key verb to serve as a model, and make a short list of the most common verbs that follow that model. Learn groups of verbs that are similar, such as those that have an irregular first person in the present tense.

go verbs	
sal**go**	ven**go**
di**go**	pon**go**
ha**go**	

Remember tips that make things simpler, like the fact that the future tense has the same endings for all three types of verbs, or that for the polite commands we use the opposite vowel in the endings to the one in the stem (**andar—ande, comer—coma**).

Make sets of verb cards and color-code them in a way that personally helps you remember. All those that change their stem from **o** to **ue** could be written in blue, the ones that change from **i** to **ie** in yellow, etc. Above all, collaborate with other students in your class. They are all facing the same task and if you can get a small study group going you can quiz one another using your verb cards. One set of cards could show an infinitive, for example, and another give the future conjugation or the present tense. Or prepare some worksheets with spaces to fill in order to test yourself or others. These can be very simple.

INFINITIVE	PRESENT	FUTURE	MEANING
poder	yo _____	tu _____	
	ellos _____	Ud. _____	*to go* _____
venir	vosotros _____	Uds. _____	

Do a number of these on a regular basis. Actually writing the tenses will help you memorize them. Try thinking of short phrases that use a conjugated form of your verbs. If possible, write a phrase that applies to your own life or that of your family.

Mi casa está en Iowa.
Iré de vacaciones a California.
Mis hermanos no saben tocar el piano.

Above all, try to work out a system for learning verbs—their forms, tense, and uses. Keep the following in mind.

1. Try to master only small amounts of information at a time.

2. Review your work regularly; don't just try to learn everything immediately before a test.

3. Be sure your material makes sense to you and is in some kind of context.

Look at the following:

7   14   28   56   112   224   448   896   1792

If these numbers mean nothing to you, then it might take you a few minutes to memorize them. As soon as you realize that each number is twice the previous one, it becomes easy. In the same way, you need to establish a personal way of systematizing your verbs. This will help you to internalize them in a way that mere learning by rote will not.

À *Activity 6* ···

Your instructor has asked you to learn the future endings, including the irregular forms, for a verb test at the end of the week, and the polite and the tú and Ud. command forms for a quiz the next week. Discuss with a partner what might be the most efficient way of studying and memorizing these forms. Compare your suggestions with those of the rest of the class.

➤ SUMMARY

We have recognized in this chapter that the Spanish verb system is much more complex than the English one, and that it requires a good deal of effort to feel at ease with it. We have also realized, though, that there are ways of attacking this problem and that it is far from insurmountable. Time and tense are important concepts and these do not always coincide in English nor in Spanish. We have examined the Spanish simple present and present progressive and have seen both similarities and differences in their uses.

We have examined some of the ways in which you can start to tackle the problem of learning Spanish verbs forms, and tried to reassure you that you are not expected to learn everything at once.

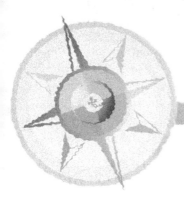

CHAPTER ELEVEN

COULD WE TALK ABOUT THE PAST?

My boy, Grand-père is not the one to ask about such things. I have lived eighty-seven peaceful and happy years in Montoire-sur-le-Loire without the past anterior verb form.

The New Yorker Magazine, 1973, *quoted by V. Fromkin and R. Rodman,*
An Introduction to Language

➤ BEFORE WE BEGIN

Most students of Spanish, like the French grandfather in the joke, don't have to worry these days about learning the past anterior verb form. Its use in modern Spanish has become infrequent enough for textbook writers to consider it safe to omit. In any event, they know that students already have sufficient problems trying to master the uses of the preterite and the imperfect, as well as the present and past perfect. In this chapter we will examine ways in which we express past time in both English and Spanish, and look at how the two languages differ.

➤ HOW WE DEAL WITH PAST EVENTS AND EXPERIENCES IN ENGLISH

We have seen that present tense and present time are not necessarily synonymous in English nor in Spanish. Something similar occurs with the past tense in English. Consider the following:

a. We *went* to the movies last night.
b. I would go on a cruise if I *had* the money.
c. He *couldn't* see without his glasses.
d. *Could* you help me?
e. David said that he *went* to the gym every evening.

177

Example *a* deals with a past event and the adverbial expression *last night* specifies when it occurred. In *b,* however, even though *had* is the past tense of the verb *to have,* we are not dealing with past time but with a supposition. In example *c, couldn't* is the past tense of *can* and is a statement about indefinite past time, yet *could* in *d* is merely a way of emphasizing a polite request. In *e* we have a past tense, *went,* in reported speech. What David actually said was: "I go to the gym every evening."

Even if our interpretation of the past tense varies in the above sentences, the form itself is straightforward: in all cases the simple past tense is used. In Spanish, however, these same situations are expressed in different ways.

   a. Fuimos al cine anoche. (preterite)
   b. Haría un crucero si tuviera el dinero. (imperfect subjunctive)
   c. No veía sin lentes. (imperfect)
   d. ¿Me podría ayudar? (conditional)
   e. David dijo que iba al gimnasio todas las tardes. (imperfect)

You cannot assume, then, that a past tense in English necessarily coincides with a similar tense in Spanish. This is why you always need to understand the underlying concept: whether you are dealing with past time or not and, if you are, how that time is viewed by the speaker.

Ᾱ *Activity 1*   ....

Look at these sentences. They all contain a verb in the past tense. Decide whether they are dealing with past time or not.

1. They *would* spend the summers in the mountains when they were children.
2. When they *finished* the meal, they went for a walk.
3. *Would* you be so kind as to direct me to the nearest bank?
4. He tried to lift the stone but he *couldn't.*
5. I think you *could* try a bit harder at school, don't you?

➤ TALKING ABOUT THE RECENT PAST

We mentioned briefly in the last chapter that English has a contrast between *perfect* and *nonperfect* verbs and that this is a question of aspect, not tense. Here we will look into this more closely, since even though Spanish also has this contrast, the usage differs.

English has the following perfective forms:

Present perfect: He has done his homework.
Past perfect: He had visited his friend.

Spanish has a tense which seems similar to the present perfect. It is formed with the verb **haber,** whereas the English present perfect is formed with the auxiliary *to have.* Both follow the auxiliary with a past participle. You will find this conjugation in your text. Remember that the participle never agrees with the subject if the auxiliary is **haber.**

The present perfect in both languages is a past tense that has reference to the present. The person speaking is viewing the event from the vantage point of the present. The present tense of the verb *to have* in English and of the verb **haber** in Spanish underlines this.

He terminado el trabajo.	*I've finished the work.*
Se ha marchado.	*He's gone.*
¿Ha visitado alguna vez España?	*Have you ever visited Spain?*

In the first two examples, we are dealing with a recent past, and in the third with an indefinite past, not at any particular point in time. There is no problem understanding these because both English and Spanish act similarly.

More problematic is a special use that English has for the present perfect: when the event, process, or state is seen as starting in the past, and leads up to and includes the present.

They have lived there for two years (and still do).
He has played the violin since he was four (and still does).
She has studied French since 1988 (and still does).

This contrasts with statements such as:

They lived there for two years (but don't anymore).
He played the violin (but now plays the guitar).
She studied French in 1988 (then gave it up).

Spanish also considers that these events start in the past and continue up to and include the present. However, the present state of these situations is emphasized to such an extent that the present tense is used to express them, whereas in English more emphasis is given to their past reference.

Viven allí desde hace dos años.
Toca el violín desde los cuatro años.
Estudia francés desde 1988.

Note particularly the use of **desde hace** and **desde** with expressions of time. They signify what in English we express with *for* and *since,* neither of which can be directly translated into Spanish in such circumstances.

If you said the following, your listener would understand that these things occurred in the past and are no longer true.

Han vivido allí.
Ha tocado el violín.

Apart from using the simple present to express such meanings, Spanish also uses the verb **llevar,** which has several senses, the most common of which is *to carry.* In expressions of time, however, this is not its meaning. The following ways of representing time are often used in conversation.

Lleva tres años estudiando alemán.
Llevan viviendo allí desde 1953.

This is equivalent to the progressive form of the present perfect, which we often use in English when we want to give greater emphasis to the duration of an event.

He has been studying German for three years.
They have been living there since 1953.

ᴺ Activity 2

Tell a partner the following in Spanish.

1. How long your parents have been living in their present home.
2. How long you have been studying Spanish.
3. How long you have been at your college/university.
4. How long you have been living in your current apartment or dorm.
5. How long you have been practicing your favorite sport.

➤ GETTING MORE REMOTE

In both languages there is a past perfect form. In English this is formed with the past tense of *to have* and the past participle, and in Spanish with the imperfect of the verb **haber** and the participle. As in the case of the present perfect, the past participle is invariable.

Lo habían hecho.   *They had done it.*
Se había marchado.   *He had left.*

In English, the past perfect refers to an event as far back in the past as we can go: the present perfect usually expresses a recent past which continues into the present, the simple past expresses past events that are over and done with, and the past perfect expresses events that occurred at a moment in time before those of the simple past.

The past perfect often contrasts with the simple past.

a. He had already washed the car when she got up.
b. They had left when Robert arrived.
c. After Joe had eaten his breakfast he went out.

In these cases, it is clear that the actions *he had washed the car, they had left, he had eaten his breakfast,* were performed first, and that they took place before she got up *a,* Robert arrived *b,* or Joe went out *c.* In Spanish, the past perfect is also used in the first two examples.

Ya había lavado el coche cuando ella se levantó.

(Notice that adverbials in Spanish cannot be placed between the auxiliary and the past participle as they often are in English: **Ya había lavado** not "**Había ya lavado**").

Se habían marchado, cuando llegó Roberto.

Example *c,* though, is different. We have the same subject in both parts of the sentence: *Joe had eaten his breakfast. Joe had gone out.* Spanish handles this kind of situation in the following way:

Después de desayunar, salió José.

You cannot conjugate the verb after **después de.** It must take the infinitive.

The past perfect is found in another special context in both languages—in reported or indirect speech.

Tom: "I went to Ecuador last year."
Tom said that he had gone to Ecuador the preceding year.

In direct speech, Tom used the simple past *(went),* but when we report what he said (perhaps the next day, the following month, or three months later), we need to shift this even further into the past. This is why this process is called *backshift.* Spanish works similarly in such contexts.

Tom: —Fui al Ecuador el año pasado.
Tom dijo que había ido al Ecuador el año anterior.

Notice that not only does the tense change, but also the adverbials (from **el año pasado,** to **el año anterior).**

The past perfect is used with certain verbs in English (expressing intention, hope, supposition, etc.) to suggest that something that was expected to happen didn't. For example:

I had intended to write the letter today, but I didn't.
We had meant to go to the lecture, but we were too busy.

Spanish tends to resolve these situations with the imperfect:

Pensaba escribir la carta hoy, pero no lo hice.
Teníamos la intención de ir a la conferencia, pero estábamos demasiado ocupados.

Finally, there is an important use of the past perfect in English which does not coincide with Spanish. We use the past perfect after *if* in conditional clauses to express something that didn't actually happen.

a. If we had known you were coming, we would have gone to the airport to pick you up.
b. The child would not have had the accident if you had been more careful.
c. If you had taken the cake out of the oven earlier, it would not have burned.

In all three examples, *if* things had been different there would have been a different result. These are all hypotheses about the past: how things might have been different if such and such a thing had been done or had happened. Spanish does not use the past perfect in these cases, but the imperfect subjunctive.

a. Si hubiéramos sabido que venías, habríamos ido al aeropuerto a recogerte.
b. El niño no se habría accidentado si hubieran tenido más cuidado.
c. Si hubieras sacado el pastel del horno antes, no se habría quemado.

You will probably learn how to use these constructions during your second year of Spanish.

Å *Activity 3* ··

In each of the following sentences, which of the two actions in each one happened first?

1. Cuando llegó Elsa al cine, Miguel ya había sacado las entradas.
2. Me dijo Roberto que Andrés había cogido el tren de las ocho.
3. Ya había llegado su madre cuando llegó al aeropuerto.
4. Antes de hacerlo, lo había meditado mucho.
5. Ramón había puesto un telegrama a su tía antes de coger el avión.

In Chapter 10 we stated that English has two kinds of aspect:

1. The contrast between *progressive* and *non-progressive* tenses.

   I study Spanish. I'm studying Spanish right now.

2. The contrast between *perfective* and *non-perfective* verbs.

Simple past (non-perfective):	I visited Germany in April.
Present perfect (perfective):	I have visited Germany.
Past perfect (perfective):	He had gone there.

Spanish has a third kind of aspect not found in English. It is the contrast between *perfect* and *imperfect* verb forms. When we talk about these forms in English, we tend to refer merely to the "preterite" and the "imperfect" as though they were two separate verb tenses. This only confuses the issue because: (1) we are talking about aspect rather than tense; and (2) there are more than two forms.

Preterite or **pretérito** simply means *past*: in other words, any verb that refers to past time. *Perfect* or **perfecto** does not have the usual sense of perfect (without blemish), but in a grammatical context means *finished, completed*. *Imperfect* or **imperfecto,** on the other hand, just means that we are not interested in when the action began or finished but in its *duration*.

One event or state of being, then, can be approached from two different perspectives in Spanish, thanks to the existence of the imperfect. And this gives it a greater richness of expression when talking about the past than is possible in English. It also means that English-speaking students of Spanish can expect to have some difficulty in distinguishing the nuances implicit in the perfect/imperfect contrast because we either do not make these differences ourselves, or we have to express them in other ways. For example:

When I entered the room, he/she was playing the piano.
entered: simple past   *was playing:* past progressive

Cuando entré en la habitación, tocaba el piano.
entré: preterite   **tocaba:** imperfect

When she was small, she used to collect stamps.
was: simple past   *used to* + infinitive: habitual action

Cuando era pequeña, coleccionaba sellos.
era: imperfect   **coleccionaba:** imperfect

I realized that he was very nervous.
realized: simple past   *was:* simple past

Me di cuenta de que estaba muy nervioso.
me di cuenta: preterite   **estaba:** imperfect

It will help you to understand that the difference between preterite and imperfect is one of aspect and not tense if you become familiar with the Spanish verb forms and their names. You do not need to learn all the Spanish names, but you will see that the true contrast is not between preterite and imperfect but between perfect and imperfect. Let us take the verb **bailar,** *to dance.*

SPANISH	ENGLISH
Pretérito imperfecto: **bailaba**	Imperfect
Pretérito perfecto simple: **bailó**	Preterite
Pretérito perfecto compuesto: **he bailado**	Present perfect
Pretérito pluscuamperfecto: **había bailado**	Past perfect
(Pretérito anterior: **hube bailado**)	Past anterior

As you see, all these tenses include the word **pretérito** because they are all ways of expressing the past. What you know as the *preterite* is called the **pretérito perfecto simple** not because it is easy, but because it consists of only one word: **bailó.** It contrasts with the **pretérito perfecto compuesto: he bailado.** (**Compuesto** means that the verb is made up of more than one word.) Other **verbos compuestos** are the **pretérito pluscuamperfecto** and the **pretérito anterior,** which is in parentheses above because it is less common.

Your instructor will probably refer to the *preterite* and the *imperfect,* and you may even have a text in Spanish that refers to **pretérito** and **imperfecto.** This is due to the wide use of the English terms in Spanish-speaking countries, to the extent that texts often translate the English terms back into Spanish. But their correct names are those listed above.

The choice between the preterite and the imperfect frequently depends on the point of view of the speaker or writer. In other words, a subjective element creeps into the narrating of past events. Although there are times when only one form or the other is correct, on other occasions either may be used but different nuances will be conveyed depending on the choice. To help you understand the different uses of the preterite and imperfect you should always focus on them when they appear in a text and analyze why you think they are there. *They are never simply interchangeable,* even in those cases where, grammatically, you could use one or the other.

You cannot study such complex issues in a vacuum. You may have a list of uses for the preterite and another for the imperfect in your textbook, but memorizing the lists will not give you the ability to use the two forms correctly nor, necessarily, to understand all the uses, since there are always many exceptions to the rules that are generally given. This is why it is very important that you habitually analyze the use of the preterite and imperfect as they appear in discourse. However, the following will help you distinguish some uses. They are not the only combinations of preterite and imperfect that you will come across, but they are among the most frequent.

Specific past events

One of the most frequent uses of the preterite is to refer to past events at a particular point in time. Sometimes adverbials of time may be employed to clarify the finished nature of the event.

Fuimos a Sevilla **en 1992**.	*We went to Seville <u>in 1992</u>.*
Estudió medicina.	*He studied medicine* (we don't know when, but he has finished now).
El avión salió **a las seis**.	*The plane left <u>at six o'clock</u>.*

This contrasts with phrases such as:

Siempre íbamos a Sevilla.	*We <u>always</u> used to go to Seville*
Estudiaba medicina **cuando lo conocí**.	*He was studying medicine <u>when I met him</u>.*
Salía de casa **todas las mañanas a las ocho**.	*He left home <u>every morning at eight</u>.*

The preterite is often used in newspaper articles where the journalist is merely concerned with reporting a series of events that are now over and done with.

> Sus Majestades los Reyes *viajaron* ayer a Ibiza y Formentera.... Don Juan Carlos y Doña. Sofía *presenciaron* un desfile militar y una exhibición de folclore ibicenco.... Por la tarde, los Soberanos *se trasladaron* a Formentera, donde *visitaron* el Ayuntamiento y *firmaron* en su libro de honor.
>
> (*ABC*, Madrid, March 22, 1994) (*Italics added.*)

> Their Majesties the King and Queen traveled to Ibiza and Formentera yesterday.... Don Juan Carlos and Doña Sofía watched a military parade and an exhibition of Ibizan folklore.... In the afternoon they went to Formentera, where they visited the Town Hall and signed the book of honor.

We are given a list of events that occurred one after the other.

viajaron, presenciaron, se trasladaron, visitaron, firmaron

All these actions took place at a certain point in the recent past: they went there yesterday **(ayer)**, and the visit to Formentera took place in the afternoon **(por la tarde)**. The journalist has no literary pretensions; he/she is merely telling us what happened from an objective standpoint. We know that all these actions convey a sense of completion: the visit to Ibiza began and finished yesterday, and the visit to Formentera began and finished in the afternoon.

Simultaneous actions

The preterite is also used in sentences that express two simultaneous actions.

Ella fregó los platos y él los secó.   *She washed the plates and he dried them.*

Again, we are focusing on the completed nature of the actions; we are not interested in drawing attention to the duration of the event, but simply in recounting what happened.

If two actions were going on simultaneously in the past and we are more interested in the duration of the events than in the fact that they are now over, we may use the imperfect for both.

Juan cortaba el césped y Teresa   *Juan cut the grass and Teresa planted*
plantaba flores.   *flowers.*

If, in English, we wanted to draw more attention to the duration of those events than to their past nature, we would have to use the progressive aspect. This is also possible in Spanish—with the imperfect combined with the progressive.

Juan estaba cortando el césped   *Juan was cutting the grass and Teresa*
y Teresa estaba plantando flores. *was planting flowers.*

The meaning is identical to the previous example, but now more emphasis is given to the duration of the event. The use of the past progressive in Spanish tends to be more emphatic than in English precisely because Spanish has the possibility of not using it, but using the imperfect instead.

One action interrupts another

The preterite is often found in a sentence in which it contrasts with another verb in the imperfect. In this case, the action that started first is expressed in the imperfect, and the action given in the preterite is understood to have interrupted it in some way.

Cuando entró Pepe en la sala, **Marisa tocaba el piano.**	*When Pepe entered the room, <u>Marisa was playing the piano</u>.*
(Yo) Preparaba la cena cuando sonó el teléfono.	*<u>I was preparing</u> the supper when the telephone rang.*

The actions that started first (*Marisa was already playing the piano; I had started to prepare supper*) are underlined.

It may help you to remember these three uses of the preterite and the imperfect if you associate them with their corresponding diagrams and examples.

• Specific points in time: **La fiesta empezó a las cinco.**

• Simultaneous actions: **Luis miraba la televisión y Juan estudiaba.**

• One action interrupts another: **Mientras Pedro se bañaba, se cayó.**

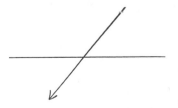

À *Activity 4*

A. Decide whether the verbs in the following sentences refer to actions that are *simultaneous* (S) or whether one interrupts the other (I). If one action interrupts the other, say which action started first.

1. Pablo limpió el garaje y su hermano cortó el césped.
2. Mientras Marita escuchaba la conferencia, tomaba apuntes (*notes*).
3. Pedro tuvo un accidente cuando conducía a clase esta mañana.
4. Elena hacía gimnasia mientras su novio jugaba al fútbol.
5. Alguien llamó a la puerta justo cuando salía de la ducha (*shower*).

B. Complete the following sentences with a suitable verb in the preterite or the imperfect.

1. Cuando salí de casa _____.
2. Enrique bebía vino _____.
3. _____ mientras yo estudiaba.

> LOOKING AT THE BEGINNING OF EVENTS

Although the preterite in Spanish most frequently focuses on the end of an action, sometimes more weight is given to the beginning.

a. Marta lo conoció el 10 de abril.
b. Enrique lo supo por su hermana.
c. Ana le dijo que llamara, pero Ramón no quiso.
d. Tuvo una niña en junio.
e. Intentó levantar la piedra, pero no pudo.

In *a*, Marta didn't know this person on April 9, but on April 11 she already knew him because she had met him for the first time on April 10. In *b*, there was something that Enrique didn't know, but thanks to his sister there was a precise moment in time when he started to know about it. In *c*, Ana wanted Ramón to phone, but this was something which he didn't want to do. The person in *d* didn't have a baby girl in May, but she did in June because that was when the child was born. Finally in *e*, someone tried to do something very specific at a special moment in time (even though there is no adverbial expression to tell us when), and was not able to do it.

Spanish is able to convey all these special circumstances through the preterite tense because it is used to refer to specific moments in past time. In English, although we are able to do the same with many verbs by using the past tense, there are some verbs that would sound strange if we used this tense to refer to specific moments in the past. For instance, we can't say:

Marta knew him on April 10 because we use the past tense of the verb *to know* in English for extended periods of time.

Marta knew him for ten years.
She knew him when she was a student.

In Spanish this would be:

Marta lo conoció durante diez años (she doesn't know him now).
Lo conocía cuando era estudiante (imprecise time).

If we want to talk about the precise moment when that knowledge or acquaintance with another person starts, we have to resort to the verb to meet.

Marta met him on April 10.

In other words, the verb **conocer** in Spanish is acting just the same as any other verb in the preterite. But because English does not have the perfective/imperfective contrast, we have to use a different lexical verb. It is not Spanish that is strange, then, it is the lack of this kind of aspect in English that makes English poorer in certain contexts.

Similarly, when we are talking about knowing facts, we cannot use the same verb *to know* to pinpoint the exact moment when we start to know something. **Enrique lo supo por su hermana** means that at a particular moment, which is not specified, he suddenly acquired knowledge which he didn't have before. Again, in English we have to use a different verb.

Enrique found it out/discovered it through his sister.

If we say **Enrique lo sabía** it knew it, but at an indefinite time in the past, with no special reference to the exact moment that knowledge was acquired.

Ana le dijo que llamara, pero Ramón no quiso.

Ramón was reacting to a specific moment and circumstance. We could say **Ramón no quería,** but the sense above is more emphatic: *Ramón refused.* This is a common translation of **no + preterite of querer.**

Tuvo una niña en junio.

If we say *She had a little girl in June,* we usually understand from the context that we are referring to a birth. We could also say *She gave birth to a baby girl in June.* English is more ambiguous here than Spanish. If we say *She had a son,* we need background information to know whether this means that she gave birth to a boy or that she had (possessed) a son. In Spanish, even out of context, this is absolutely clear.

Tuvo un hijo.
Tenía un hijo.

In the first phrase, the preterite makes it clear that the emphasis is on a process that began and finished *(the birth)*, whereas in the second the reference is to an ongoing past event, so it must refer to possession.

Intentó levantar la piedra y no pudo.

Once more, we are confronted with a specific situation in the past, an event that occurred and was over and done with, as made clear from the preterite. In English we could say *He/She tried to lift up the stone and was unable to* or *He/She tried to lift up the stone and couldn't manage it.*

Ṅ Activity 5

Underline the appropriate form of the verb in each sentence below.

1. Yo (sabía/supe) la noticia porque me llamó Berta.
2. Invitamos a Juan a la fiesta pero no (quería/quiso) venir.
3. No (sabíamos/supimos) que te habían dado una beca. ¡Enhorabuena!
4. El asesino dijo que no la (quería/quiso) matar.
5. Esteban trató de decírselo a David, pero no (podía/pudo).

➤ NUTS AND BOLTS

We have discussed many ways of expressing the past in this chapter, and now you may feel that you will *never* master the numerous verb forms in Spanish. As we stated in Chapter 4, it is very important that you devote time to learning the verb tenses as they come up in your course. You will find that familiarity with one verb form will probably help you learn another, and gradually you will start to see each verb form as part of a bigger picture that makes sense, rather than as an isolated fragment.

Let us look at some verb forms and ways in which you can make them more meaningful for you.

Present perfect

Keep in mind the following guidelines.

> 1. The present perfect is formed with the present tense of **haber +** *past participle.*
>
> 2. For regular verbs, the participle follows the vowel theme of the stem: **-ar** verbs **-ado; -er and -ir** verbs **ido.**
>
> 3. The past participle is *invariable,* that is, it *never* agrees with the subject.
>
> Ella ha comprad**o** un vestido. Ellos han comid**o**.

Some very common verbs have irregular past participles. Look at the following verbs and discuss with a partner what you might do to try and memorize these forms more easily.

abrir: **abierto**   cubrir: **cubierto**
decir: **dicho**   escribir: **escrito**
hacer: **hecho**   morir: **muerto**
poner: **puesto**   romper: **roto**
ver: **visto**   volver: **vuelto**

Some of the following observations may prove helpful.

1. Notice that **morir** and **volver** have the same vowel change in the past participle that they have in the present (**él muere/vuelve**).
2. For **decir** and **hacer** you could learn the saying: **Del** *dicho* **al** *hecho,* **hay gran trecho.** *(There's many a slip 'twixt the cup and the lip.* That is, it's not the same to talk about doing something as to do it—things may go wrong).
3. For **escribir** you can think of the TV program *Se ha escrito un crimen* (*Murder she wrote*).
4. You can make up a sentence with each of the forms which makes sense to you or has some relevance to your life.

5. Look the above forms up in the dictionary. You will find that some of them are used in colloquial sayings or may be other parts of speech, as well as participles, and this may suggest a phrase that will help you learn it more easily. For example: **Está mal visto no saber "visto"** (*It's frowned upon not to know "visto."*).

Notice that the following verbs have an accent in the participle:

caer: **caído**   creer: **creído**
leer: **leído**   oír: **oído**
reír: **reído**   traer: **traído**

Look at the infinitives of these verbs. What rule or rules do you think lie behind the reason to add an accent.

The past perfect

Remember the following about the past perfect.

1. It is formed with the imperfect of the verb **haber.**

2. All the imperfect forms of **haber** have a written accent.

3. As in the case of the present perfect, the past participle is invariable.

The preterite

It is very important that you devote enough time to learning the preterite forms of verbs as it is not only a verbal form that you will use frequently, but you need to know it in order to form the imperfect subjunctive. Try saying the endings aloud several times to yourself in a rhythmic way and write them out a number of times. Try writing out the preterite forms of as many regular verbs as possible until you have no doubt about them. When studying the forms, remember the following:

1. There is one set of endings for **-ar** verbs and another for **-er** and **-ir** verbs.

2. There are no accents on the **vosotros** form: **comprasteis**.

3. The **nosotros** form of **-ar** verbs is the same in the preterite as in the present tense. This is not likely to cause confusion because it will be clear from context whether you are talking about the present or the past.

   Nosotros cantamos en un coro todos los domingos.
   Cantamos anoche en la iglesia.

4. It is important to stress the right syllable (the last) in the first- and third-person singular forms, particularly with **-ar** verbs. Failure to do so may lead to confusion with other verb forms: **canté, cante, cantó, canto, etc.**

There are many irregular preterites and you should learn these as they come up in your text. One that you should learn early on is the preterite for the verb **ser** as this is identical to that of the verb **ir** and they are both high frequency verbs. You will find these verbs in your text. As in the case of the shared form for the first person plural of **-ar** verbs in the present and preterite, this does not cause confusion because the sense is always clear from context:

Ayer fuimos al cine.	*Yesterday we went to the movies.*
Su padre fue abogado.	*His father was a lawyer.*

The preterite of the verb **dar** is easy to remember because it consists simply of the endings for an **-er** or **-ir** verb, plus **d**.

di	dimos
diste	disteis
dio	dieron

Why are there no accents on the first- and third-persons singular? (Compare **comí, comió**).

The imperfect

This is the easiest of all the verb forms to learn because of the following:

1. There are only three irregular verbs in the imperfect: **ir, ser,** and **ver.**

2. There is one form for **-ar** verbs and another for **-er** and **-ir** verbs.

3. Only the **nosotros** form of the **-ar** verbs has a written accent: **tomábamos.**

4. All forms of the **-er** and **-ir** verbs have a written accent.

The three irregular forms are easy to learn. **Ir** has the same endings used with **-ar** verbs with **i** placed in front. Only the **nosotros** form has an accent.

iba	íbamos
ibas	ibais
iba	iban

The verb **ver** loses the final **r** and adds the endings for the **-er** and **-ir** verbs. It is not really so irregular.

veía	veíamos
veías	veíais
veías	veían

The other irregular verb is **ser,** which adds the endings of the present tense of **-ar** verbs to the stem **er-,** except for the first person, which takes **-a** instead of **-o.** Notice that the **vosotros** form does not have a written accent for the imperfect of **ser** and that the **nosotros** form *does* have a written accent.

Ӑ Activity 6

Decide whether the following verbs have been conjugated in the present tense or in the preterite. What clues help you decide? Look up the meaning of any verbs you don't know.

1. Cenamos en un restaurante argentino el sábado.
2. Alquilamos un apartamento en la costa el verano pasado.
3. Pasamos por la calle Belén siempre que vamos a casa de mi suegra.
4. Lo pasamos fenomenal en la boda de Enrique.
5. Tomamos unas copas en el bar "Los tres hermanos" cuando nos visitó Moncho.

➤ SUMMARY

In this chapter we examined ways of talking about the past. We have seen that, as with the present, past time and past tense are not necessarily the same thing. We have looked at some of the ways in which English expresses past time, as well as how past tenses in English are often used to express things other than past time. We then compared these with Spanish and saw some similarities, but also some clear differences. We mostly concentrated on what, in English, is called the preterite and imperfect, and saw that this is really an inaccurate way of naming these verb forms, since it is not a question of a different verb tense but one of aspect, that is, the way we view an event. The speaker's or writer's view of a past event or state will influence how he/she speaks or writes about it. And often in Spanish there are at least *two* ways of talking about the same event. Finally, we looked at ways in which you can become more sensitive to these nuances, which are either not expressed at all in English or expressed in a different way, sometimes through the use of the progressive forms.

CHAPTER TWELVE

EXPRESSING SPATIAL AND TEMPORAL RELATIONS

*It is said that one of Winston Churchill's papers was altered by a secretary to avoid
ending a sentence with a preposition and Churchill, restoring the preposition to its
original place, wrote: "This is the kind of pedantry up with which I will not put",
and there is the story of a little girl who finding her mother had brought up a book
that she did not like, said, "What did you bring that book I didn't want to be read
out of up for?"*

Frank Palmer, Grammar

➤ BEFORE WE BEGIN

If he/she had been Spanish, Winston Churchill's secretary would have
been even more upset to find prepositions at the end of a sentence. In
English, formal style usually requires prepositions not to be placed in final
position, but it happens frequently in informal English. In Spanish, whether
speech is formal or informal, prepositions *never* go at the end of a sentence.

In this chapter we will talk mainly about expressing place, direction, destination, and time in Spanish, as well as other relationships. The class of
words we will be talking about are prepositions. In your textbook you probably will not find a chapter that deals exclusively with prepositions, although
you will be gradually introduced to the most common ones. This is a complicated aspect of Spanish, mainly because it often differs greatly from
English. Even those with a high level of competence in Spanish often give
themselves away because of their use of prepositions.

One difficult aspect is that English frequently makes use of a combination
of verb plus preposition or adverb in everyday expressions: *to sit down* (**sen-
tarse**), *to catch on* (**comprender**), *to wash up* (**lavarse**), *to do in* (**matar**), etc.
These verbs are extremely difficult for foreign students of English because
frequently a translation of the individual parts will give no clue at all to the

meaning (as in the last example). For English-speaking students of Spanish, the difficulty resides in the temptation to translate word for word. You should never assume that a verb like this (called a phrasal or prepositional verb, depending on the function of the particle that accompanies it) has an exact equivalent in Spanish. You will need to learn the Spanish equivalents of these verbs as they arise.

Now let us look at prepositions more closely.

➤ WHAT IS A PREPOSITION?

A preposition, both in English and in Spanish, is a word that joins two elements, expressing a relationship between the two. In Spanish, the element that comes before the preposition can belong to various parts of speech. It may be:

- noun:

    Vendió **el ordenador** por $1.000.
    He sold the computer for $1,000.

- verb:

    Soñó con ella.
    He dreamed about her.

- adjective:

    rico en grasa
    rich in fat

- adverb:

    Prefiere sentarse **lejos de** él.
    She prefers to sit far away from him.

The element that comes *after* the preposition in Spanish is also important. It can be:

- noun:

    Fue al colegio con **su hermano.**
    She went to school with her brother.

- pronoun:

    He traído esto para **Ud.**
    I've brought this for you.

- infinitive:

    Esto te pasa por **gastar** tanto dinero.
    That's what you get for spending so much money.*

- a subordinate clause:

    Sueña con **que lleguen pronto las vacaciones.**
    He's dreaming about the vacations coming soon.

- an adjective = noun:

    Con **tontos** no trato.
    I don't deal with stupid people.

*Note that English uses a gerund, not an infinitive, here.

The element that comes before the preposition has so much influence on it that frequently only one preposition can be used; for example, **hombre** *de* **pocas palabras** *(a man of few words)*. No other preposition is possible here. There are other initial elements, however, that can take several prepositions: **miedo** *al* **examen,** or **miedo** *del* **examen** *(fear of the exam)*. There are also many verbs in Spanish that can be followed by only one preposition; this preposition may be totally different from the one used in English: **soñar** *con* *(to dream of)*, **depender** *de* *(to depend on)*. In some cases, an accompanying preposition may not be required in English: **casarse** *con* **alguien** *(to marry someone)*. In others, as mentioned before, there may be a preposition in English but not in Spanish: **Fuimos al cine** *el* **sábado** *(We went to the movies* <u>on</u> *Saturday;* **Busco mi reloj** *(I'm looking* <u>for</u> *my watch).*

Ä Activity 1 ···

Find the prepositions in the following sentences and give the part of speech that precedes it. In some cases there may be more than one preposition.

1. La actriz Assumpta Serna anuncia su boda con Scott Cleverdon.
2. La belleza es el fruto de un frágil equilibrio.
3. Trabajar en una película de Trueba es maravilloso.
4. Mi decisión fue venirme a Madrid por cuestiones profesionales.
5. Burt Reynolds aceptó pagar a Loni 260 millones de pesetas.

➤ LEARNING TO CLASSIFY REALITY IN A DIFFERENT WAY:
   SPACE, DIRECTION, AND DESTINATION IN ENGLISH AND
   SPANISH

It is useful to see how in English spatial notions are expressed because it will help us understand some of the problems with Spanish prepositions. Look at the following examples:

a. La comida está en la mesa.	*The meal is* <u>on</u> *the table.*
b. El niño está en la playa.	*The child is* <u>on</u> *the beach.*
c. La foto está en la pared.	*The photo is* <u>on</u> *the wall.*
d. Están andando en el parque.	*They are walking* <u>in</u> *the park.*
e. Están en el cine.	*They are* <u>at</u> *the movies.*
f. Está en la parada del autobús.	*He's* <u>at</u> *the bus stop.*
g. ¿Cómo vas a San Francisco? Voy en avión/en tren.	*I'm going* <u>by</u> *plane/train.*
h. Colocó el regalo en la caja.	*He put the present* <u>in</u> *the box.*
i. Tiene un grano en la nariz.	*He has a pimple* <u>on/in</u> *his nose.*

Although all these examples use **en** in Spanish, English uses different prepositions because of the way space is envisaged. In *a* and *b* we are dealing with horizontal, flat surfaces with no clear boundaries, except their own: table, beach. Note these examples:

There is a plate on the table.
There is a woodworm in the table.

By using *on* and *in*, English makes absolutely clear whether we are talking about something on the surface or something within the actual material of which the table is made. In Spanish, these expressions would be:

Hay un plato *en* la mesa.
Hay carcoma *en* la mesa.

Spanish is less precise in these cases, yet the context makes it clear whether we are talking about on or inside.

In *c,* we are also dealing with a flat surface (wall), but this time it is vertical. However, we still use *on.* In *d* we again have a flat surface, but now it is restricted; there are boundaries of one sort or another so we deal with this by using *in. In* is also used for interiors of buildings.

Juanito está en la escuela.	*Johnny is in the school* (in the building).
María está en la clínica.	*Mary is in the hospital* (she has appendicitis).
El padre de Tomás está en la cárcel.	*Tom's father is in prison* (he robbed a bank).

Notice, however, that by changing the preposition in English and, in some cases, by adding the definite article *the,* we can give a totally different slant to these sentences:

Johnny is <u>at</u> school (it's his first day of class).
Mary is <u>at</u> the hospital (she's taking her mother some flowers).
Tom's Dad is <u>at</u> the prison (he's visiting his brother).

These sentences would be translated the same in Spanish as those above, and we would need to rely on context to clarify the sense. Spanish does, however, have other forms of expression. For example:

María está ingresada en la clínica.	*Mary is in the hospital.*
El papá de Tomás está encarcelado.	*Tom's Dad is in prison.*

A verb then, in both these cases, clarifies what we express in English by means of a preposition.

Example *e* uses *at* to express the fact that the people are at a function (the movies). We are not interested in their physical presence in the movie theater (they are in the theater), but in the fact that they are there watching a film. Similarly:

Luisa está en un concierto.	*Louisa is at a concert.*
Marcos está en el circo.	*Mark is at the circus.*
Mamá está en la peluquería.	*Mom is at the hairdresser's.*

In example *f* we are concerned with a specific point on an imaginary line—the bus stop. Similarly:

Espérame en la puerta.	*Wait for me at the door.*
Te esperaré en la taquilla.	*I'll meet you at the box-office.*

Example *g* deals with transport, and expressions of this kind tend to use *by* in English and *en* in Spanish. Other examples of this usage are:

Fui en bici.	*I went by bike.*
Fuimos en autobús.	*We went by bus.*

Note, however, the following: *to go on foot,* **ir a pie,** *to ride a bike,* **montar en bicicleta.**

In example *h* we are dealing with volume. This is a common context where English uses the preposition *in*. Note also the following:

Andrés lo puso en el cajón.	*Andrew put it in the drawer.*
Carmen metió la ropa en la lavadora.	*Carmen put the clothes in the washer.*

Example *i, He has a pimple on/in his nose,* demonstrates the English concept of space. We use *on* if we are thinking of the nose as a flat surface with a protuberance on it, and *in* if we are thinking in terms of a space with volume (inside the nose). This distinction is not made in Spanish, so **en** will do for either.

As you can see, it is not possible to give a single translation of even the most common Spanish prepositions, since the meaning will change according to context and interpretation.

To sum up

En is used for expressing:

- points in space on a horizontal flat surface: **La taza está**
  en **la mesa.**

- points on a vertical flat surface: **Hay una mosca** *en*
  la pared.

- points within a bounded surface (park, garden, etc.):
  Luis está *en* **el jardín.**

- points within a volume (box, drawer, bath, etc.): **El**
  regalo está *en* **la caja.**

- points on a line (bus stop): **María está** *en* **la parada del**
  autobús.

- the interior of buildings: **Hay muchos estudiantes** *en* **el aula.**

- place: one that offers services or entertainment (at the supermarket,
  hairdresser's, movies, theater, etc.): **Juan y Miguel están** *en* **el**
  cine.

- idiomatic meanings with certain verbs: **pensar en, echar en falta,**
  concentrarse en, etc.

Never think of *in* as the only, or even most frequent, translation of **en.**

Ṅ *Activity 2* ....

Look at the following sentences in Spanish and decide how you would
translate **en:**

1. El cordero, cortado **en** trozos, se sazona (*is seasoned*) con sal y pimienta.

2. **En** una sartén se derrite (*is melted*) la manteca.

3. El príncipe Felipe de Borbón y Grecia, hijo del rey Juan Carlos I, estudia
   en la Universidad Americana de Georgetown, **en** Washington.

4. Durante nueve años, Jill Whelan apareció **en** la pequeña pantalla interpretando el papel de Vicki, la hija del capitán Stubing, **en** la serie "Vacaciones **en** el mar".

5. A los veintisiete años, Jill se ha casado con un hombre de negocios **en** una ceremonia celebrada también a bordo de un barco **en** el lago californiano Arrowhead.

6. Al terminarse la serie en 1988, Jill estuvo **en** un colegio **en** Inglaterra.

7. La actriz Deborah Kerr ha recibido un Oscar **en** seis ocasiones.

8. **En** la foto está la duquesa de York con sus hijas, **en** unas vacaciones **en** Suiza.

9. Los duques de York volvieron a cenar juntos **en** un restaurante **en** Winkfield Rd, Berkshire.

10. Había una vela roja encendida **en** la mesa.

(Adapted from *Hola,* Madrid, April 21, 1994 and February 10, 1994)

> MORE ABOUT SPACE: DISCUSSING TIME AND DESTINATION

In Spanish there is a relatively small group of what are called *simple prepositions,* which consist of one invariable word. There is also an extensive number of prepositional phrases made up of two or more words. The following are the most common simple prepositions: they always have the same form, with no distinction of gender or number.

a, ante, bajo, con, contra, de, desde, en, entre,
hacia, hasta, para, por, según, sin, sobre, tras

Notice that **bajo** can behave as an adjective or preposition. If it functions as an adjective, it agrees in number and gender with the noun to which it refers.

Eduardo es bajo; Marisa también es baja.	*Edward is short; Marisa is short too.*

If it is a preposition, however, it does not vary.

Ana está bajo un árbol.	*Ana is beneath a tree.*

Now let us look at how simple prepositions are used to express space, time, and destination, three concepts that you will need to handle frequently.

The preposition *a*

Location

El árbol está a la derecha de la casa.	*The tree is to the right of the house.*
La ventana da al mar.	*The window looks out on the sea.*
La oficina que busca está al fondo del pasillo.	*The office you're looking for is at the end of the corridor.*

Time

La clase es a las diez.	*The class is at ten o'clock.*

Notice that this is different from:

Son las diez.	*It's ten o'clock.*
Ocurrió al atardecer/amanecer.	*It happened at dusk/dawn.*

But:

Ocurrió por la tarde/mañana/ de noche.	*It happened in the afternoon or evening/ morning/at night.*

Destination

A number of verbs of movement take the preposition **a**, such as **llegar a, ir a, volver a, regresar a, volar a.**

Va a París.	*He's going to Paris* (and staying there).
El avión vuela a México.	*The plane flies to Mexico.*
Felipe vuelve a su casa.	*Philip is going home.*
Llegaron a la estación.	*They arrived at the station.*

Note that **a** can mean *at* only when referring to time.

El concierto es a las siete.	*The concert is at seven o'clock.*

It does *not* mean *at* when referring to space, in which case you will usually use **en**.

Roberto está en casa/en el trabajo/en la escuela.	*Bob's at home/at work/at school.*
La exposición está en el ayuntamiento.	*The exhibition is at the town hall.*

The most common use of **a** is when it is placed immediately before a direct object referring to a person. In this case it is known as the personal **a**. English does not have an equivalent. (Note that personal **a** is not used after the verb **tener: Consuelo tiene tres hermanos.)**

Vi a tu hermano anoche.   *I saw your brother last night.*

Here are some very common verbs that take **a**:

acercarse a alguien/algo   *to draw near to someone/something*
Pepe se acercó al niño.   *Pepe got close to the child.*

parecerse a alguien/algo   *to look like someone/something*
Teresa se parece a su madre.   *Teresa looks like her mother.*

jugar a (las cartas)   *to play cards*
Jugaron a las cartas durante   *They played cards for two hours.*
dos horas.

oler a   *to smell of*
La casa huele a rosas.   *The house smells of roses.*

saber a   *to taste of*
La comida sabe a ajo.   *The food tastes of garlic.*

To sum up:

A is used in the following situations:

- for destination: **Voy a Roma.** *I'm going to Rome.*

- time: **El partido es a las ocho.**
  The game's at eight o'clock.

- in certain specific expressions of location:

  a la derecha/izquierda *(on the right/left)*, **al fondo** *(at the back)*

- as a personal **a** before a human direct object: **Vi a Pablo.**

Note also:

- It is frequently translated by *to*.

- It is not translated when used as a personal **a**.

- It is rarely translated by *at* in expressions of space.

Activity 3

What would be the English equivalent of **a** in the following sentences?

1. Harrison Ford es una potencia mundial del cine de aventuras, comparable únicamente **a** Sean Connery.
2. Su público está dispuesto **a** viajar con él hasta el fin del mundo.
3. **Al** final de la película *Unico testigo*, Ford deberá abandonar el pueblo y volver **al** mundo **al** que pertenece.
4. La profesora preguntó **a** su hijo más pequeño **a** que se dedicaba su padre y dijo, "es actor y unas veces hace de bueno y otras de abogado."
5. El periodista le pregunta: —Cuando tiene que estar lejos varios meses, ¿lleva **a** sus hijos consigo? Ford contesta: —Lo intento.
6. Dice Ford: —Admiro enormemente **a** mucha gente que trabaja en Hollywood, que trabaja muy duro y por muy buenos motivos.
7. Ford no ha ganado un Oscar, y le preguntan: —¿Es **a** causa del tipo de películas que usted hace?

(Adapted from *Cambio 16*, Madrid, August 9, 1993, pp. 62–63)

The preposition *de*

Time

De indicates time in expressions such as:

Se despierta todos los días de madrugada.	*He wakes up every day at dawn.*
El padre de Antonio trabaja de noche.	*Antonio's father works at night.*

The normal English translation in this context is *at,* although in other time expressions it may be *from.*

La tienda abre de cinco a ocho.	*The shop opens from 5 to 8.*

Origen

De indicates origen, as opposed to destination, in phrases such as:

Manuel es de Sevilla.	*Manuel is from Seville.*
El avión viene de Estados Unidos.	*The planes comes from the United States.*

Possession

The most frequent use you will have found for **de** so far is to indicate possession. In English this is expressed by the possessive.

El coche es de Marta.	*It's Marta's car.*
Es el marido de mi amiga.	*It's my friend's husband.*

Common verbs with *de*

Here are some common verbal expressions that use **de**.

alegrarse de algo — *to be pleased about something*
Se alegró de recibir la noticia. — *He was pleased to get the news.*

tener miedo de — *to be afraid of*
Tengo miedo de las arañas. — *I'm afraid of spiders.*

depender de — *to depend on*
Mis planes dependen de mis notas. — *My plans depend on my grades.*

ir de compras — *to go shopping*
Siempre vamos de compras los sábados. — *We always go shopping on Saturdays.*

De + adverbials

De is combined with certain adverbial expressions such as:

antes de (que)	*before*
después de (que)	*after*
a pesar de (que)	*in spite of*

You need be careful with these expressions because in English their usage is more straightforward. In English, if you have two actions and both refer to the same subject, you can use a combination with *ing*.

a. Before going to bed, he cleaned his teeth.
b. After finishing work, he went out for a meal.

In Spanish, the adverbial expression uses **de** followed by an infinitive.

a. Antes de acostarse, se limpió los dientes.
b. Después de terminar el trabajo, salió a comer.

If you have two actions and two different subjects, in English you conjugate the verb.

a. After you've finished dessert, I'll make coffee.
b. Before you leave, I'll call a taxi.

If there is a change of subject in Spanish, you need to add **que** plus a conjugated verb. If what comes after **antes de que** or **después de que** refers to future time, the verb will be in the subjunctive, as in these examples.

a. Antes de que te vayas, llamaré a un taxi.
b. Después de que hayas terminado el postre, prepararé café.

De, of course, can also be used immediately before nouns.

Antes del concierto, tomaron unas copas.	*They had a few drinks before the concert.*
Después del partido, fueron a celebrar.	*After the match, they went out to celebrate.*

To sum up:

De is frequently found in expressions of:

- origin: **Es *de* Venezuela.**

- possession: **El libro es *de* Juan.**

- time: **Trabaja *de* noche.**

ᴺ
Ӑ *Activity 4* ···

How would you express **de** in English in the following sentences?

1. Consigue un gran premio **de** treinta millones.
2. Es el perfume **del** que están vestidos los sueños.
3. ¿Por qué uno **de** cada tres americanos compra un No Frost General Electric?
4. Sea lo que sea, fíese **de** los americanos.
5. Rodéate **de** belleza: cerámica **de** color.
6. Cuanto más entienda **de** whisky escocés, más apreciará Ballantine's.
7. Semana Internacional **de** Palma **del** 31 **de** julio al 8 de agosto. Copa **del** Rey.

Two prepositions that will create special problems for you are **por** and **para**. As you have already seen, it is best not to try and equate Spanish prepositions with a single English preposition because this does not work. There is a tendency for English speakers to equate both **por** and **para** principally with *for*. But this does not always hold, particularly with **por** which, unfortunately, is similar only in its spelling to English *for*. Bear in mind that **por** and **para** are not interchangeable. You have to be specially careful because your grammatically correct sentence may not mean what you think it does, and a lot of confusion could arise. If you make a mistake, however, a Spanish speaker will make allowances for you and try to understand what you are saying. Consider the following:

Rosa trabajaba para su hermano.	*Rosa worked for her brother* (he was the boss).
Rosa trabajaba por su hermano.	*Rosa worked instead of/in the place of her brother.*
Por perder el trabajo, pasó hambre.	*Because he lost his job, he went hungry.*
Para perder peso, pasó hambre.	*In order to lose weight, he went hungry.*

Direction

Both **para** and **por** can be used to express spatial relationships and direction, but in different ways. **Para** suggests movement toward a destination you have not yet reached.

Salimos para Madrid esta tarde.	*We're leaving for Madrid this afternoon.*
No están aquí. Se marcharon para la estación.	*They're not here. They left for the station.*

Por, with an appropriate verb, also indicates movement, but through something or somewhere.

Pasamos por París cuando fuimos a Bruselas.	*We passed through Paris when we went to Brussels* (we don't know whether they stopped or not).
El ladrón entró por la ventana.	*The thief entered through the window.*

Indefinite location

Por is also used in expressions of place of an indefinite nature, when the exact location is not known or may not be important.

La secretaria estuvo por aquí hace un momento.	*The secretary was around here a moment ago.*

Time

Both **por** and **para** can also be used in expressions of time. The latter is used when looking ahead to something that is not done or is not yet here.

Acábalo para las nueve.	*Finish it by nine o'clock.*
La casa estará terminada para Navidad.	*The house will be finished by Christmas.*

Por can express times in the year when something occurs:

Les visitamos por Navidades.	*We visited them around Christmas time.*

This is different from:

Les visitamos para las Navidades.	*We visited them for Christmas (we spend Christmas with them).*

Por can also refer to the duration of an event.

Hablaron por tres horas.	*They talked for three hours.*

But note the following:

Perdió el avión por cinco minutos.	*He missed the plane by five minutes.*

Por is the preposition you find in some of the most common expressions of time.

Practica karate por las tardes.	*He practices karate in the evenings.*
Por la mañana tengo un examen.	*I have an exam in the morning.*

Final clauses

One very frequent use of **para** that does not coincide with English is when it is used immediately before an infinitive to express *in order to*. English expresses concepts like this merely with the infinitive.

| Compró carne para hacer hamburguesas. | He bought meat to make hamburguers. |
| Vendió su coche para obtener dinero. | He sold his car to get money. |

Another common use of **para** is with the verb **estar** to give the sense of being about to do something.

| Parece que está para llover. | It looks as though it's about to rain. |

Por is also used with **estar** to suggest that the subject is thinking about doing something.

| Estoy por no ir. | I'm thinking about not going. |

Por may also be used to express something that has not yet been done.

| Es tardísimo y tengo la comida todavía por hacer. | It's very late and I still haven't made lunch. |

Other uses of *por*

Por has the sense of *for* in phrases that express going to get something from somewhere (or asking someone to go for it).

| Vete por más tabaco. | Go for some more cigarettes. |

It means *in favor of* in expressions such as:

| Estamos todos por la democracia. | We're all for democracy. |

Por expresses the means of doing something.

| Lo mandó por avión. | He sent it by air. |

It is found in passive constructions to indicate who or what has done the action.

| La ley fue aprobada por el Congreso. | The law was passed by Congress. |

It expresses quantity or price.

| Me lo vendió por cien dólares. | He sold it to me for a hundred dollars. |

There are many verbs in English that always take *for*, and you must avoid trying to translate these directly into Spanish with **por** or **para.**

| Buscó su corbata. | He looked for his tie. |

Set phrases

There are some contexts in which **por** or **para** are used that can be analyzed, yet there are many specific uses or phrases that have become set in time, and you will need to learn them individually. **Por,** in particular, appears in a number of very common expressions, and you should learn some of these.

por ello	*because of that*
por cierto	*certainly*
por fin	*at last, in the end*
por supuesto	*naturally*
por ejemplo	*for example*
por lo menos	*at least*
por aquí	*around here*
¿por qué?	*why?*

Å Activity 5

Decide whether you would complete the following phrases with **por** or **para.** If either could be used, how would the sense change? What is **por** or **para** being used to express in each case (time, direction, imminence, a final clause, etc.)?

1. En España consumen tres litros de helado *(por/para)* persona.
2. Hace unos días, miles de espectadores acudieron a New Jersey *(por/para)* escuchar un macroconcierto de música *grunge*.
3. *(Por/Para)* ayudar a un amigo, tuvo muchos problemas.
4. Tendré que ir *(por/para)* más pan si vienen tus amigos a cenar.
5. Ahora *(por/para)* solamente 350 ptas. recibirá un Compact Disc con esta revista.
6. María del Mar abandonó los estudios *(por/para)* cuidar el ganado.
7. En la costa del Mediterráneo hay muchas playas no aptas *(por/para)* bañarse.

Now read over the **por/para** section again and briefly sum up the main uses of both in a chart similar to the ones that appear in this chapter for the other prepositions.

You have now seen that the meanings of prepositions in Spanish and English frequently do not coincide. You cannot learn just a single translation for a Spanish preposition, since it may have different meanings in English depending on context. This is a complicated aspect of Spanish and one which will require several hours of study. So you should now start thinking about the best way to learn how to use these expressions. You may do this in several ways.

1. Read back through this chapter and see if you understand what is meant by a *preposition*. Write out a few sentences of your own in English which contain prepositions. Look quickly through a journal or newspaper article and underline the prepositions.

2. Look through articles in a Spanish magazine or newspaper and locate as many sentences as you can that use the prepositions treated in this chapter. Classify them in groups according to the preposition used, and see if you can understand the basic concept behind their use (location, direction, time, etc.).

3. Think about the concept of space in English. Look back particularly at pages 198–201. Do you understand the concepts of horizontal and vertical surface and volume?

4. Do drawings (simple stick drawings will do) of people going into, toward, or being on surfaces. What Spanish prepositions would you use to describe these motions?

5. Get together with some of your classmates from Spanish class. Let each person take charge of one preposition and find as many examples of its use as possible. Then let the whole group decide why the preposition is used in those examples.

6. Learn a few set phrases or verbs with prepositions every night.

Here is some additional practice with prepositions.

Ṅ *Activity 6* ··

As you read the following advertisements, underline all the prepositions; then decide whether you would use the same prepositions in English. Finally, translate the texts into English.

1. Hasta hoy sólo utilizábamos el agua de colonia "4711" para sentir frescor en la nuca (*nape of the neck*) y en las manos. Ahora tenemos la oportunidad de refrescar todo nuestro cuerpo con la esencia de "4711."
2. El Speedmaster Professional Jubilee es una edición limitada que ha realizado OMEGA para conmemorar el XXV aniversario de la llegada del hombre a la Luna. El reloj está realizado en oro de 18 quilates.
3. Cuando entres en tu farmacia para comprar un endulzante (*sweetener*) sin azúcar ni calorías, acuérdate de pedir Acofarinas. Porque ahora, al comprar Acofarinas 500 comprimidos, tu farmacéutico te obsequiará con Acofarinas 100 comprimidos y Acofarinas Líquido. ¡Tres presentaciones por el precio de una!

➤ SUMMARY

We have seen in this chapter that not all languages express concepts of place, time, or destination in the same way. Spanish and English frequently use different prepositions to express these concepts. Understanding how reality is divided in English helps us understand the underlying differences. The concept of space is particularly striking because of the very precise way English has of dealing with it. It is not possible to give a single translation into English of any one Spanish preposition. You need to understand and learn contexts in which the prepositions occur in order to find the exact English equivalent. We have looked particularly at **en, de,** and **a,** and also **por** and **para,** which, we have said, are never interchangeable. Whenever you read Spanish, be particularly aware of the use of prepositions: seeing how they function in discourse, both written and oral, will help you incorporate prepositions successfully into your own use of Spanish.

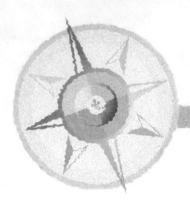

CHAPTER THIRTEEN

LOOKING TO THE FUTURE

...y no hablar es morir entre los seres.

Pablo Neruda, "La palabra"

➤ BEFORE WE BEGIN

In this chapter you are going to try to evaluate your progress not just in acquiring the Spanish language, but in your attitudes towards both the language and the people who speak it. You are going to look back at the goals you set yourself at the beginning of the book, and decide whether these need modifying and, if so, in what way. You are going to think about how you feel toward learning Spanish: whether you feel more at ease now in the classroom or if you feel just as anxious, or perhaps even more so, than when you started out. Finally, you are going to think about ways in which you can continue to help your own learning process, and what things you can do to promote your own success.

➤ LOOKING AT HOW FAR WE'VE COME

If you have worked your way systematically through this book, in conjunction with a textbook, you will have come a long way since Chapter 1. You were starting a new language at the beginning of the book, or perhaps one that you had studied before but without reaching any depth. You have gone from expressing ideas in the present and mastering concepts such as the agreement of nouns and adjectives, to probing the interesting but complex world of the preterite and imperfect. Do the following activity and then compare your answers with a partner. You may want to do a class survey and put the results on the board.

Ā Activity 1

1. How difficult have you found Spanish pronunciation?
   a. extremely difficult
   b. moderately difficult
   c. fairly easy
   d. extremely easy

2. Would you say that your progress in pronunciation since you started your Spanish course
   a. has improved dramatically?
   b. has improved noticeably?
   c. has improved somewhat?
   d. is about the same?

3. Which of these sounds in Spanish do you still find very difficult to pronounce correctly:
   a. vowels   b. **rr**   c. ñ   d. **ch**   e. **j**   f. other (specify)

4. When you listened to Spanish at the beginning of the semester did you
   a. understand nothing?
   b. understand the main points?
   c. understand a few words?
   d. understand practically everything?

5. If you had to rate your listening comprehension skills now on a scale from 1 to 5, with 5 being the top score, how would you rate yourself?

6. Of the amount of time that your instructor speaks in Spanish, what percentage would you say that you understand?
   a. 90–100%
   b. 80–90%
   c. 70–80%
   d. 60–70%
   e. 50–60%
   f. less than 50%

7. What percentage would you say you understood at the beginning of the course when your instructor spoke in Spanish?

8. What techniques would you say have helped you most in acquiring listening comprehension skills?
   a. listening to tapes at home
   b. taking part in a structured lab program with an instructor
   c. talking to Hispanics on campus or in the community
   d. watching videos on my own or in class
   e. other (specify)

9. What techniques have you used to help you study grammar?
   a. mnemonic devices (give examples)
   b. cooperative study with your peers
   c. flashcards
   d. other

10. Check off the kinds of things you have written in Spanish since you started this course.
    a. shopping lists   d. descriptions   g. poetry
    b. telephone messages   e. instructions   h. other (specify)
    c. letters to friends   f. creative paragraphs

11. Which of the following techniques do you find most helpful when reading in Spanish?
    a. skimmming for the general meaning
    b. scanning for specific information
    c. detailed reading for information
    d. examining illustrations before reading
    e. thinking about the context and predicting
    f. other (specify)

12. What kind of dictionary (or dictionaries) are you using to help you in your studies?
    a. only a bilingual dictionary
    b. a bilingual and a monolingual Spanish dictionary
    c. only the glossary at the back of the textbook
    d. none of the above

13. How do you feel your dictionary skills have improved in the last three months?
    a. dramatically   b. considerably   c. somewhat   d. not at all

14. Check off those items below that you feel you still have trouble with when writing Spanish. Under "other," add any that are not on the list. Some of the items may not be pertinent to your present level of Spanish or course work.

agreement of gender and number   verb conjugations
prepositions   use of the present tense
expression of the future   preterite forms
preterite/imperfect contrast   **ser/estar**
subject pronouns   direct object pronouns
indirect object pronouns   double object pronouns
demonstrative adjectives and pronouns   accents
use of personal **a**   reflexive passive **se**
comparisons and superlatives   impersonal **se**
impersonal verbs like **gustar**   present subjunctive
commands   stem-changing verbs
other (specify)

15. How do you view your oral skills in Spanish now compared with three or six months ago? Do you...
    a. feel much more comfortable now speaking Spanish in front of the class?
    b. feel more comfortable when speaking in pairs or small groups, but clam up in class?
    c. feel you are making good progress when you speak Spanish to Hispanic or American friends in informal situations outside of class, but feel uncomfortable participating in the classroom?
    d. feel that you have made no progress whatsoever in oral presentations?
    e. If *d*, to what do you attribute this?

Once you have compared your list of problems in item 14 with your partner's or with the rest of the class, in groups of three or four discuss strategies that you think would help you overcome these difficulties. For example:

- Holding small peer-group sessions (four or five people) where at least one person in the group feels confident enough that he/she can help explain the concept(s) to the others. Your class may choose to draw up a list of students and, by each name, place two or three of the above concepts (or any other) that each person feels comfortable with and think they could help the others with. This will help you organize work-study groups in which you help one another. You may go to one group-study session, for example, where you help explain the use of direct object pronouns, and attend another where a fellow student explains the passive construction.

- Working with a partner. You may find it easier to discuss your problems with just one other person in your class. Even if that person also has problems with a given concept, the two of you should be able to work it out.

- Working solo on a concept. It may help you to write down an explanation of the grammatical concepts you have studied, and prepare brief study notes as though you had to explain them to someone else. Imagine that you have to give a class presentation on the preterite and the imperfect. Study notes might include:

What points do I think are the most important? How can I express these concepts in simple language that my peers will understand? What do I find confusing? I may be able to explain only part of something. If I try to separate the things I know from the ones I don't, I will have more precise questions to ask my instructor and this will help my own learning process .

- If you have a final exam (or midterm) to prepare for, which you know will ask you to complete exercises on a number of grammatical questions that you still have not fully understood or assimilated, make sure you organize your schedule well. Remember that you cannot learn a language by staying up half the night (or all night!) before an exam. It is a very slow process and daily study sessions, preferably of a length that fits your concentration span, are much more helpful than long periods at infrequent intervals. You need first of all to fully understand the concepts you have to study. This may be obvious, but a surprising number of people try to learn concepts parrot-fashion, even if they don't understand what they are trying to memorize. This is of no use to you in studying a language because at some point in the future you will have to use what you have learned in a meaningful context. You need to understand the concepts in order to fully assimilate them. Only then will you be able to really make them yours and start using them. You should also remember that at this stage you will have partial control of some concepts; but you cannot expect to have full control of them—this will require more instruction in the language and contact with Spanish than you have had so far.

Of all the skills you have been developing in Spanish—reading, writing, speaking, listening comprehension—which one(s) has caused you the most difficulty? Discuss this with a partner and see if you agree. Poll the rest of the class and find out who finds it easiest to speak and understand Spanish, who finds it easiest to read, and who finds writing the easiest. Are there people who feel comfortable speaking Spanish but have difficulty understanding when they are spoken to? With listening comprehension, are there notable differences when you try to listen to your instructor in Spanish, a tape, a video, or a conversation with a Hispanic person? Which is most difficult? What is easiest to understand? Discuss ways in which, in pairs, in groups, or as a whole class, you think you can improve each of these skills.

➢ CHANGING ATTITUDES

You will have discovered by now that learning a language is not merely an intellectual pursuit: it is something that engages your emotions and can change your whole outlook on life. Contact with another culture can also make you evaluate your own culture and values, perhaps in a way that you had never thought possible. You have not just acquired a number of verb tenses, grammatical concepts, and vocabulary in your new language, your eyes have been opened to a whole different world: that of Spanish-speaking peoples. Let us look back at some of the things you have learned.

Å Activity 2

Before your next Spanish class, answer as many of the following questions as possible.

1. Write the names of twelve countries where Spanish is spoken, and the name of the capital city of each one.
2. Could you have done this when you started studying Spanish?
3. Is there a country that you didn't know was Spanish-speaking? Is there a country where you thought Spanish was spoken but have since found out that it is not?
4. Write down four nouns in Spanish (for example, **el desayuno, la familia, el vino, la boda**) where you think that the English translation of the word does not convey the cultural differences that exist. For the words that you have chosen, briefly explain what you think these differences are.
5. Write a short paragraph on one aspect of Hispanic life that you have learned about and that has surprised you because it is very different from your culture.
6. Write a short description of one aspect of Hispanic culture that you have learned about and that has struck you as being very similar to your own culture.
7. What values would you say are highly esteemed in Hispanic culture? Do any of these enjoy the same esteem in your own culture?
8. In what way would you say that your perception of your own culture has changed because of your contact with Hispanic culture? Are there any values in your own society that you would now call into question? Why?
9. What would you say were your perceptions of Spanish-speaking people before you started to learn Spanish?
   a. positive attitude
   b. negative attitude
   c. neutral—didn't know anything about them
10. What areas in this country have a large Hispanic population?
11. Can you name the geographical origins of the Hispanic populations in several parts of the United States (for instance, the origins of the majority of Spanish speakers in Chicago, New York, Los Angeles, etc.)?
12. How would you say that these Hispanic communities differ? Apart from differences caused by their geographical origins, are there any marked social differences?
13. Can you name any important Hispanic people (in the administration, local politics, etc.)?

14. For what jobs do you think it will be an advantage to know Spanish by the beginning of the twenty-first century? Did you think about this before you started to study Spanish?

15. Have you considered taking your studies in Spanish beyond the basic level, even if you are not majoring in the subject? Do you now think that a greater knowledge of Spanish may be advantageous to you in your future profession or daily life?

16. Are there any aspects of Spanish art, music, history, etc., that you did not know about before and have started to become interested in?

17. Do you think that your contact with Hispanic culture has started to enrich you in any way? If so, how?

18. Since learning more about Hispanic culture, are there any things you have learned that have made a negative impression on you? What are they?

19. Have you become more aware of traces of Hispanic culture or life in your own community? What influences of Hispanic culture have you discovered that you didn't know were there?

20. Have you made the acquaintance of any Hispanic students or people in the community since you started studying Spanish? Have you discovered a Hispanic background of any students in your Spanish class or in other classes? Have you talked to them about what being Hispanic means?

21. Have you had the opportunity to watch videos about different aspects of Hispanic life and culture? What things have you seen that have surprised you? What things have you noticed about the way in which Spanish-speaking people converse and relate to one another?

22. What have you found out about stereotypes? Do you think you now have a more realistic idea of what Spanish culture is and is not? What stereotypes of your own did you have that you have now eliminated?

23. Do you think that the media encourage the propagation of stereotypes of Hispanic people? In what way? Draft a letter to a television company complaining about the stereotypes of Hispanic peoples in a particular program. Say why these are stereotypes and why it is important to show Hispanics in a truer light.

> REASSESSING OUR GOALS

When you started reading this book you were asked to define your goals for studying Spanish. It may well be that your goals have now changed after coming into contact with the Spanish language and culture. In the previous section we asked whether you are considering the possibility of continuing your studies in Spanish. It may be that you are not, but the reasons why you don't want to continue with Spanish may have little to do with the possible impact of Spanish on your life and future career, and a lot to do with difficulties you may have experienced so far with the language.

Å Activity 3

1. Do you know any people in your class who are majoring or thinking of majoring in Spanish?
2. If so, what reasons do they give for wanting to do so?
3. Are there any students in your class who intend to work in the future in any of the health-care professions or in social work? Do they see Spanish as an asset?
4. Are there any students in your class specializing in business who think that their knowledge of Spanish will be considered an asset by future employers?
5. Is there anyone studying criminal justice? What kind of profession does he/she intend to go into, and how will he/she be able to use Spanish?
6. How many students are studying journalism or communication? Why do they think Spanish will be useful to them in those disciplines?
7. How many people are studying education? Do they intend to teach high school or elementary school children? Do they think they will have any difficulty finding a teaching job in your state teaching Spanish? Find out how many high school Spanish teachers there are in your state.
8. What other disciplines are people majoring in? Do any see Spanish as being relevant to them?
9. Think of at least one profession in which you now realize that knowing Spanish will be advantageous, although you did not think this when you started studying Spanish?
10. Find out what the most common language taught in high school is. How many high school Spanish students are there in your state?
11. Is Spanish taught at an elementary school level in your state or in a neighboring state? How do you think this will affect the number of Spanish speakers in your state in the future?
12. Solicit opinions from at least five people in your class regarding their motives for learning Spanish.
13. Even if you are having difficulty learning Spanish, do you think that it is worth the effort so that you can tell your future employer that you have not simply taken a few courses in the language, but that you have attained a certain degree of proficiency?

14. What have you particularly enjoyed about studying Spanish? Are there any aspects worth pursuing for pleasure, rather than for professional or commercial reasons?

> AFFECTIVE REACTIONS

Learning a foreign language, as we said earlier, can be a threatening experience for many people. It is normal, moreover, to feel apprehensive about performing in front of your peers and instructor. We talked about several ways in which anxiety may spoil your performance in the language and some of the things you could do to alleviate this. Now work through the following activity.

Å Activity 4 ···

1. How would you rate your degree of anxiety when you started to study Spanish?
   a. extremely high   c. moderate   e. I was not at all anxious
   b. high   d. low
2. How do you feel now when you go to Spanish class?
   a. considerably less nervous than before
   b. more comfortable, but still nervous for certain activities
   c. very relaxed
   d. much more apprehensive than before
3. If you answered *a,* what factors have helped lessen your apprehension?
   a. the personality and techniques of the instructor
   b. growing confidence in my own ability
   c. the knowledge that my peers, on the whole, don't know any more than I do
   d. I'm more motivated because of my awakened interest in the language
   e. other (specify).

   If you answered *b,*
   a. what activities do you particularly enjoy and feel relaxed about doing?
   b. what activities do you still feel anxious about?
   c. do you think your anxiousness stems from the way in which your instructor corrects you, or because you know you are not going to the class well-enough prepared? (Be honest your grade will not be affected by admitting the last point!)
   d. What steps do you think you need to take in the future to try to remedy this situation?

If you answered c,

a. what factors have contributed to you feeling so good in your Spanish class?
b. do you feel like this in all your classes, or is there something different about the way your Spanish classes are set up?
c. what are the things that you most enjoy about learning Spanish?

If you answered d,

a. if you feel more apprehensive about going to Spanish class now than you did before, do you think this is due to unrealistic expectations you had of yourself?
b. has your rapport with your instructor been less than ideal? (You may want to think about this privately or consider the possibility of telling your instructor how you feel, if not directly, on an evaluation form, since your instructor will want to know how to adjust his/her teaching strategies and manner for future classes.)
c. were there aspects of the course that were too difficult so that you got increasingly behind your peers? What aspects?
d. have you had a good relationship with your peers? If not, has this considerably affected your attitude toward the class? What things do you think you can do in the future to avoid this negative influence?
e. do you think that the course moved too quickly for you?
f. had you had an unsuccessful language learning experience before?
g. have there been personal factors that have negatively influenced your progress?
h. what things do you think you need to do to overcome this anxiety in the future?
i. have you done fairly well in day-to-day classwork but not so well in tests? Does formal testing make you particularly nervous? Do you have access to general counseling regarding stress control and examination techniques?

Now look back at the expectations you had for yourself when you worked through the first chapter of this book and ask the following of yourself and a partner:

1. To what extent have you reached those expectations?
2. Were your expectations realistic or, now that you know more about the language learning process, do you think that you were too ambitious?
3. Have you kept to the study schedule that you drew up for yourself?
4. If not, to what do you attribute your failure?
5. If you have devoted regular periods of time to Spanish, in what ways do you think this has paid off?
6. What goals are you going to set for yourself now?

Studying a language is really a life-long activity. Take a look at your knowledge of your own language and you are sure to recognize that even with your native language there is much that you do not know—vocabulary that you sometimes have to look up in a dictionary, or turns of phrase that you may find difficult when you write formal English. Now let us discuss how you are going to continue to plan your studies in Spanish.

You may or may not have the opportunity to continue with formal study. If you do, it will be much easier for you because you will simply have to hone the skills you have already started to master. You will have plenty of support from your instructor too. If you are unable to continue to attend classes, yet still want to improve your Spanish, there is much you can do.

One thing you need to realize is that just as you can see that you have learned a lot in a short time, unfortunately you can also forget practically all of it in an equally short period. Sometimes people are surprised at the rate at which they forget a language. They think that once they have mastered certain concepts like verb conjugations, or vocabulary—even things like the subjunctive—that they will retain this knowledge for the rest of their lives. In a way you do. If you have really understood the concepts as you have been meeting them in your text, it will be fairly easy to refresh your memory, even if you seem to have forgotten many of them. However, understanding the grammar of a language is not the same as being capable of reading, writing, listening, and speaking. Language is a practical skill and has an intellectual side to it as well. You have to understand how it fits together. But however well you understand it, if you don't practice it, you will not be able to use it. It's like ice skating. You may have learned how to skate as a child and may always remember what to do, but if you spend years without skating, the first few times you may fall down.

There are many things you can do to stop yourself from forgetting. The easiest of all is reading. With the reading skills you have already acquired, you can continue to improve your reading level in Spanish. You can add to your vocabulary and, not only that, seeing the language in action will help you remember the structures you learned in a meaningful way. It will also keep you in contact with Spanish culture, and enable you to continue to expand your knowledge of the Spanish-speaking world.

A good way to practice writing is by setting up a pen-pal relationship with someone residing in a Spanish-speaking country, or a Hispanic here who would be willing to correspond with you. Letter writing, perhaps on the computer through internet, is an interesting way to make new friends and to find out about another country.

Practicing speaking may not be such a problem in some parts of the United States where there are large communities of Spanish-speaking people. In some areas it may be possible to get involved with some kind of community work where your knowledge of Spanish, however basic it may seem to you, is a distinct advantage. In many areas there are special social programs for migrant workers who are only in the country for short periods and have great difficulty understanding English. You may be able to help with migrant children, particularly if you are also studying education. They often have a hard time adjusting to school in this country, and you may be able to get involved with programs that exist in some areas to help them.

There may be churches in your area where there is a religious service or mass in Spanish. Try attending and offer your services to the priest; if you are able to devote a few hours a month you will no doubt be made very welcome.

You should be on the lookout all the time for opportunities to use the language. Even in areas without a large Hispanic population, there may be more opportunities than you realize to use your Spanish and improve it in meaningful ways.

On your campus make contact with the international office or Hispanic culture office, if there is one. Go to Spanish-speaking films, or rent Spanish-speaking videos. If you were living in a Spanish-speaking country, you would be surrounded by opportunities and could not avoid using them. Here you have to look for the opportunities, but they are there and are not too difficult to find.

You should carefully consider spending a period of time in a Spanish-speaking country. For various reasons many people do not even consider this. You may be afraid that such a stay would lengthen the time you are going to take to get your degree if you are studying for one. You may think that the cost will be so exorbitant that you cannot afford it. You may also be more than a little afraid, for the thought of going to live in a foreign country can be frightening. Even your short contact with Spanish culture will have shown you that, although there are many things that are similar to American culture, especially with regard to the life style of young people, there are also many things that are different: social values, etiquette, the family structure, traditions, education, etc. The thought of being immersed in a country where there is no escaping from these things can be daunting. However, you should bear in mind the following:

- There are numerous programs in Spanish-speaking countries organized by colleges and universities in this country. Your own school may have several or, if not, will be able to give you information about others. These programs are set up with American students in mind, so even though classes are usually given by Spanish-speaking instructors from the host country, or in some cases from the United States, they are structured so that American students can cope with them.

- The cost obviously has to be taken into account, and will vary considerably depending on whether you go for a summer, a semester, or a full year. It will also depend on where you go, and whether the program is organized by your school or by another school or organization. Sometimes the costs are much lower than you may think. The advantages, in any event, more than compensate for the expense.

- You should look on going abroad not as merely a chance to upgrade your language skills, but as a true learning experience that may well change your outlook on life. Even if you only go for the summer, you will come back a different person. Finding that you can cope in a foreign culture and in a land where you often have to communicate with people who may have absolutely no knowledge of your language can be a very satisfying experience. Merely working out on your own how to catch a bus or the subway, or finding the right shop for a product, is much more educational than learning about how to do these things in a classroom setting.

- In the classroom, you have no real need to communicate in Spanish because everyone, including your instructor, speaks English. You are all involved, then, in a kind of pretend situation where you artificially create communication activities. However, when you discover in Mexico that you must change some travelers checks and you don't know whether the banks are still open or not, or someone steals your passport when you are on a subway platform in Madrid, you not only find out whether you know enough Spanish to cope with things like this, but whether you are a resourceful enough person and have enough maturity. If you don't, you acquire it rather quickly!

  The things you learn from practical experience are those that usually stay with you for years, if not for life. Many years later you will remember the vocabulary you had to learn to survive in all kinds of situations. Often you will find yourself associating words with certain people, events, places, or even smells, and these will never leave you. Amy, writing about a recipe for Spanish potato omelette, says:

  > Esta receta es muy especial porque la aprendí de una persona muy importante y especial para mí, mi madre anfitriona, y por eso, tengo algo de ella. Cada vez que hago tortilla me acuerdo de ella. Los olores me recuerdan la cocina en Segovia y a veces puedo cerrar los ojos y casi puedo estar allí.

> SUMMARY

We have looked back at what you have learned since you first started using this book. You reviewed your goals and decided whether or not you have met them and if not, why. We looked at your attitude toward Spanish and the people who speak it and tried to decide whether this has changed after more contact with Spanish language and culture. We have also looked at the anxiety factor and at some of the reasons why you may still be suffering from anxiety.

We have considered ways in which you can now continue to upgrade your language skills in Spanish, even if you are not continuing with your classes, and have placed emphasis on the value of studying Spanish in a Spanish-speaking country.

As you know, Spanish is a world language. You have made a great deal of headway with making this language your own. In the future, if you continue studying Spanish, you will enjoy many successes but also suffer some failures and frustrations. Indeed, learning a language *can* be a very frustrating experience. After a time, you may feel that you have reached a plateau and seem to be making no progress. This in fact is not true. It is just that when you first start a language, since you know nothing, you seem to learn an awful lot in a very short time. Once you have mastered the very basic concepts, your learning curve slows down because you are now into more difficult aspects of the language that cannot be mastered in a matter of weeks or even months. Some things will take years before you fully master them, but this should not detract from your enjoyment of the language nor deter you from continuing.

Spanish is without doubt a beautiful language with many nuances that often cannot be found in English, another world language. By taking Spanish, you have already expanded your cultural horizons. Consider your entry into the Spanish-speaking world a privilege: not everyone is able to do this. The famous American poet, Carl Sandburg, once wrote:

> There are no handles upon a language
> Whereby men take hold of it
> And mark it with signs for its remembrance
> (Carl Sandburg, "Languages")

By studying Spanish, though, you have indeed gotten "a handle on it." **Buena suerte y, ¡a seguir!**

ANSWER KEY

Not all the activities in the book have a single answer. Below are the answers for those that do.

CHAPTER 1

Activity 1

1. T   2. F   3. F   4. T   5. T   6. T
7. T   8. F   9. F   10. T. However, it is spoken in more.   11. F   12. F   13. F
14. T   15. F   16. T   17. F   18. T
19. F   20. T

Activity 3

1/k   2/h   3/g   4/h   5/f   6/i   7/j
8/l   9/b   10/d   11/c   12/a

Activity 7

el: cuaderno, libro, muchacho, amigo, hermano, perro, gato, pescado
la: silla, puerta, casa, lámpara, hamburgesa, pluma, ventana, mesa, mochila, profesora

CHAPTER 2

Activity 8

A. 1. la   2. el   3. el   4. la   5. la
   6. la   7. el   8. el   9. la   10. la
B. 1. el   2. el   3. el   4. Masculine
   5. Feminine (plural)

Activity 9

A. 1. los   2. los   3. las   4. las
   5. las
B. 2. unos   2. un   3. unas   4. un
   5. unas

CHAPTER 3

Nuts and bolts

Subject (noun)	Direct object (noun)	Indirect object pronoun	Subject pronoun	Conjugated verb
			I	am
			I	cannot*
Mtazi Mtsweni			I	wanted
				wanted
				could*
			She	were
the families			she	had been living
	their homes		She	had made
	plumbing, water, and electricity		They	lacked
The company the authorities	a house	him		wanted
			She	had bought
				would*

*These verbs strictly speaking are not conjugated as they are examples of what are sometimes called anomalous finites. They only have one form.

CHAPTER 4

Activity 1

Conjugated verbs: continues, faces, decreased, are. *Could* and *should* are anomalous finites.
Infinitives: to decline, to determine, to learn, bring back, vanish.

Activity 2

-*ar* infinitives: ahorrar, llamar; -*er* infinitive: poder; -*ir* infinitive: recibir

Activity 3

-*ar*: 1, 3.   -*er*: 6   -*ir*: 2, 4, 5.
If you didn't know that *compartes* is from *compartir,* you might think that it was an -*er* verb, because the *tú* forms have the same endings for both kinds of verb. Similarly, if you didn't know *discutir,* you might think that it was from a different conjugation because the *–o* is common to all three forms.

Activity 4

Madrid (**proper noun**); visitors (**common noun**); Much (**indefinite pronoun**); Those (**demonstrative pronoun**); The calendar (**common noun**); art galleries (**common noun**); the choice (**common noun**); The Teatro de la Zarzuela (**proper noun**); Eating (**gerund**); The problem (**common noun**).

Activity 5

we are; **we** love; **She** is; **she** refuses. None of them can be omitted.
nosotros contamos; nosotros tenemos;

Activity 6

1. Los niños seropositivos
2. nosotros (omitted)   3. El virus del SIDA. Él (=el virus) ataca   4. La destrucción del sistema....   5. el beso
6. Los animales domésticos...
7. pruebas; ellas (las pruebas)   8. El sarcoma de Kaposi; él (el sarcoma).

Activity 7

1. a letter   2. a large steak and fries
3. a new car   4. that toy   5. John and his brother (personal a would be necessary)

Activity 8

1) a large mouse; it
2) an atom of fear; a desire

Activity 9

1. me   2. Juan; lo   3. tu falda; la   4. tu periódico; lo   5. los

Activity 10

1. us   2. the dog   3. me   4. him
5. you   6. us   7. the child   8. her

Activity 11

1. le (It's enchanting to her= Mari Paz loves potato omelette).
2. les; (It's annoying to them=They hate studying...)

3. le; to him (Federico has $100 left in the bank).
4. le; to her
5. te; to you (Do you find those books interesting?)

Activity 12

1. Se lo doy.   2. Se los traigo.   3. Se la busco.   4. Se lo devuelvo.   5. Se las reservo.

Activity 13

C. Direct object: 1. the bad news   2. a bike   3. a present   4. a dress
5. some flowers. Indirect object:
1. Mark   2. his brother   3. her friend
4. her daughter   5. Jennifer
D. 1. him it   2. him it   3. her it (or it for her)   4. her it (or it for her)
5. her some.   1. se la dieron (la mala noticia)   2. se la vendió (la bicicleta)
3. se lo compró (el regalo)   4. se lo hizo (el vestido)   5. se las dio (las flores).

CHAPTER 5

Activity 4

Antonyms: morir/nacer; rubio/moreno; ancho/estrecho; abierto/cerrado; acostarse/levantarse; líquido/sólido.
Synonyms: contento/feliz; despacio/lento; lívido/pálido; enfadado/enojado.

CHAPTER 6

Activity 2

1. that   2. house   3. you   4. establish
5. this   6. said   7. it   8. the   9. wine-shop   10. would   11. declared   12. on
13. father's   14. open   15. with   16. at
17. then   18. simply   19. observed
20. growl   21. with   22. up
23. was   24. drew   25. must
26. You   27. we   28. This   29. We
30. to   31. say   32. don't   33. But
34. it   35. exercise   36. wisdom

37. be   38. was   39. deference   40. then   41. manner   42. the   43. it   44. how   45. am   46. different   47. all   48. differently   49. there   50. going   51. have   52. invite   53. late   54. her

Activity 6

1. a) durante siglos, la Iglesia católica ha considerado a la mujer la guardiana de sus ritos y creencias
   b) los insistentes mensajes de Juan Pablo II no responden a los tiempos que vivimos
   c) su vida ahora es mucho más compleja.
2. a) Un Crédito Personal que te financia la compra de tu ordenador, tu moto, tu equipo de música o de deportes   b) Un Master 20 que te financia los gastos y la estancia de todo tipo de master   c) Estamos abiertos hasta las 19:00 horas.
3. a) Si Vd. quiere acabar con la inmoralidad y la violencia en la TV...   b) Si Vd. quiere que los programas de TV respeten la moral, la religión y la Iglesia Católica.   c) Por favor, remítanos urgentemente su cupón-respuesta.
4. a) una federación territorial cuya superficie sólo alcanza el 30 por ciento de Bosnia-Herzegovina.
   b) convencer a los serbios para que se integren en la nueva fórmula política.   c) Espero que los serbios se unan a este esfuerzo por una paz amplia.

Activity 9

1) estrella (noun)   2) muy (adverb)
3. planetas (noun)   4. la (definite article)
5. con (preposition)   6. una (indefinite article)   7. vemos (verb)   8. nosotros (personal pronoun).

Activity 10

1. to infiltrate   2. discreetly   3. disciple   4. inflammatory   5. null
6. to hold responsible   7. satisfactory
8. to carbonize   9. demoralized
10. volcano

CHAPTER 7

Activity 1

B. 1/e   2/d   3/b   4/f   5/a   6/c

Activity 2

Once upon a time there was a little girl who lived with her mother in a little cottage on the edge of a large, dark forest. This little girl often wore a pretty little red cloak with a little red hat, and for this reason people called her Little Red Riding Hood.

One morning, Little Red Riding Hood's mother called her inside, "Little Red Riding Hood, here's a little basket with some bread and butter and sugar cookies. Take this little basket to the cottage of your grandmother who lives on the other side of the forest. Shake a leg! Don't stop along the road! Don't stop to pick flowers! Don't stop to talk with strangers!"

"OK, mother," replied Little Red Riding Hood, and took the little basket and started off.

On the road to the cottage of her grandmother, Little Red Riding Hood met an enormous wolf.
"Well, well, well", said this wicked wolf, "If it isn't Little Red Riding Hood! Where's our pretty little girl going with her little basket?"

"I'm a-going to my grandmother's," replied the little girl. "Grandma's sick in bed. I'm a-taking her some bread and butter and sugar cookies."

"Oh, ho! Have a nice walk," said the wicked wolf, but he thought to himself, "I'll take a short cut to the cottage of her grandmother. I'll catch up with her later, and then—Oh boy!"

CHAPTER 9

Activity 8

1. bar-ba-ri-dad
2. man-te-qui-lla
3. an-tro-po-lo-gí-a
4. be-bé
5. his-to-ria
6. or-de-na-dor
7. co-rre-o
8. fi-ló-so-fo

Activity 9

1. bailó ends in a vowel. Without the accent it would be pronounced with the stress on bai.
2. ímpetu ends in a vowel. Without the accent it would be pronounced with the stress on pe.
3. geográfico ends in a vowel. Without the accent it would be pronounced with the stress on fi.
4. Belén ends with n. Words which end with a vowel, n or s, have the stress on the second syllable from the end. It would be pronounced with the stress on Be.
5. compás. The same reason as number 4. It would be pronounced with the stress on com.

Activity 10

—¿Por qué hiciste esto Pedro? Quedamos en ridículo aceptando la boda con Rosaura. ¿Dónde quedó pues el amor que le juraste a Tita? ¿Qué no tienes palabra?

—Claro que la tengo, pero si a usted le negaran de una manera rotunda casarse con la mujer que ama y la única salida que le dejaran para estar cerca de ella fuera la de casarse con la hermana, ¿no tomaría la misma decisión que yo?

Nacha no alcanzó a escuchar la respuesta porque el Pulque, el perro del rancho, salió corriendo, ladrándole a un conejo al que confundió con un gato.

CHAPTER 10

Activity 1

1. Present tense/future time
2. Present tense/past time
3. Present tense/past time (nos informan); present tense/future time (sale)
4. Present tense/future time
5. Present tense/present time

Activity 3

1. I'm expecting... 2. will place himself under the orders of 3. you will receive 4. is going to be
5. intends to spend

Activity 4

1. Tendrá dolor de cabeza.
2. Mariana estará enfadada conmigo.
3. Será su madre. 4. Estará en las páginas amarillas. 5. Estará cansada de la prensa.

CHAPTER 11

Activity 1

1. Past time. 2. Past time.
3. Polite request. 4. Past time.
5. Conditional.

Activity 3

1. Miguel ya había sacado las entradas.
2. Andrés había cogido el tren.
3. Había llegado su madre.
4. Lo había meditado mucho.
5. Había puesto un telegrama.

Activity 4

1. S 2. S 3. I conducía 4. S
5. S. Notice that here you have one in the preterite and the other in the imperfect, but the two actions coincided.

Activity 5

1. supe   2. quiso   3. sabíamos
4. quiso   5. pudo

Activity 6

1. Preterite. Clue: el sábado.
2. Preterite. Clue: el verano pasado.
3. Present. Clue: a habitual action.
Note vamos.   4. Preterite. Clue: la
boda.. a past event.   5. Preterite.
Clue: nos visitó

CHAPTER 12

Activity 1

1. con; noun (su boda)   2. de;
noun (el fruto)   3. en; infinitive
(trabajar); de; noun (una película)
4. a: infinitive (venirme); por: proper
noun (Madrid)   5. a: infinitive
(pagar); de: noun (millones)

Activity 2

1. in   2. in   3. at; in   4. on; in; at
5. in; on   6. at; in   7. on   8. in; on;
in   9. at; in   10. on

Activity 3

1. to   2. to (the "to" is implicit in the
infinitive, viajar).   3. at the end; to
the world, to which   4. a su hijo –
not translated; what his father worked
at   5. a is not translated.   6. a is
not translated.   7. a causa de—
because of, due to

Activity 4

1. of   2. in which   3. out of
4. not translated   5. with; not translated   6. about   7. The International
Week of/in Palma from July 31
through August. The King's cup.

Activity 5

1. por   2. para   3. por (on account
of).   4. por   5. por   6. para (in
order to); por (on account of)   7. para

Activity 6

1) Prepositions: de; para; en; en; de;
con; de.
Until now, we only used to use "4711"
eau de cologne to feel freshness on the
nape of our neck and on our hands, but
now we have the opportunity to refresh
our whole body with "4711" perfume.
2) Prepositions: para; de; del; a; en; de.
The Speedmaster Professional Jubilee
is a limited edition made by OMEGA
to commemorate the XXV anniversary
of the arrival of man on the moon. The
watch is made (out) of 18 carat gold.
3) Prepositions: en; para; sin; de; a(l);
con; por; de.
When you go to your pharmacy to buy
a sweetener without sugar nor calories,
remember to ask for Acofarinas.
Because now, when you buy 500
tablets of Acofarinas, your pharmacist
will give you 100 tablets of Acofarinas
and Liquid Acofarinas free of charge.
Three packages for the price of one!

INDEX

a, pp. 203–204
a, personal, p. 61
accents, pp. 158–159
adverbs, p. 151
adverbial expressions,
    p. 151
adverbials + de, p. 206
agntonyms, p. 77
article,
    definite, pp. 35–36
    indefinite, p. 36
aspect, pp. 166–167, 183
assimilation, p. 117

circumlocution, p. 130
classroom expressions,
    pp. 13–14, 80
cloze, p. 83
cognates, p. 93
commands, see imperative
composition, p. 95
computer programs,
    pp. 74–75
conjunctions,
    pp. 150–151
conocer, pp. 188–189
content words,
    pp. 92, 103
culture, p. 17–32

de, pp. 205–207
derivation, pp. 94–95
desde (hace),
    pp. 179–180
dictionaries, pp. 79–80
direct object, pp. 60–64

e-mail, p. 149
en, pp. 198–201
error correction,
    oral production,
    pp. 136–138
    writing, pp. 154–156

falsos amigos, p. 93
fillers, p. 103
flashcards, pp. 73–74
free writing, p. 147

future,
    expression of,
    pp. 169–170
    of supposition, p. 170
gender, pp. 14–15, 32–34
gestures, pp. 29–30, 118
goals, setting, pp. 10–11
grammar,
    and ambiguity,
    pp. 43–44
    deductive, p. 41
    feelings about,
    pp. 39–41
    importance of,
    pp. 43–46
    inductive, p. 41
gustar, pp. 66–67

haber, pp. 133,
    179–180
Hispanic (as an American
    creation), p. 24

illustrations, use of,
    pp. 95–97
imperative, pp. 171–172
imperfect,
    definition, p. 183
    forms, p. 194
    uses of, pp. 185,
    186–187
infinitives, pp. 52–53
interrupted actions, p. 187
intonation, p. 106
ir a + infinitive, p. 169
it, pp. 59, 60

jabberwocky, p. 87

language,
    nonverbal, p. 118
    and social class,
    pp. 106–107
learning styles, pp. 72–73
linking, pp. 115–117
llevar (expression of
    time), p. 180

meaning, understanding,
    pp. 82–88

nonverbal language,
    p. 118
nouns,
    masculine and
    feminine, pp. 32–35

o, p. 151
object, direct, pp. 60–64
objectives, setting of,
    pp. 11–12
oral expression,
    attitudes to,
    pp. 121–122
    strategies for,
    pp. 125–127
os, pp. 68–69

para, pp. 208, 209
parts of speech,
    pp. 99–100
past,
    expression of,
    pp. 177–190
    interrupted actions
    in, p. 187
    simultaneous actions
    in, pp. 186–187
past perfect, pp.
    180–182
past, recent, pp.
    178–180
pen pals, p. 224
perfective/non-
    perfective,
    pp. 178–180
pero, pp. 150, 151–152
personal a, p. 61
phonemes in Spanish,
    pp. 112–115
phrasal verbs,
    pp. 196–197
pluperfect, see past perfect
poder, p. 190
por, pp. 208–211
prefixes, p. 94
prepositions,
    definition, p. 197
    simple, p. 202

strategies for learning,
p. 212
present perfect,
pp. 178–180, 191–192
present progressive,
pp. 168–169
present tense,
pp. 167–169
preterite,
definition, p. 183
forms, pp. 192–193
uses of, pp. 185–190
progressive/non-
progressive,
pp. 166–167
pronouns,
direct object,
pp. 61–63
double object,
pp. 67–69
indirect object,
pp. 64–67
it, pp. 59–60
subject, pp. 57–58
pronunciation,
pp. 112–115
b, d, g, p. 115
d, t, p. 135
j (jota), p. 134–136
l/ll, p. 113–114
n/ñ, p. 113
p, t, k, p. 114
r/rr, p. 113
s/z, p. 114
errors of, pp. 134–136
vowels, pp. 115,
135–136
punctuation, pp. 160–161
purr words, p. 99

reader, role of, pp. 92–93
reading, pp. 81–101
attitudes, pp. 81–83
reduction, vowel, p. 132
regional Spanish,
pp. 108–109
rephrasing, pp. 130–131

saber, p. 189

scanning, pp. 90–91
schwa, p. 132
simple present, uses of,
pp. 167–169
skimming, pp. 89–90
snarl words, p. 99
social courtesies,
pp. 104–105
Spanish, varieties of,
pp. 108–109
speech, socially
appropriate,
pp. 128–129
stereotypes, pp. 23–25
stress, pp. 131–133
and auxiliaries, p. 133
and prepositions,
p. 133
and pronouns, p. 133
stress-timed language,
p. 131
study abroad,
pp. 225–226
subject, pp. 56–57
suffixes, pp. 95
syllabification,
pp. 156–158
syllable-timed language,
p. 131
synonyms, p. 77

tener, pp. 189–190
tense, pp. 163–164
tiempos verbales, p. 163
time,
and tense,
pp. 163–164
future, pp. 169–170
present, pp. 167–169
titles, understanding,
p. 88
tú, pp. 30–31

usted, pp. 30–31

verbs,
activity, p. 164
-ar, pp. 54–55

classification of,
pp. 164–166
conjugated, pp. 53–56
-er, p. 54–55
intransitive, p. 165
-ir, pp. 54–55
memorizing,
pp. 172–176
process, p. 164
regular, pp. 54–56
transitive, p. 165
with indirect object
pronouns, pp. 66–67
video, p. 118
vocabulary, classification
of, pp. 75–77
voice, p. 51
vos, p. 31
vosotros, pp. 31, 66
vowels
diphthongization of,
p. 135
pronunciation of,
pp. 115, 135

word,
classes. See parts of
speech
division, pp. 156–158
words,
cultural association
of, pp. 26–28
families of, p. 79
purr, p. 99
snarl, p. 99
writing,
accounts, pp. 144–145
advertisements, p. 150
diary, p. 147
historical events, p. 145
poetry, p. 147
recipes, p. 146
schedules, p. 144
shopping lists, p. 143
style, pp. 148–149
telephone messages,
p. 144
y, pp. 150–151